Cross Reference Guide & Index

OTHER BOOKS BY

DANIEL J. SHEPARD

YOU & I TOGETHER - HAVE A PURPOSE IN REALITY

IN THE IMAGE OF GOD

STEPPING UP TO THE CREATOR

Cross Reference Guide & Index

Daniel J. Shepard

Stephen Moore

PROCTOR PUBLICATIONS, LLC
Ann Arbor, Michigan

- First Edition -

Library of Congress Catalog Number: 98-65128
ISBN: 1-882792-61-0

Proctor Publications
PO Box 2498
Ann Arbor, MI 48106
(800) 343-3034

Book designed and edited
by Stephen Moore

Please visit our companion web sites:

www.panentheism.com & www.wehope.com

Dedicated to

Brian Peterson & Amy Grossberg

Contents

Introduction ix

Questions Addressed 13

- You & I Together 15
- In the Image of God 48
- Stepping Up To The Creator 81

Flowcharts 111

- You & I Together 113
- In the Image of God 146
- Stepping Up To The Creator 179

Thematic Index 209

Index 245

Glossary 277

Introduction

Welcome to the *Cross Reference Guide & Index*. This volume is intended as a companion to the trilogy; *You & I Together - Have a Purpose in Reality*, *In the Image of God*, and *Stepping Up To The Creator*.

This fourth volume has been included in order to assist the reader in exploring the trilogy. It contains five distinct sections; Flowcharts, Questions Addressed, Thematic Index, Index, and Glossary of Terms. These allow the reader to locate, through different means, particular points of interest within the trilogy.

The subject of the trilogy is the development of a universal philosophy. Particular emphasis is placed on symbiotic panentheism as one such philosophy, and how it could provide a perceptual shift for humankind. This perceptual shift could have enormous benefits for us as individuals, as members of society, and as an entity within the universe.

Social dilemmas, both present and future, are addressed and the consequences of not resolving these dilemmas are explored. Many fields of enquiry are included within the discussion, including; religion, science, philosophy, and prophecy. The merits of each are examined and their historical conflicts with each other are addressed. Using the *Cross Reference Guide & Index*, the reader is able to explore the benefits and disadvantages of these various belief systems. Consideration is given to a unification of these diverse beliefs in order to attain a particular goal - that of achieving a universal and constructive philosophy for humankind.

Because the trilogy covers such a broad range of topics, the *Cross Reference Guide & Index* should be an invaluable tool in gaining the most from the series.

Cross Reference Guide & Index

Questions Addressed

Volume I

You & I Together

- Have a Purpose in Reality -

Volume II

In the Image of God

Volume III

Stepping Up To The Creator

Volume I - You & I Together - Have a Purpose In Reality
Chapter 1: God

Why has the question of God, and His relationship to Mankind, always been with us?

What do we find when we subtract myths and superstitions from our thinking?

Is it hope, fear or intelligence that drives our belief in God?

What do we mean by atheism?

What or who is God?

Does God conform to the view we have of Him or is He independent of us?

Is the God of Christianity, Islam, and other religions really that different? Is He everyone's God?

Why must we be tolerant?

Who created God?

Who is the God of God?

What do we, as a species, need to do to understand God's nature?

Why do we need to search for the answer to God?

Should we stop believing in God?

Are some religions more true than others?

How does our misunderstanding of God influence our behavior?

Volume I - You & I Together - Have a Purpose In Reality
Chapter 2: Quadratic vs. Linear Philosophies

What is Mankind's purpose?

What is Quadratic and Linear Philosophy? How do they differ?

How do contradictions in our thinking interfere with our lives?

How can we solve the problem of Mankind's existence?

What form does God take?

Is our present thinking too simplistic to solve Mankind's problems?

What do we need to do to solve Mankind's problems?

How can we obtain a more cohesive picture of reality?

Why should we think quadratically?

Volume I - You & I Together - Have a Purpose In Reality
Chapter 3: B.E.G.A. Begins

What does science tell us about the structure of the Universe?

How is our Universe constructed?

What prevents our Universe from destroying itself?

What is symmetry?

What are the different forms of energy in the Universe?

What is nothingness and how could it explain God's presence?

What is omniscience?

What do we mean by dual universes?

What are parallel universes?

How do we obtain an understanding of the true nature of the Universe?

Volume I - You & I Together - Have a Purpose In Reality
Chapter 4: Sets of Four Parallel Universes

What does science tell us about the structure of the Universe?

How is our Universe constructed?

What prevents our Universe from destroying itself?

What is symmetry?

What are the different forms of energy in the Universe?

What is nothingness? How does it explain God's presence?

What is omniscience?

Volume I - You & I Together - Have a Purpose In Reality
Chapter 5: The Universe

What can God know?

Can God increase His knowledge?

What is the soul?

Is predestination and free will compatible? How could God resolve the issue?

Where is the Universe located?

Volume I - You & I Together - Have a Purpose In Reality
Chapter 6: The Universes

Does our Universe have a boundary?

What are the implications for us as a species if the Universe is bounded?

If the Universe is bounded, and therefore has limits, what is on the other side of that boundary?

How does logic address the issue of the boundary of the Universe?

How are the Universe and the new knowledge related?

What types of knowledge are there?

What does physics tell us about the symmetry of the Universe? What are the implications?

Why should we be humble?

Are we the only intelligent species in the Universe?

Are we replaceable as a species?

What do we first need to do in order to accomplish our purpose in reality?

If our Universe has limits, are we also limited?

Who is God?

Volume I - You & I Together - Have a Purpose In Reality
Chapter 7: The Ripple Effect

What might be Mankind's purpose in reality?

Understanding and action: how do we resolve the issue of responsibility?

How are we limited in our efforts to understand?

What is the Ripple Effect and how can we learn its lessons?

What consequences, both good and bad, follow from our actions?

By taking responsibility, what do we and others need to do?

What are the consequences of hedonism?

What role does religion play in our lives? What are its positive and negative consequences?

What role should society play in our lives?

If the Universe will destruct someday, can we still have meaning in our lives?

Volume I - You & I Together - Have a Purpose In Reality
Chapter 8: The Mechanism

If the Universe can be destroyed, what purpose do we have in its existence?

What is the nature of the Universe?

How do we begin to address the problem of the Universe?

What is the creation process?

Why was the Universe created?

How can Mankind achieve a better understanding of its role within the Universe?

What is the 'missing link' to Mankind's understanding of itself?

What is the Creative Force, and what is its nature?

Does the destruction of the Universe undermine our purpose and value in existence?

Why do we as a species continue to be violent? Is there a solution to the problem?

Volume I - You & I Together - Have a Purpose In Reality
Chapter 9: The Missing Link

How are religion, philosophy, and science intertwined?

Are we, as a species, at a dangerous point in our history?

Why is there now an urgency for change for Mankind?

Why is there now a greater need for tolerance?

How can Mankind break the cycle of destruction that has been a significant part of its history?

What is Mankind's purpose, and what can we do as a species to facilitate it?

How are Mankind's and God's purposes interconnected?

Volume I - You & I Together - Have a Purpose In Reality
Chapter 10: Omnipotent/Omnipresent/Omniscience

If one possessed complete knowledge, what would be the consequences?

What are the three paradoxes of possessing complete knowledge?

What are the positive and negative aspects of faith and how do they relate to Mankind's future?

Why must we first take responsibility for our own lives?

How can Mankind eliminate the paradoxes of omnipotence, omnipresence, and omniscience?

What does Mankind first need to do in order to change?

What is the nature of the Creator? Is it compatible with Mankind's perceptions?

What role does Mankind play in the Creator's development and growth?

Volume I - You & I Together - Have a Purpose In Reality
Chapter 11: In Summary

What are the seven basic assumptions of 'the Philosophy'?

What impact does 'the Philosophy' have?

How does 'the Philosophy' address the question of Mankind's existence?

Present and future faith: what will be the effect on our self-perception?

What is the function of faith?

Volume I - You & I Together - Have a Purpose In Reality
Chapter 12: Man's Inhumanity To Man

What have been the greatest crimes of the 20th century?

What are the consequences of the Ripple Effect on Mankind's history?

What is the purpose of Mankind?

Does life have meaning?

How could a universal philosophy change our existence?

What do we need to do in order to attain a universal philosophy?

Volume I - You & I Together - Have a Purpose In Reality
Chapter 13: Man's Good Side

What does it mean to be 'good'?

What is Mankind's function in life?

What can Judas teach us about good and evil?

How do we begin building a better foundation for Mankind?

What are the implications of the Ripple Effect?

How would 'the Philosophy' change our perceptions?

Does Mankind possess a 'good' nature?

Volume I - You & I Together - Have a Purpose In Reality
Chapter 14: Is It Worth It In The End?

Do heaven and hell exist?

Is our present conception of heaven and hell an accurate representation of reality?

Is there life after death?

What are the implications of accepting life after death?

What are the consequences for us and God of living a 'good' life?

Volume I - You & I Together - Have a Purpose In Reality
Chapter 15: Is There Hope For You As An Individual?

Is there hope for you as an individual?

How does 'the Philosophy' approach the question of Mankind's purpose?

Is there hope for Mankind?

What are the consequences of the Ripple Effect?

Why do we need to be responsible for our actions?

What negative effects have the mass media had on Mankind?

Does religion have limits? How can it grow and change?

Volume I - You & I Together - Have a Purpose In Reality
Chapter 16: Is There Hope For Mankind?

Is there hope for Mankind?

Are we insignificant, or do we possess a higher purpose?

Do we control our destiny?

What are the pillars of a society?

What has history shown us? How can we learn its lessons?

Volume I - You & I Together - Have a Purpose In Reality
Chapter 17: Religion Is It: Significant/Necessary? Which One?

Is religion significant or necessary?

Which myths do we perpetuate within our society?

Are myths harmful?

What does Mankind need to do to reform religions?

How does Mankind's present perception limit God?

What do we need to do in order to find our purpose in reality?

Does Mankind have a purpose?

Volume I - You & I Together - Have a Purpose In Reality
Chapter 18: In Summary: The Soul

What is Mankind's nature?

What problems continue to plague society?

Are hierarchy and class distinctions necessary within a society?

What are the problems associated with hierarchy and class distinctions? Is there a better alternative?

Is there a solution to Mankind's problems?

What is Mankind's purpose? How can it be attained?

How are Mankind and the soul intertwined?

What is God's nature?

Volume I - You & I Together - Have a Purpose In Reality
Chapter 19: Class Status: Social/Occupational/Economic

Status - social, economic, and occupational - why has Mankind needed such labels and hierarchies?

Are hierarchies and labels necessary? What are the alternatives?

Why is status an illusion?

Why are all men ultimately equal?

Why does everyone make a contribution to life?

What is Mankind's purpose in life? How can it be best achieved?

Why must we help others find their purpose in life?

Should we dismantle status systems? What are the dangers in doing so?

What is meant by 'the journey of the soul'?

What can we learn about status and its relationship to the Ripple Effect?

Volume I - You & I Together - Have a Purpose In Reality
Chapter 20: Atheism

What do we mean by atheism?

Do atheists have a function in reality?

How do atheists contribute to our understanding and growth?

Should society discourage atheism?

Should atheists respect religious doctrines?

Atheism and the Ripple Effect: What are the consequences for the soul?

What is psychological violence?

How can a universal philosophy help solve the problem of psychological violence?

What does Mankind need to do now?

Volume I - You & I Together - Have a Purpose In Reality
Chapter 21: War/Abortion

Is it right or moral to interfere with another person's life and decisions?

Why are moral issues so difficult to resolve?

How does 'the Philosophy' approach the question of moral choices?

Is war ever just? What are the repercussions?

Is it ever right to take the life of an unborn baby?

What can Mankind do to help resolve the issue of abortion?

Why should we protect the rights of all souls?

What do we know about the soul and its relationship to the body?

Why must we have faith?

Volume I - You & I Together - Have a Purpose In Reality
Chapter 22: Suicide

Is suicide ever justified?

Do we have a right to interfere with another person's decisions about life and death?

Is suicide a solution to despair and sadness? What are the alternatives?

Is there an afterlife?

What are the implications of an afterlife for Mankind?

How are suicide and the Ripple Effect interconnected?

How does 'the Philosophy' approach the question of suicide?

Volume I - You & I Together - Have a Purpose In Reality
Chapter 23: Capital Punishment/Life Incarceration

Capital punishment or life incarceration? What are the consequences for the soul?

What is meant by 'debt to society'?

How has society responded to the question of crime and its punishment? Are there better alternatives?

Does punishment harm criminals or society most, or both?

What can we do to ensure the safety of other souls?

How does 'the Philosophy' approach the question of capital punishment and life incarceration?

Capital punishment or life incarceration: how do they relate to the Ripple Effect?

What can society do, other than enforce capital punishment or life incarceration, to ensure its own safety and protection?

What can society do to help other souls?

Do we have the right to end the life of another?

What are the rights of criminals? Do they outweigh those of victims?

Volume I - You & I Together - Have a Purpose In Reality
Chapter 24: Letting Go/Forgiving

What is our nature? Are we God or are we just human? Are we both?

What are the repercussions of crime within society? Who are the real victims?

Why does society need to reevaluate its treatment of both criminals and victims?

How could a universal philosophy, such as 'the Philosophy', help victims of crime?

Why must we always accept responsibility for our actions and their consequences?

How would 'the Philosophy' force us to reassess society's rules and laws?

What are the responsibilities of parenting? What is meant by 'letting go'?

How does 'letting go' relate to our behavior within society?

Volume I - You & I Together - Have a Purpose In Reality
Chapter 25: Missionary Work/Helping Others

Are we all missionaries?

How does 'the Philosophy' relate to missionary work?

What is the relevance of missionary work? Is it necessary?

How do we ensure the safety of the soul?

Is the soul a part of God? Why would He allow the soul to be harmed?

How does God increase His omniscience, omnipotence, and omnipresence? Does He need the soul to do so?

What is the purpose of life?

Is Mankind suffering from an overload of information within society? What have been the effects?

Why is there a need for a universal philosophy?

How does 'the Philosophy' relate to religion?

How does 'the Philosophy' provide a foundation to build on?

Why is everyone unique and important?

Volume I - You & I Together - Have a Purpose In Reality
Chapter 26: In Summary: Intolerance Is An Outmoded Term

How does intolerance create social dilemmas?

Why doesn't society accept differences and unique qualities in individuals?

Why should people from all religions, races, and genders be given equal respect and consideration?

What is the function of religion? How does it relate to the soul?

What must society do to become more tolerant?

What is a universal philosophy? How could it be successfully applied to our present society?

What is the purpose of the soul? Is society, in its present form, hindering the soul's growth?

Volume I - You & I Together - Have a Purpose In Reality
Chapter 27: God/gods

Does God conform to the definitions we have of Him?

Why are all religions important?

Is one definition of God more true than another?

What relationship does our past history have to our future?

Why is it so important that we examine our past behavior? What lessons can it teach us?

Regardless of Mankind's origin, why is our future so important?

What is God's nature?

What are the consequences of the Ripple Effect?

What is the function of the soul?

Do we have a commonality with our fellow man?

Volume I - You & I Together - Have a Purpose In Reality
Chapter 28: Good/Bad: Misnomers

What function have the concepts of good and evil played in Mankind's history?

Why is it necessary for Mankind to move beyond labels of good or evil, moral or immoral, right or wrong?

What is sin?

Why is it necessary for us to take responsibility for our actions?

What is the Ripple Effect?

How will our behavior affect the future?

Volume I - You & I Together - Have a Purpose In Reality
Chapter 29: Heaven and Hell

What is heaven and hell?

How are Mankind's and God's purposes interconnected?

What are the consequences of the Ripple Effect?

Why is it necessary for Mankind to be responsible?

What are the limits of Mankind?

What repercussions do positive and negative actions have on the soul?

Does God punish?

Does heaven and hell exist?

Volume I - You & I Together - Have a Purpose In Reality
Chapter 30: 'God Is Going To Get You For That'

Why does Mankind believe that vengeance is God's way?

Why do religions perpetuate the belief that God is vengeful?

What contradictions are there in the belief that God is vengeful?

What is God's nature and essence?

Why do we believe that personal tragedies and dilemmas are God's way of punishing us?

What do religions need to do to guide Mankind?

How can 'the Philosophy' provide a foundation for religions?

What are the consequences of the Ripple Effect?

Who are we? Who is God?

What does Mankind need to do now?

Volume I - You & I Together - Have a Purpose In Reality
Chapter 31: Christianity/Religion

How do Christianity and 'the Philosophy' differ?

Are all religions truly religions?

What is 'the Philosophy'? Is it a religion?

What does 'the Philosophy' seek to do?

How are 'the Philosophy' and religion interconnected?

What do religions need to do in order to maintain their beliefs and traditions?

What is Mankind's purpose in reality?

Why should we encourage religious diversity?

What do religions need to do now?

Volume I - You & I Together - Have a Purpose In Reality
Chapter 32: Jesus Christ

Who was Jesus Christ?

Why did God send Jesus Christ?

What did Jesus Christ wish to achieve?

Are different religions compatible?

Should we accept and encourage religious differences?

Why should we be tolerant of other religious beliefs?

What is the function of religion?

What does 'the Philosophy' say about the purpose of the soul?

Do Christianity and other religions have the same purpose?

Volume I - You & I Together - Have a Purpose In Reality
Chapter 33: In Summary

What role do the past, present, and future play in our lives?

Why is it important to study the past?

Why should we maintain and encourage religious traditions and beliefs?

Why is it important that we now develop a universal philosophy?

What are the consequences of the Ripple Effect on our souls?

What is Mankind's purpose in reality?

What are some of the most important questions facing Mankind? How can we best address them?

Volume II - In the Image of God
Chapter 1: To Begin

How do 'social' and 'moral' laws interfere with making ethical and moral choices?

In making an ethical decision, what are the three guides available to us?

What is social morality?

What is religious morality?

•

How can contradictions occur in deciding moral issues?

Why is Humankind's present understanding of reality inadequate in dealing with moral and ethical decisions?

Are there moral contradictions within religion?

•

How would a universal philosophy resolve moral issues?

What is Humankind's purpose?

What is the soul? What is its function?

What is the relationship between the soul and God?

Volume II - In the Image of God
Chapter 2: Only Words

What do we mean by the terms 'life' and 'death'? How can we arrive at a clear definition of both?

Why is the issue of abortion such a controversial issue within society? Who has suffered as a consequence?

When does life begin and end?

What does science tell us about life and death?

•

Why has our present theistic approach to the question of life and death been unsuccessful?

What does theism tell us about the relationship between God and Humankind?

•

How does symbiotic panentheism differ from theism in its approach to the question of Humankind's existence and purpose?

Does symbiotic panentheism undermine established religions?

If the basic tenets of symbiotic panentheism were adopted, who would benefit?

Volume II - In the Image of God
Chapter 3: The Choice

What can social science tell us about human nature? How would its conclusions influence Humankind's self-perception?

In accepting a limited self-perception, how would Humankind and God lose?

•

How does theism define God?

What is the nature of reality? Is Humankind's present understanding of it accurate?

What are the dangers of continuing a theistic philosophy?

•

If Humankind adopted symbiotic panentheism, what would be the consequences?

What is God's nature? Why is Humankind an integral part of God's existence and growth?

Are God and Humankind interconnected? Does Humankind share a symbiotic relationship with God?

Does Humankind have a higher purpose?

Volume II - In the Image of God
Chapter 4: Slavery Is Slavery

Is Humankind's belief in its origins accurate? Are we native to the Earth or did we originate elsewhere?

How do our present beliefs limit our freedom and growth?

What is the nature of slavery? How does Humankind's present self-perception enslave it?

Why was Humankind created? Does it have a higher purpose?

•

If we perceive ourselves to be servants of God, what are the consequences for Humankind?

How does maintaining a belief in theism limit our growth? Would symbiotic panentheism resolve the problem?

What is the nature of reality? How do theism and symbiotic panentheism differ in their approaches to the question?

•

How would symbiotic panentheism resolve Humankind's greatest challenges?

How would adopting symbiotic panentheism liberate us from the dangers of slavery?

In not possessing a universal philosophy, what limitations are imposed on Humankind?

If Humankind adopted symbiotic panentheism, how would God's omnipotence, omniscience, and omnipresence expand and grow?

Volume II - In the Image of God
Chapter 5: Humanity Sentenced To Life

Where did Humankind originate? Are we native to the Earth, or were we placed here for a reason?

How can we explain our propensity for violence and conflict?

Are we inferior as a species?

•

Why does Humankind allow itself to maintain a subservient position to God?

How can Humankind break free from the stigmatizing, degrading, and shallow-minded philosophy of theism?

If theism places a limit on Humankind's growth, does it also hinder God's growth?

If Humankind maintains its present theistic beliefs, what effect will it have on the future?

•

How would symbiotic panentheism alter our relationship to God?

How would a universal philosophy alter Humankind's self-perception?

Who would benefit from the adoption of symbiotic panentheism?

Volume II - In the Image of God
Chapter 6: Trapped

How does the structure of a Klein bottle help explain the structure of the Universe?

If the Universe possesses a boundary, what does it imply for Humankind's presence and value within it?

In a bounded Universe, could Humankind still have a purpose in reality?

•

How do our present theistic beliefs ultimately limit God's omnipotence, omnipresence, and omniscience?

Is Humankind insignificant to God?

What are the dangers, both for Humankind and God, of possessing a flawed perception of reality?

•

In terms of the Universe, what is the difference between emptiness and nothingness?

How does Humankind's presence within the Universe help increase God's omnipotence, omnipresence, and omniscience?

How would symbiotic panentheism alter Humankind's perception of itself?

In adopting symbiotic panentheism, how would Humankind move from its position of subservience to one of magnificence?

Volume II - In the Image of God
Chapter 7: Collapse

If the Universe is bounded, what would be the nature of its structure?

How does the structure of a Klein bottle resemble the structure of the Universe?

Why does Humankind's faulty self-perception ultimately limit God's omnipotence, omnipresence, and omniscience?

•

How do theism and symbiotic panentheism differ in their approaches to Humankind's value and purpose?

What is God's relationship to reality?

How do theistic beliefs limit God's growth?

•

What does symbiotic panentheism tell us about Humankind's future?

What is the difference between emptiness and nothingness in terms of the Universe?

If Humankind's future will eventually end, can it still find meaning in its temporary existence?

What does symbiotic panentheism tell us about Humankind's symbiotic relationship with God?

Volume II - In the Image of God
Chapter 8: The Nightmare

What is the nature of reality? Is it a dream? Is it imagination?

If reality is a dream, what can it tell us about Humankind's self-perception?

Is it possible for Humankind to find a purpose within this reality?

•

How does theism lead us to a flawed perception of ourselves and of our purpose in reality?

How do flawed self-perceptions enslave and limit us?

•

Can Humankind attain a higher significance and purpose?

How does Humankind's present self-perception limit God's omnipotence, omnipresence, and omniscience? Is there a solution to the problem?

Who is the Creator? What relationship does the Creator share with Humankind?

How can we best reap the benefits of symbiotic panentheism? How can we attain our true significance in reality?

Volume II - In the Image of God
Chapter 9: A Toy

What is the fundamental building block of the Universe?

If Humankind could create matter, would it then have attained the status of God?

In creating matter, how would science and religion respond to the consequences? Would Humankind be elevated as a species or would it be undermined?

•

Is Humankind God's toy? Does it have a higher value and purpose?

Is Humankind a servant of God?

How would our present theistic beliefs limit Humankind's and God's growth and development?

How would religion, in its present form, perpetuate the problem of Humankind's status with God?

•

How would symbiotic panentheism address the issue of Humankind's purpose within the Universe?

How does symbiotic panentheism elevate Humankind to an equal status with God?

Why is Humankind so important to God?

In adopting symbiotic panentheism, what benefits would there be for Humankind?

Volume II - In the Image of God
Chapter 10: Growing

Does the Universe remain in a state of equilibrium or does it change and grow?

If the Universe were in a state of equilibrium, what would be the negative consequences?

Why is it necessary for the Universe to change and grow?

•

Does religion need to examine and change its present perception of reality? If it does not, what will be the consequences for Humankind?

In their present form, do religions hinder Humankind's growth and future?

Why does religion allow Humankind to see itself as inferior to God? Why is this wrong, for both Humankind and God?

•

How would symbiotic panentheism address the issue of Humankind's negative self-perception?

Does symbiotic panentheism wish to eliminate religion?

How is symbiotic panentheism important in addressing Humankind's uniqueness and value?

Why should Humankind see itself as equal, and not subservient, to God?

What does symbiotic panentheism say about God's nature and essence?

Volume II - In the Image of God
Chapter 11: "Typhoid Mary"

Why has Humankind been unable to change its viewpoint regarding its relationship to the Creator?

Why does Humankind accept a position of subservience to the Creator?

How does Humankind's limited self-perception ultimately limit other species? How does it limit the Creator?

•

What danger does theism pose for both ourselves and other species?

Why have the basic assumptions of theism had such destructive effects on Humankind's history?

Does theism undermine Humankind's potential for growth? Would it also undermine another species?

•

How would adopting symbiotic panentheism change Humankind's self-perception, and ultimately, its future?

In adopting symbiotic panentheism, how would other species in the Universe benefit? How would the Creator benefit?

In accepting ourselves as part of the Creator, what would be the consequences for Humankind?

Volume II - In the Image of God
Chapter 12: Twins

What is the universal sound 'Om'? What is its significance?

What is the nature of the Universe?

What is the nature of reality?

How does the structure of a Klein bottle resemble the structure of the Universe? What importance does it have for Humankind's understanding of reality and of its place within the Universe?

•

How do our present theistic beliefs respond to the fact that the Universe will eventually be destroyed?

Why do our theistic beliefs continue to place Humankind in a subservient position to God?

How can our theistic beliefs be harmful? What can we do to avoid undermining Humankind's importance in reality?

•

What does symbiotic panentheism tell us about the Universe and Humankind's importance within it?

Why can we find meaning and purpose within a Universe that will ultimately be destroyed? What does symbiotic panentheism tell us about our value to God?

Why are we so important to God? Why is it dangerous to see ourselves as subservient, rather than equal, to God?

How could symbiotic panentheism enable us to grow and evolve within the Universe? How could it enable God to also grow and evolve?

Volume II - In the Image of God

Chapter 13: Contact

If new life forms were discovered in our Universe, what effect would this discovery have on Humankind?

What are the positive and negative issues involved in dealing with another intelligent species? How would we have to reevaluate our present values and beliefs?

How could a new species undermine our values and cause dissent among particular social, racial, and religious groups within our society?

•

In which ways would our present theistic beliefs put us at a disadvantage in dealing with other intelligent, but not benevolent, species in the Universe?

How does our present understanding of reality affect our self-esteem and value?

Why do we continue to endorse a belief system that weakens our ability to attain our purpose in reality? Are there more constructive alternatives available?

•

How would symbiotic panentheism approach the issue of other intelligent life forms in the Universe?

In which ways would symbiotic panentheism allow Humankind to attain its purpose in reality, and to maintain its self-esteem and dignity as a species?

What does symbiotic panentheism tell us about Humankind and its relationship to God? How do our beliefs affect the future of both Humankind and God?

Volume II - In the Image of God
Chapter 14: Quadruplets

What is the structure of the Universe? What can it tell us about our place within it, and of our value?

Does a self-destructive Universe imply that Humankind's existence lacks value?

Does Humankind have a finite or infinite future? In which ways do we have both? What does the question tell us about Humankind's relationship with God?

•

Is it possible to find meaning in a finite Universe? How is our self-esteem undermined by limited perceptions?

How is Humankind, and ultimately God, affected by our limited self-perception?

Why do our present concepts of theism and pantheism limit our ability to reach our full potential?

•

How would symbiotic panentheism free us from our limited self-perception?

If symbiotic panentheism were adopted by Humankind, what would be the immediate benefits? What are the long-term benefits for both Humankind and God?

How would other species in the Universe be affected by Humankind's adoption of symbiotic panentheism?

What are the immediate and long-term dangers of continuing to choose theism, rather than symbiotic panentheism, as the foundation for our beliefs?

Volume II - In the Image of God
Chapter 15: A Doorway

What are the dangers for Humankind of discovering that the Universe is structured differently than was previously believed?

Is Humankind at a stage in its development whereby it could adapt its self-perception in response to new scientific knowledge concerning the structure of the Universe? Could Humankind retain its dignity as a consequence of such knowledge?

•

If the structure of the Universe was different than was previously assumed, would Humankind's present theistic beliefs help to maintain its dignity or would it undermine it?

What are the dangers for Humankind of continuing theistic beliefs? Is there a better belief system that would enable Humankind to retain its dignity unconditionally?

What are the dangers for other species if we continue to maintain, and spread, our theistic beliefs?

•

How would Humankind benefit from changing its perception from theism to symbiotic panentheism? How would Humankind grow as a species?

How would symbiotic panentheism help to maintain Humankind's dignity and purpose in reality?

What would be the universal benefits of Humankind's adoption of symbiotic panentheism? How would alien species also benefit?

Volume II - In the Image of God
Chapter 16: Perfection

What ethical and moral issues are involved in communicating with other species in the Universe?

What are the dangers, for both Humankind and alien species, of spreading our present beliefs and values into the Universe?

How could Humankind become enslaved by another species as a consequence of our present perceptions?

•

In which ways does theism force Humankind into lowering its self-perception and value? What are the alternatives?

How would our present theistic beliefs put us at a disadvantage in our dealings with other species in the Universe?

How is God affected by our negative belief systems? What are the consequences for the soul?

•

How would symbiotic panentheism approach the question of contact with other species in the Universe?

In which ways does symbiotic panentheism allow Humankind to retain its dignity within a self-destructive Universe?

What is Humankind's purpose? How does it relate to God's growth and exploration of reality?

Volume II - In the Image of God
Chapter 17: More . . .

What is Humankind's status within the Universe?

If the Universe will finally self-destruct, do we still have purpose and meaning within it?

If the Universe will finally end, does this mean that our lives, and our worship of God, has had no value? Has God betrayed Humankind?

•

What will be the negative consequences for society in maintaining our belief in theism?

In which ways does theism trap Humankind into continuing to perpetuate hierarchy and status within society?

What will be the cost, to Humankind, God, and the soul, of continuing to adhere to theistic beliefs?

•

What does symbiotic panentheism tell us about finding meaning within a self-destructive Universe? Is it possible to have a meaningful existence? What is our purpose?

What does symbiotic panentheism tell us about Humankind's relationship with God? How are they both interconnected in reality?

Do God and Humankind share an equal status with each other? What is the purpose of Humankind and the soul?

How can Humankind find purpose and significance in a self-destructive Universe?

Volume II - In the Image of God
Chapter 18: The Fall

What is "The Great Debate?"

What is our purpose in reality?

Could we be surpassed, and enslaved, one day?

•

How does our self-perception affect our future?

Why is all life of equal importance?

Should we allow ourselves to be dominated by another species?

•

How would symbiotic panentheism address the issue of justice and equality?

Why is all life in the Universe worthy of respect?

Why should we be treated with respect and dignity?

Volume II - In the Image of God
Chapter 19: Solitary

What are the implications for Humankind of existing within a bounded Universe?

What are the consequences for Humankind of continuing its linear perception of reality?

How could an alien species enslave Humankind? Why would our present beliefs allow this to happen?

•

Why does theism allow Humankind to perceive itself as inferior to God, and inferior to other species?

How would quadratic thinking allow Humankind to break free of its present and limited self-perception?

What is Humankind's future if it continues to adhere to its present perception of reality?

•

What does symbiotic panentheism tell us about existing within a bounded Universe?

What is the nature and purpose of the soul?

How can Humankind attain its full potential and purpose in reality?

Why is Humankind important and vital to God's existence?

Volume II - In the Image of God
Chapter 20: The Light

Why is it so important that we develop a universal philosophy for Humankind?

How will our self-perception affect Humankind's future? How will it affect the soul? How will it affect God?

What are the three philosophical perceptions of reality that have been so influential in Humankind's history? Why are their similarities and differences so important and consequential?

•

How does theism define Humankind's place in reality? How does pantheism?

In which way does theistic beliefs lead to a self-perception of inferiority and subjugation to God?

What is pantheism, and how does it differ from theism and symbiotic panentheism?

•

What are the subtle, but extremely important, differences between theism and symbiotic panentheism?

In which way is our reality only temporary? How is it separate from eternity?

How does our negative behavior damage us? How does it affect the soul; how does it affect God?

What is Humankind's purpose in reality? How would a universal philosophy help achieve it?

Volume II - In the Image of God
Chapter 21: The Point

Why is it necessary for Humankind to achieve a universal perception of morality? Why has it been so difficult to do so?

In which ways could mathematics and geometry lead to the formulation of a universal philosophy, and a universal morality?

How are logic and morality interconnected?

•

Why are our current perceptions of 'right' and 'wrong' inadequate?

How do our present theistic beliefs limit our perception of the value and importance of Humankind, and the soul, to God?

•

How would symbiotic panentheism provide a foundation for making moral decisions?

What is Humankind's purpose in reality? How would a universal philosophy help attain this purpose?

What are the limits of symbiotic panentheism? Is it a comprehensive philosophy or a foundation for more growth?

Volume II - In the Image of God
Chapter 22: A Sigh

Is Humankind's journey at an end or is it just beginning?

Why is it necessary for us to change our behavior and take responsibility for our lives and our destiny?

Why is the future important? What can we do, in the present, to ensure that the future will be good and fruitful?

*

Why does theism hinder our purpose and journey in reality?

In which ways do status and hierarchy hinder our ability to grow and achieve our purpose in reality?

How is the soul, and ultimately God, affected by our theistic beliefs?

*

What does symbiotic panentheism tell us about our actions, and the effect they have on the future?

Why is it vital that we participate fully in the journey of life?

Why is it important that we reject passivity and submission?

Why should we all be visionaries?

What does symbiotic panentheism tell us about the significance of every life and soul?

Volume II - In the Image of God
Chapter 23: Reflections - 3000 A.D.

Why must Humankind take responsibility for its actions?

What is meant by 'free will'? Do we have a choice in our actions and behavior?

How can we use our free will to choose constructive, rather than destructive, actions and behavior?

How does our self-perception influence our actions, both towards ourselves and towards others?

•

How do our present theistic beliefs, with their emphasis on Humankind's inferiority to God, limit both Humankind and God?

Why is violence and abuse a direct result of our belief in hierarchy and status?

How is the soul diminished by theistic beliefs and perceptions?

What is social morality? How is it influenced by our present self-perception?

•

What does symbiotic panentheism tell us about Humankind's status with God?

Why is the soul so important to Humankind and to God?

How would status, hierarchy, and abuse be eliminated by the adoption of symbiotic panentheism?

Volume II - In the Image of God
Chapter 24: Companions

Why is changing our perceptions and behavior difficult? Why is it feared?

What is meant by 'logic and faith'? Are logic and faith compatible with religion? How would symbiotic panentheism address the issue?

•

Why do present theistic beliefs reject the concept of a companion in reality? Why would symbiotic panentheism be a good companion?

In which ways are religion and symbiotic panentheism different? In which ways are they similar?

•

How would symbiotic panentheism elevate the importance of the Creator?

Why should we strive to maintain our religious beliefs?

In which way is religion our first mentor?

Why is a universal philosophy for Humankind important? How would symbiotic panentheism facilitate it?

In which ways does symbiotic panentheism add to, rather than diminish, present religions?

Volume II - In the Image of God
Chapter 25: Understanding

Why do violence and conflict continue to inflict society?

Why do our present beliefs set the foundation for conflict and abuse within society?

In which ways do our beliefs give rise to an acceptance of hierarchy and status? What is the alternative?

•

Why is theism resistant to embracing symbiotic panentheism?

Why is it difficult to change our perceptions and the actions that follow them?

What will be the consequences of resisting symbiotic panentheism and continuing our theistic beliefs?

•

How would symbiotic panentheism address the issue of status, hierarchy, and power within society?

How could embracing symbiotic panentheism create a universal philosophy - one of equality and tolerance for all Humankind, and all species?

What will be the consequences, for Humankind and for God, of resisting symbiotic panentheism?

Why is Humankind and God of equal importance and status? Why are they both important to each other?

Volume II - In the Image of God

Chapter 26: Panentheism, the Soul, Reality

Understanding pantheism, theism, and panentheism: What do they tell us about God and Reality? What do they tell us about ourselves?

How does panentheism differ from both theism and pantheism? Why is the difference important for our understanding of Humankind's value and purpose?

Why is it vital that we now develop a universal philosophy? How would the adoption of symbiotic panentheism achieve this universal philosophy?

What have been the arguments both for and against the existence of God? Which is true?

Why was our Universe created? How does it relate to God's omniscience and growth?

What are the dangers for Humankind of continuing to adhere to theistic perceptions and beliefs?

What is the Ripple Effect? Why is it so important to Humankind's purpose in reality?

Why is it necessary that we take responsibility for our actions and behavior?

How are Humankind, the soul, and God interdependent?

Volume II - In the Image of God
Chapter 27: The Soul

What is Humankind's purpose in reality?

Do we need to change our perception of our value?

Why is every life, and every soul, significant?

How are Humankind and God interdependent? Why are they important to each other?

What can physics tell us about the nature of the Universe, and Humankind's existence within it?

•

Why are our present theistic beliefs so limited by comparison to what they could be?

How does our limited self-perception influence our actions? What are the consequences for society?

•

How would symbiotic panentheism set the foundation for resolving our social problems and dilemmas?

Why is Humankind of phenomenal value and significance to God?

What does symbiotic panentheism tell us about our present actions and behavior? What is the significance of the Ripple Effect?

How does our positive and negative actions affect God? How would symbiotic panentheism address the question?

Volume II - In the Image of God
Chapter 28: . . . Ism's

What kind of abuses are perpetrated within society? How can we successfully eliminate them?

Why is power and control such pervasive factors in the behavior of many social institutions and groups?

Who is truly exploited within society? Who are the real victims?

•

In which ways does our present perception of reality hinder our ability to resolve society's most pressing dilemmas?

Why is there so much intolerance and injustice within society?

Are there any groups within society who cannot contribute to life's journey? Is everyone unique and valuable?

•

What does symbiotic panentheism tell us about the importance of every life and soul? Why are we all unique and valuable?

How would a universal philosophy address the issue of social injustice?

Why do we need to resist, both for our own sake and for God, intolerance and bigotry? In which way is the individual, and their soul, so important to God?

What is the soul's purpose in reality? How does it relate to Humankind's actions? How does it relate to God?

Volume II - In the Image of God
Chapter 29: The Circle

Why is everyone's journey through life important and valuable? Why are we all unique?

What is the relationship between the Ripple Effect and the soul's journey?

What is meant by the "significance of reality"?

How can our limited perceptions lead to self-violence?

•

Why are we often tempted to accept a limited and restrictive view of life's importance?

How can our principles be compromised by a limited perception of reality?

How does theism limit our ability to see the importance of each life and soul?

•

What does symbiotic panentheism tell us about the importance of attaining a universal philosophy?

Why is it vital that we accept responsibility for our life's journey?

What does symbiotic panentheism say about the importance of every soul?

How are the soul and God interrelated?

What does symbiotic panentheism say about the soul and the consequences of the Ripple Effect?

Volume II - In the Image of God
Chapter 30: Your Essence

Why is it important that we continue to seek truth and knowledge?

Why is some research so controversial? Why is it often rejected, rather than embraced and understood?

Is there such a thing as 'exploitative' research?

Why is it always necessary to question our status within society? How are we all equal, irrespective of race, class or gender?

•

How does theism limit our ability to achieve our full potential?

Why is Humankind often intolerant with respect to differences among different racial, economic, and social groups?

In which ways does Humankind limit its own potential and purpose in reality? How does it limit the soul? How does it, ultimately, limit God?

•

Why is it necessary for Humankind to move beyond intolerance and instead embrace the importance of every individual and soul? In which ways are we all important?

What does symbiotic panentheism offer us in terms of a universal philosophy?

Why does symbiotic panentheism stress the importance of each soul's journey? What does it tell us about reaching our full potential?

Volume II - In the Image of God
Chapter 31: The Glue

Why are women relegated to a position of subservience and inferiority within society?

What are the consequences, both for Humankind and the soul, of accepting subservience within society? How is God affected?

Why is it necessary for Humankind to have a universal philosophy? How would it help resolve social dilemmas?

•

Why do our social institutions allow problems within society to continue? Is their role to alleviate problems temporarily, or instead to solve them completely?

Are social institutions a reflection of society?

•

What does symbiotic panentheism tell us about subservience within society? Does it endorse or reject it?

Why is it important that we understand who we are and what our purpose is in reality?

Why are we all responsible for improving society?

How can we aid the soul's journey?

Why is it necessary for Humankind to change its perception regarding status and hierarchy? If it does not, how will the soul, and God, be affected?

How would symbiotic panentheism help to revolutionize society and its institutions?

Volume II - In the Image of God
Chapter 32: Points

What are the ultimate consequences of our negative actions?

Why does our flawed and limited perception of reality hinder our ability to attain our purpose in reality?

What does the Ripple Effect tell us about our actions?

•

In which ways does theism allow us to continue our negative behavior?

Why does theism see Humankind as subservient to God?

How will maintaining our theistic beliefs allow crime, poverty, and abuse to continue? Is there a better alternative?

How do our theistic beliefs limit God?

•

What does symbiotic panentheism tell us about a universal philosophy? What benefits would that philosophy have for Humankind?

What does symbiotic panentheism say about Humankind's relationship to God?

In which way would symbiotic panentheism allow all of Humankind to share a common goal and purpose in reality?

Volume II - In the Image of God
Chapter 33: It's Time

Why has the issue of partial-birth abortion been controversial? What mistakes have been made regarding this issue?

Why is it difficult to find the truth within society?

If partial-birth abortion continues, what will be the consequences for the soul, and ultimately, God?

•

Why do our theistic beliefs hinder our ability to attain a new perception of reality?

How and why do social institutions resist changing their destructive behavior?

In which ways do our present theistic beliefs limit the soul and God?

•

How would symbiotic panentheism address the issue of partial-birth abortion?

Why is it necessary for Humankind to redefine its purpose in reality? What will be the benefits if it does? What will be the consequences if it does not?

Why is Humankind, and the soul, important to God?

Volume III - Stepping Up To The Creator
Religion: Hinduism - 1500 BC *# 100-109*

In which way has Hinduism provided the foundation for other religious faiths?

Why is the Hindu concept of monotheism so important for Humankind?

What does Hinduism tell us about the nature of the soul and its relationship to the Causative Force?

How are Humankind and science in agreement with regards to the nature and structure of the Universe?

How does Humankind's negative behavior affect the Causative Force? In which way does Hinduism address the problem?

What does Hinduism tell us about our existence both within and outside of the Universe? In which way do we all possess significance in eternity?

Why is it necessary that we treat all life forms in the Universe with equal respect?

What does Hinduism tell us about the soul, and our awareness, after our death?

What will happen to our soul if the Universe is destroyed?

Why is Hinduism so important to the concept of symbiotic panentheism?

Volume III - Stepping Up To The Creator
Religion: Judaism - 1000 BC *# 110-119*

In which way did Judaism bring the concept of monotheism to the West?

What have been the effects of Judaic teaching on the modern world?

What does Judaism tell us about the Causative Force?

What are the differences between Judaism and panentheism? What have they both in common?

What does Judaism tell us about the immortality of the soul?

Why is humanitarian behavior a natural outcome of Judaic and panentheistic beliefs?

What does Judaism tell us about the nature of the Universe and our perception of reality?

Why is Humankind, and the soul, so important to the Causative Force?

What has been the global significance of Judaism?

Why is Judaism so important to the concept of symbiotic panentheism?

Volume III - Stepping Up To The Creator
Religion: Buddhism - 500 BC *# 120-129*

Why is the elimination of suffering such an important aspect of Buddhist philosophy and teaching?

Why does Humankind's acceptance of status and hierarchy systems lead to abuse and suffering?

How does our behavior, both positive and negative, affect the Causative Force?

Why is it so important that we as a species eliminate suffering within society?

How can our actions, both good and bad, have such a significant effect on the future? What do we mean by 'the Ripple Effect'?

What is the significance of all life? How is the soul and eternity interconnected?

How will our experiences affect the Causative Force?

Why should Humankind respect all other life forms in the Universe? Why should they, in turn, respect us?

What are the consequences and responsibilities of possessing free will?

Why is Buddhism so important to the concept of symbiotic panentheism?

Volume III - Stepping Up To The Creator
Religion: Christianity - 0 BC *# 130-139*

In which ways did Christianity expand the concept of love to include all of Humankind?

Why is the concept of universal love so important to us as individuals? Why is it so important for society?

How do our positive and negative actions affect the Causative Force? How will they affect our own future in eternity?

What will happen to our soul after our death? How will it affect the Causative Force?

Why is our understanding of our relationship to the Causative Force so important? How will it influence the way we treat each other?

In which way are we all a part of the Causative Force?

How will our acceptance of universal love affect our perception of, and actions towards, other life forms in the Universe?

How is our soul, and its significance, tied to eternity?

Why should the elimination of suffering be Humankind's greatest priority?

Why is Christianity so important to the concept of symbiotic panentheism?

Volume III - Stepping Up To The Creator
Religion: Islam - 500 AD *# 140-149*

Why is the elimination of suffering such an important aspect of Islamic teaching?

What role does justice play in Islamic teaching?

Why is it so important that Humankind attain social justice?

What will be the consequences of Humankind's negative and positive behavior on the Causative Force?

Why are we all finally responsible for our behavior and actions?

Why is the Ripple Effect so important in how we perceive our actions towards each other?

What is the nature and destiny of the soul in eternity?

How will our perception of each other affect our treatment of other life forms in the Universe?

Why is life, all life, important and valuable?

Why is Islamic teaching important to the concept of symbiotic panentheism?

Volume III - Stepping Up To The Creator
Religion: Ontological Argument - 1000 BC *# 150-159*

Why do we believe that a Causative Force exists?

What is an ontological argument? What are its repercussions for Humankind?

Why does Humankind seem to constantly seek a Causative Force?

What is the nature of the Universe?

What are the consequences of an omnipresent Causative Force?

Why would the Causative Force have created the Universe?

Why is it vital that we establish a clear definition of life?

Why does Humankind possess significance within the Universe?

What is the relationship between Humankind and the Causative Force?

Why is ontological argument important to the concept of symbiotic panentheism?

Volume III - Stepping Up To The Creator
Religion: Modern Science - 1500 AD *# 160-169*

Why has science played such a significant role in our understanding of the Universe and our place within it?

What is the nature of the Universe? What exists outside of its boundary?

What is the significance of Humankind within the Universe?

Why should other life forms in the Universe be treated with equality and respect?

What is the nature and function of the soul?

How is Humankind, and other life forms within the Universe, interconnected and interdependent?

Why is it so important that we eliminate suffering?

What is the Ripple Effect? How does it affect our future?

In which way are we all a part of the Causative Force?

Why is modern science important to the concept of symbiotic panentheism?

Volume III - Stepping Up To The Creator
Religion: Atheism *# 170-179*

What does atheism imply about the nature of the Universe?

What are the ultimate consequences of atheistic beliefs?

Does the Universe have a beginning and end? Does it possess a boundary?

Is life significant? What is its significance under atheism?

In which ways does atheism limit Humankind? How does it also limit the Causative Force?

What does atheism imply about Humankind's significance in eternity?

What relationship is there between atheism and the Causative Force?

How is the Causative Force and Humankind interdependent?

Who created the Causative Force?

Why is atheism important to the concept of symbiotic panentheism?

Volume III - Stepping Up To The Creator
Religion: Classical/Traditional Theism *# 180-189*

If the Causative Force is omnipresent, are we then a part of the Causative Force?

Why is 'transcendence' a contradiction of the idea of an omnipresent Causative Force?

What exists outside the boundary of the Universe?

How does classical theism help us to understand the Causative Force's relationship to the Universe and to Humankind?

Why is Humankind, as well as other life within the Universe, so important to the Causative Force?

What relationship does life have to eternity?

What roles do religion, philosophy, and science play in our understanding of ourselves and our destiny?

Why are our actions, both positive and negative, important?

Why is it necessary for Humankind to eliminate hierarchy and status within society?

Why is classical/traditional theism important to the concept of symbiotic panentheism?

Volume III - Stepping Up To The Creator
Religion: Panentheism - 2000 AD *# 190-199*

Under panentheism, what is Humankind's relationship to the Causative Force?

Why will it be necessary to modify some of our present religious perceptions?

How does panentheism show that we have meaning and purpose, even within a Universe that will eventually be destroyed?

How are panentheism and omnipresence interconnected?

Why is Humankind important and valuable to the Causative Force?

How does Humankind affect the Causative Force?

Under panentheism, why is all life within the Universe vital and important?

What is Humankind's purpose in reality?

How could panentheism provide solutions to present and future social dilemmas?

Volume III - Stepping Up To The Creator
Science: Entropy *# 200-209*

How does entropy relate to the destruction of the Universe?

What happens to our soul after death?

Is the Universe alive?

What exists beyond the boundary of our Universe?

How does entropy reinforce the concept of panentheism?

Where is the Universe located?

Why is all life within the Universe vital and sacred?

How can entropy help explain the nature of the Universe? How can it help explain the nature of life?

If our Universe will finally end, as entropy implies, can Humankind still find meaning and purpose in reality?

Why is entropy important to the concept of symbiotic panentheism?

Volume III - Stepping Up To The Creator

Science: The Big Bang *# 210-219*

What does The Big Bang tell us about the origin and future of our Universe?

In a fundamental sense, what are the three choices we possess in conducting our behavior?

Why is growth and change such an important aspect of our journey through life?

Is awareness eternal or does it end after we die?

If awareness is eternal, where does it go after our death?

How are awareness and the soul interconnected?

What will be the effects of our behavior, both as individuals and as a species, on eternity?

Why is all life of equal value?

Why is Humankind and the Causative Force interdependent?

Why is The Big Bang important to the concept of symbiotic panentheism?

Volume III - Stepping Up To The Creator
Science: Symmetry *# 220-229*

How does the concept of symmetry help us to understand the structure of the Universe?

How is it possible that our Universe could be created from nothingness?

How does panentheism relate to the concept of symmetry?

What exists outside the boundary of the Universe?

Is it possible for Humankind to find meaning, even within a Universe that will finally dissolve into nothingness?

How is awareness interconnected with eternity?

What happens after our death?

Why is every life unique and important?

How would Humankind benefit from a universal philosophy?

Why is symmetry important to the concept of symbiotic panentheism?

Volume III - Stepping Up To The Creator
Science: Topology *# 230-239*

How can Humankind adapt its approach to topology and mathematics to questions regarding religious and philosophical concepts?

Why should religion, science, and philosophy unite in order to answer Humankind's quest for knowledge and purpose?

How does our present understanding of reality interfere with our purpose in reality? Why do we need a perceptual shift in our understanding?

How does topology help us to understand the structure of the Universe?

Why is it so important to find universal truths? How will they affect our understanding and behavior?

How can philosophy help Humankind in its quest for universal truths?

Is it possible for Humankind to find purpose and value within a bounded and limiting Universe?

How would our understanding of reality also relate to other life forms within the Universe?

How is an 'outside' to our Universe possible?

Why is topology important to the concept of symbiotic panentheism?

Volume III - Stepping Up To The Creator
Science: Set Theory *# 240-249*

What are the four 'theisms' and what can they tell us about our existence within the Universe?

Why is free will important?

How can set theory help us to understand our relationship to the Universe and to the Causative Force?

How could symbiotic panentheism provide us with a model of reality?

What is the significance of life?

Under symbiotic panentheism, how does the importance and significance of the individual become absolute?

How can set theory help us to understand our place and purpose in reality?

Do modern theisms fully accept the concept of omnipresence?

How does symbiotic panentheism reinforce science, religion, philosophy, and prophecy?

Why is set theory important to the concept of symbiotic panentheism?

Volume III - Stepping Up To The Creator
Science: Space - The Null Set *# 250-259*

Questions Addressed

How are matter, energy, and time interconnected?

If the Causative Force is omnipresent, isn't it reasonable to conclude that Humankind is located within the Causative Force?

What can symbiotic panentheism tell us about our relationship to the Causative Force?

How could the Causative Force use Humankind as a means to change and grow?

Why is it vital that we become responsible for our behavior and actions?

Why is attaining a universal philosophy important for Humankind?

Why should we respect other life forms within the Universe?

What is the relationship of the soul to eternity?

Does awareness continue after death?

Why is space - the null set important to the concept of symbiotic panentheism?

Volume III - Stepping Up To The Creator
Science: Ecological Niche *# 260-269*

What is an ecological niche?

How does Humankind fill an ecological niche within the Universe?

Why is Humankind's constant search for knowledge and meaning important?

What is Humankind's relationship to the Causative Force?

What is, or could be, the significance of life?

How could Humankind tie its significance to eternity rather than to mortality?

Why are ecological niches temporary in nature?

Are we important to the Causative Force?

In which sense is Humankind interconnected with the Universe and with the Causative Force?

Why is ecological niche important to the concept of symbiotic panentheism?

Volume III - Stepping Up To The Creator
Science: Homo- ... *# 270-279*

What is the fundamental difference between the human species and the rest of the Earth's creatures?

How is Humankind capable of filling an ecological niche, one which is unaffected by time?

If we are the only inhabitants of the Earth who possess free will, what are our choices and responsibilities?

How could symbiotic panentheism lead us towards an understanding of our purpose in reality?

How could symbiotic panentheism help us to achieve a universal philosophy?

What is the purpose of awareness?

What is the significance of Humankind in eternity?

How does symbiotic panentheism differ from atheism, pantheism, and classical/traditional theism?

What will be the consequences, both for Humankind and the Causative Force, if we do not achieve a universal philosophy?

Why is homo- important to the concept of symbiotic panentheism?

Volume III - Stepping Up To The Creator
Science: Palaeomagnetism *# 280-289*

What can palaeomagnetism tell us about the geological history of the Earth?

Using palaeomagnetism, how can we predict what will happen to the Earth in the future?

Will the Earth be destroyed one day?

Why is it so vital that Humankind prepare for the future?

Why do we now need a perceptual shift in our understanding?

How could a universal philosophy help us to reach our full potential?

What is Humankind's purpose? Do we still have meaning and value, even within a Universe that will eventually be destroyed?

How are Humankind and the Causative Force interconnected?

How could Humankind have a purpose in eternity?

Why is palaeomagnetism important to the concept of symbiotic panentheism?

Volume III - Stepping Up To The Creator
Science: Symbiosis ***# 290-299***

How do we share a symbiotic relationship with the Causative Force?

Why does our Universe exist? What is its purpose?

How are the Universe and Humankind located within the Causative Force?

How does our behavior, both positive and negative, impact the Causative Force?

Is life eternal?

How can the past help us to understand and shape our future?

Where does our significance, both as individuals and as a species, lie?

Why is it vital that we accept responsibility for our actions?

How do science, religion, and philosophy help us to understand who we are?

Why is symbiosis important to the concept of symbiotic panentheism?

Volume III - Stepping Up To The Creator
Philosophy: Unified View *# 300-309*

What is the first aim of philosophy?

How can philosophy make people more critical thinkers?

How can philosophy help us to understand the function of the Universe?

What have been the limits of philosophy?

Why is it important that we achieve a 'unified view' or universal philosophy for our species?

What would be the benefits of a universal philosophy?

How can philosophy help us to understand the significance of life?

Why is it important that we find a comprehensive definition of life?

What is the function of the soul?

What happens to us after death?

Volume III - Stepping Up To The Creator
Philosophy: Philosophy, Religion, and Science *# 310-319*

How have philosophy, religion, and science attempted to understand reality?

How do philosophy, religion, and science reinforce each other?

How can philosophy help us to define the truth of reality?

Why do we as individuals, and as a species, need to be responsible for our actions?

If the Universe is in a constant state of change, isn't the Causative Force also changing?

How is panentheism interconnected with philosophy, religion, and science?

Why does life exist?

What is the difference between reality and Reality?

How could the merging of philosophy, religion, and science help us to achieve an understanding of our purpose in reality?

What would be the benefits of a universal philosophy?

Volume III - Stepping Up To The Creator
Philosophy: Confucianism *# 320-329*

What is Confucianism?

Why does Confucianism emphasize sincerity in personal and public conduct?

What have been the positive influences of Confucianism?

How could Confucianism be made stronger?

What are rules of behavior?

How does Confucianism reinforce the concept of an omnipresent Causative Force?

Why does society remain in a state of confusion and conflict?

What have been the failings of philosophy?

If rules and laws are necessary for an orderly society, how can we find out what these rules and laws should be?

Why is free will an essential aspect of our lives?

Volume III - Stepping Up To The Creator
Philosophy: Taoism *# 330-339*

What is Taoism?

How does Taoism differ from Western philosophy?

Why does Taoism place an emphasis on the 'whole' rather than on individual aspects of our existence?

How are panentheism and Taoism alike?

In which ways does Taoism teach us tolerance?

Why does Taoism emphasise the rights of the individual over the demands of conformity imposed by society?

What is free will?

Why is it essential that we have a choice over our own behavior and destiny?

Why does our species need a sense of purpose?

How do symbiotic panentheism and Taoism support each other?

Volume III - Stepping Up To The Creator
Philosophy: Ancient Philosophy *# 340-349*

In which way did Ancient Philosophy initiate a debate over the nature of reality?

What is the function of philosophy?

Why is a universal philosophy important for our species?

How are faith and reason interconnected?

How can something physical be generated from something non-physical?

How are many of our present beliefs in agreement with Ancient Philosophy?

What is the nature of the Universe?

In which way are we a part of the Causative Force?

Why is it important that we define who we are and our reason for existence?

Why is it vital that we accept responsibility for our actions?

Volume III - Stepping Up To The Creator
Philosophy: Early Christian Philosophy *# 350-359*

How did Early Christian philosophy undermine and surpass Ancient philosophy?

Why did Early Christian philosophy reject science and reason?

Why was the concept of panentheism considered such a threat to Early Christian philosophy?

Why is life significant to the Causative Force?

What did Early Christian philosophy imply about the nature of the Universe?

What is Humankind's significance in eternity?

If the Causative Force is omnipresent, are we not then located within the Causative Force?

How have Western/Middle Eastern religions expanded our understanding of the Causative Force?

Why is a universal philosophy important? How would it affect the behavior of our species?

How does symbiotic panentheism reinforce the concepts embraced by Early Christian philosophy?

Volume III - Stepping Up To The Creator
Philosophy: Renaissance Philosophy *# 360-369*

How does ontology and Renaissance philosophy differ?

Why has ontology not provided the answers to our fundamental questions?

In which way does faith provide a foundation for knowledge?

What do we first need to do in order to achieve a universal philosophy?

What would a universal philosophy have to provide?

Why is existence significant?

If the Causative Force is omnipresent, are we not then located within the Causative Force?

In which ways has Renaissance philosophy failed to provide answers to Humankind's questions?

Why is it reasonable for religion and science to unite?

What would be the advantages of a universal philosophy?

Volume III - Stepping Up To The Creator
Philosophy: Appeal to Reason and Experience *# 370-379*

What are epistemology and metaphysics?

How can philosophy, religion, and science help us to understand reality?

What is the nature of the Causative Force?

What is the function of awareness? What is the function of life?

Why is change important?

Why is all life significant?

What happens to us after death?

What is the significance of every individual on eternity?

What does philosophy need to do to achieve a unified view?

Why is a Causative Force significant to our understanding?

Volume III - Stepping Up To The Creator
Philosophy: Appeal to Humanism/Adjustment *# 380-389*

Why did philosophers turn their attention to the importance of the individual?

What is humanism?

How was religion ahead of both science and philosophy in exploring the importance of the individual?

Why must we never hide from our past?

What is the significance of life?

What is philosophy built upon?

Why is the concept of equality important?

What is life?

What must we do as a species?

What are the rights of the individual?

Volume III - Stepping Up To The Creator
Philosophy: Symbiotic Panentheism *# 390-399*

What does symbiotic panentheism tell us about the Causative Force?

Is symbiotic panentheism a model of a universal philosophy, or is it the first step?

How would a universal philosophy affect our past, present, and future?

Who will benefit from a universal philosophy?

Why are freedom and free will important?

What is life?

What is the function of philosophy?

Why should we be proud as a species?

What are universal truths?

How does symbiotic panentheism offer us hope?

Flowcharts

Volume I

You & I Together

- Have a Purpose in Reality -

Volume II

In the Image of God

Volume III

Stepping Up To The Creator

Volume I - You & I Together - Have a Purpose In Reality

Chapter 1: God

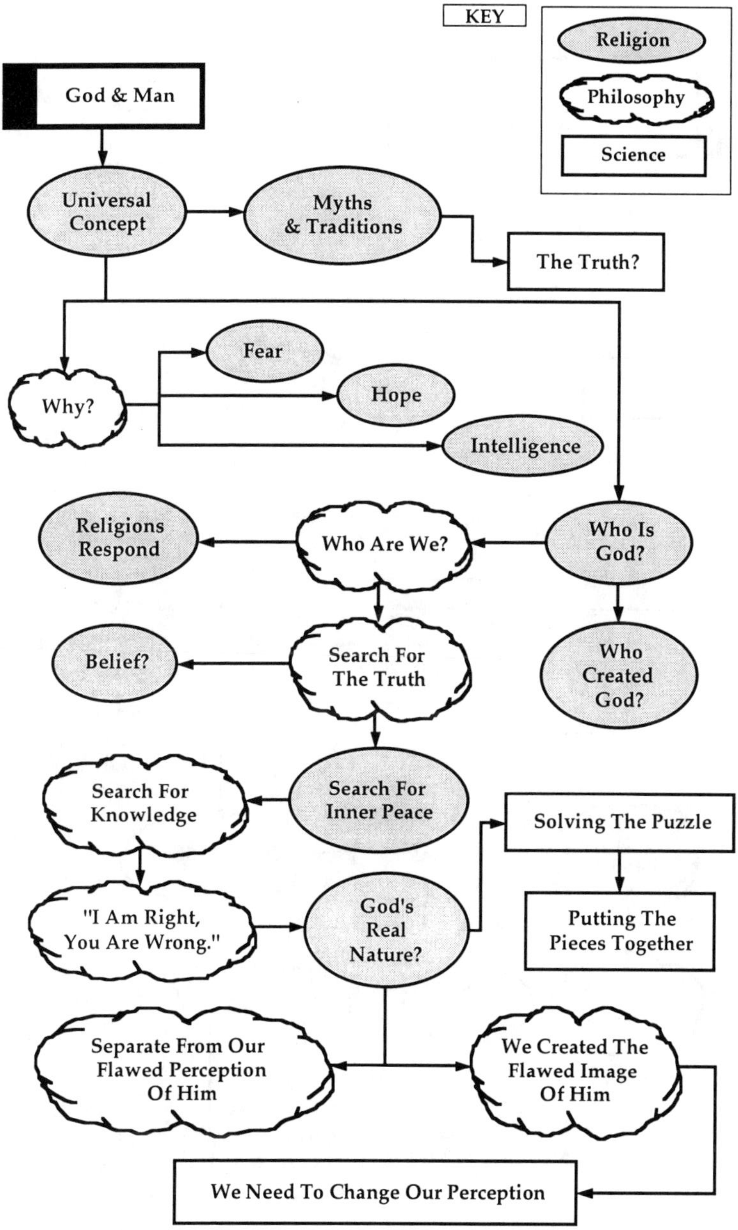

Volume I - You & I Together - Have a Purpose In Reality
Chapter 2: Quadratic vs. Linear Philosophies

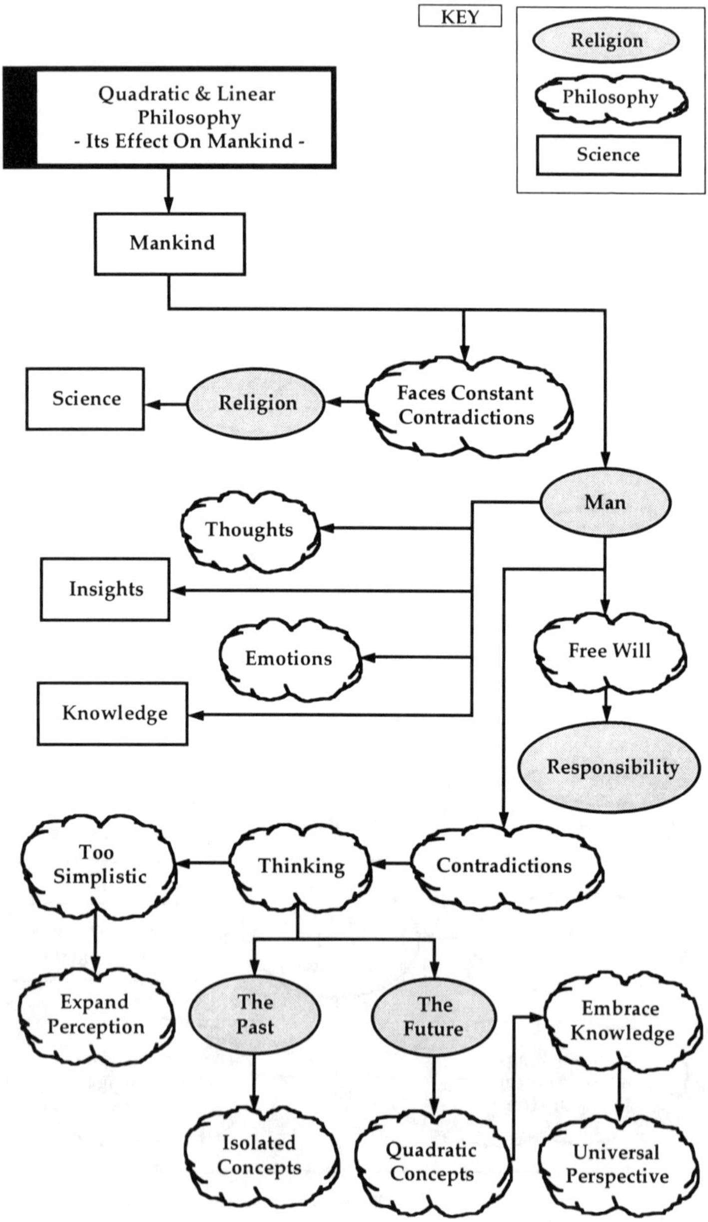

Volume I - You & I Together - Have a Purpose In Reality
Chapter 3: B.E.G.A. Begins

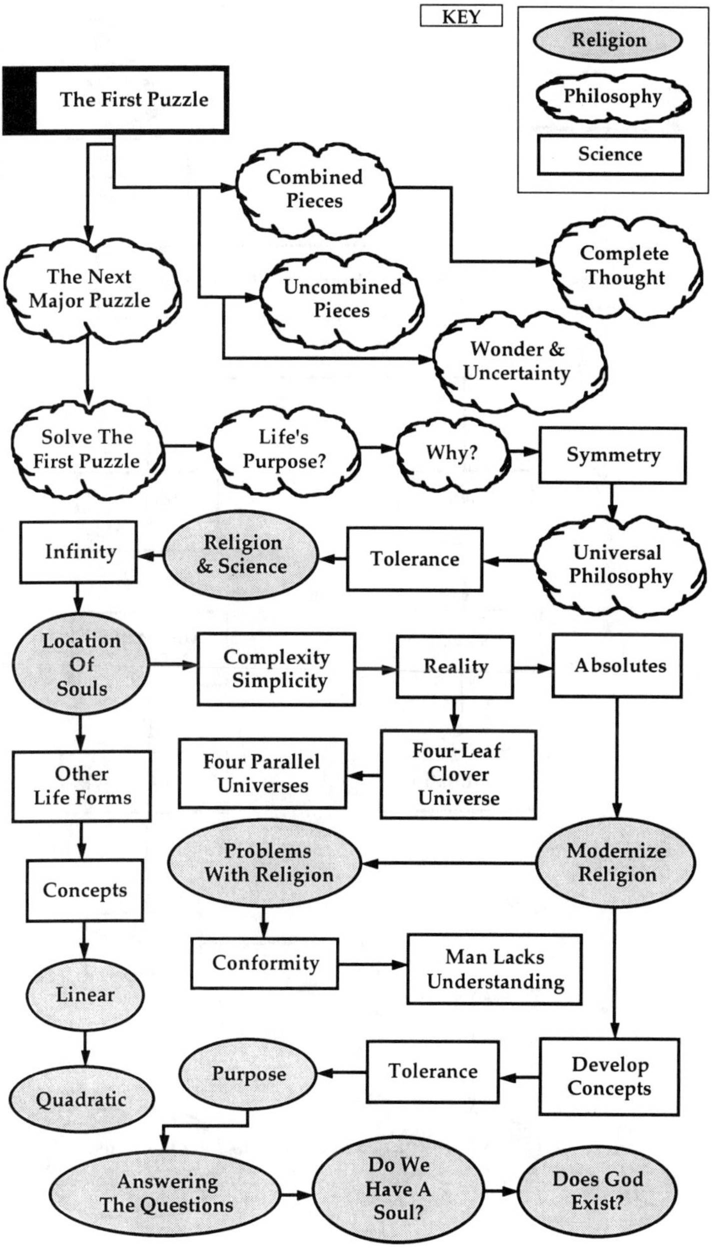

Volume I - You & I Together - Have a Purpose In Reality
Chapter 4: Sets of Four Parallel Universes

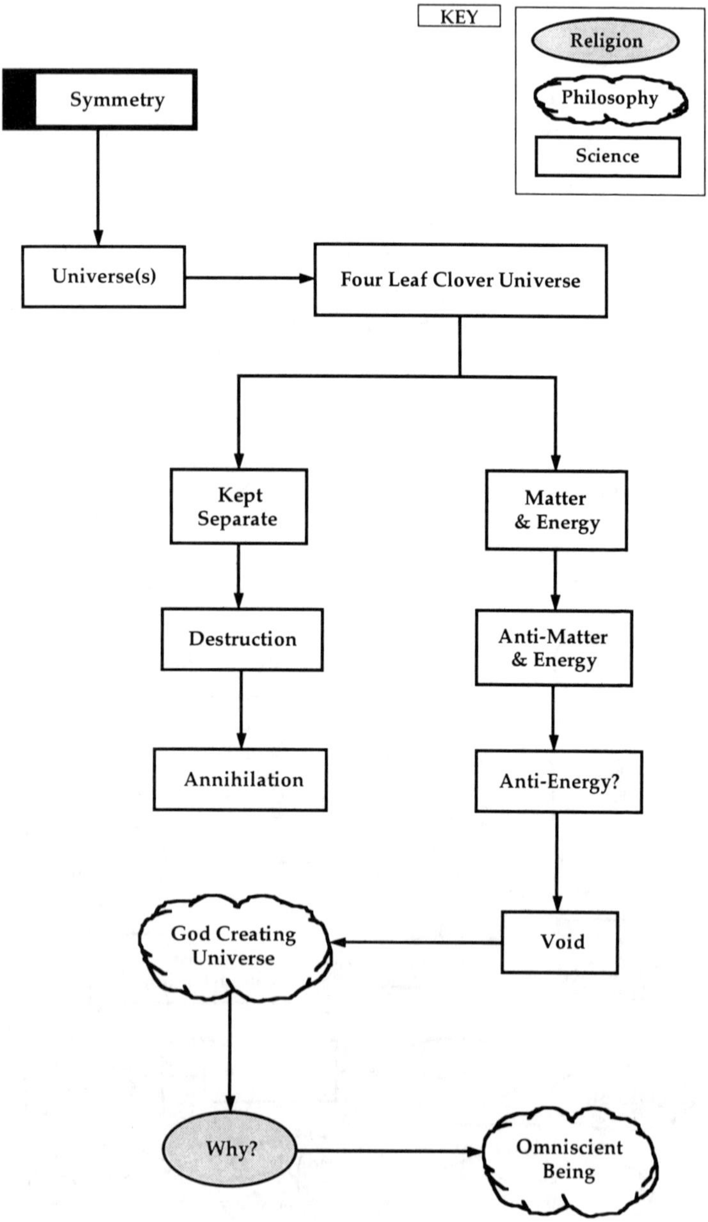

Volume I - You & I Together - Have a Purpose In Reality
Chapter 5: The Universe

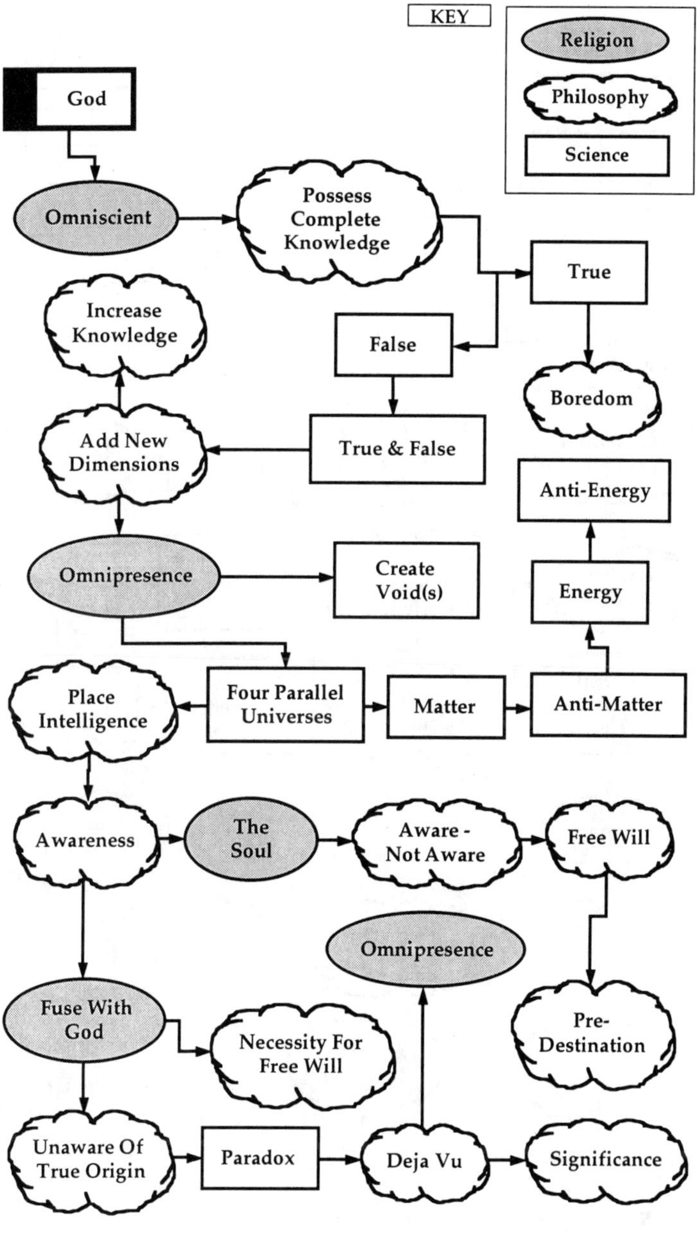

Volume I - You & I Together - Have a Purpose In Reality
Chapter 6: The Universes

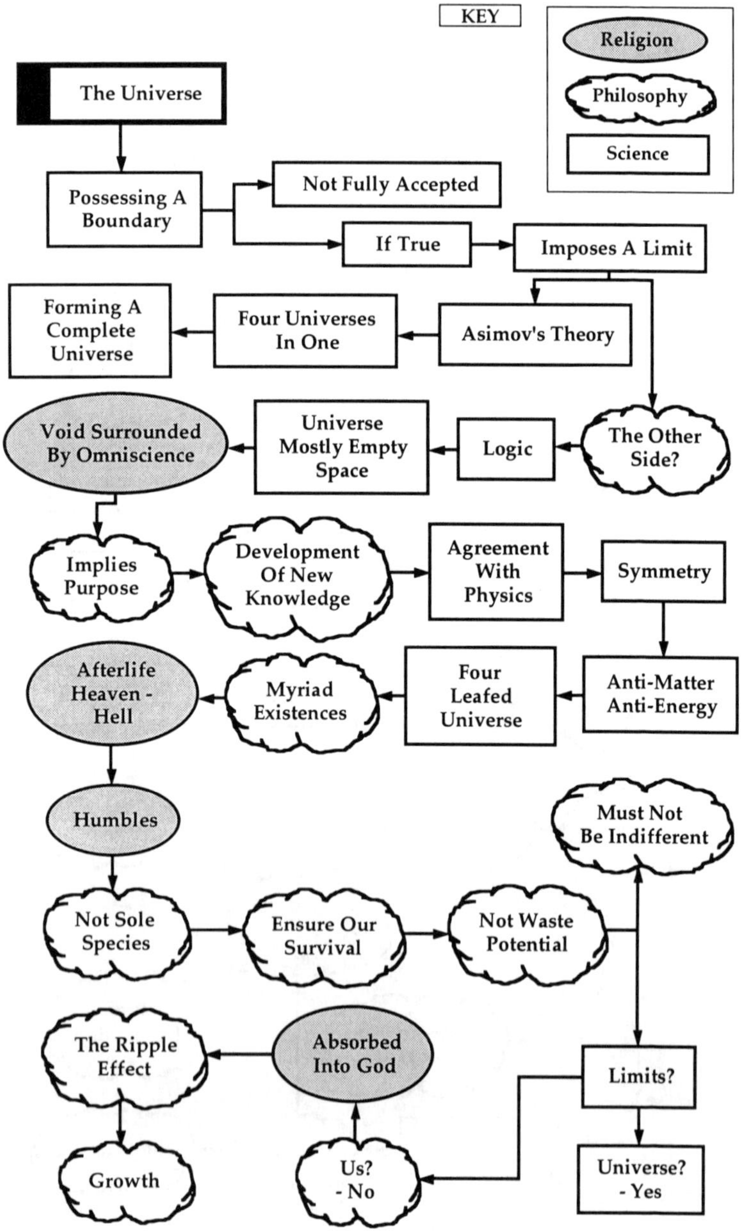

Volume I - You & I Together - Have a Purpose In Reality
Chapter 7: The Ripple Effect

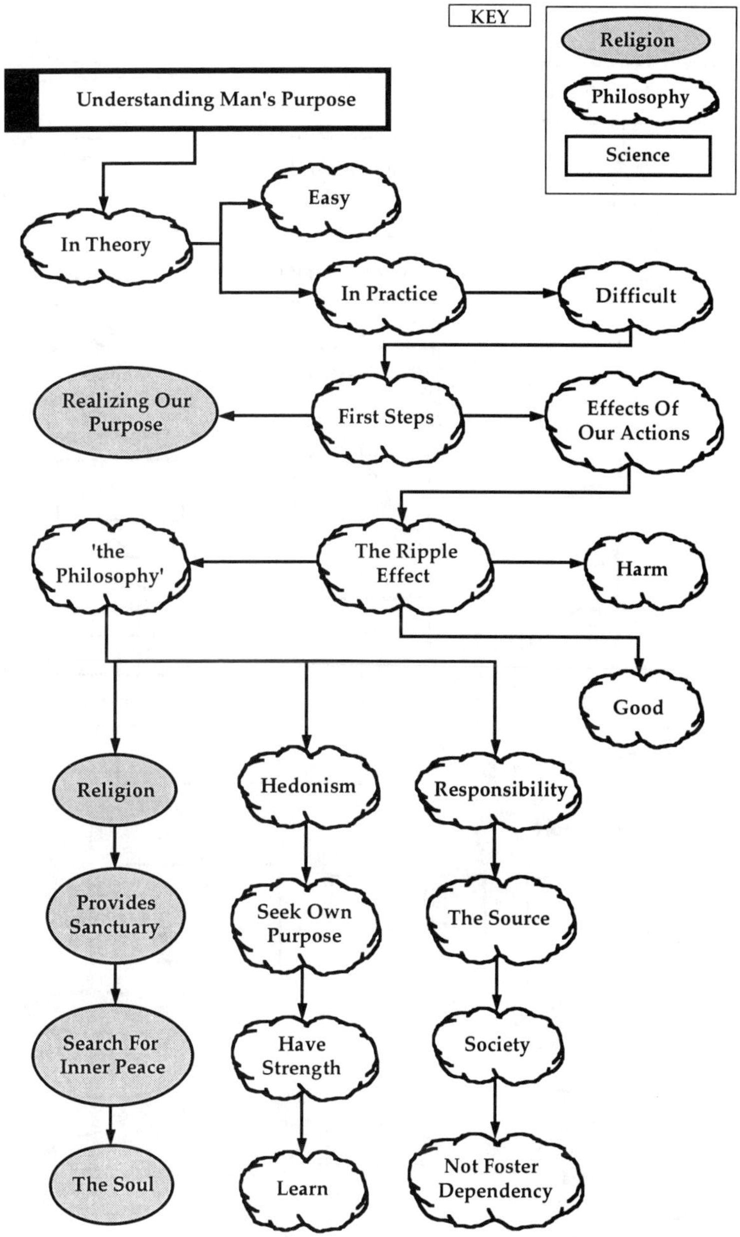

Volume I - You & I Together - Have a Purpose In Reality
Chapter 8: The Mechanism

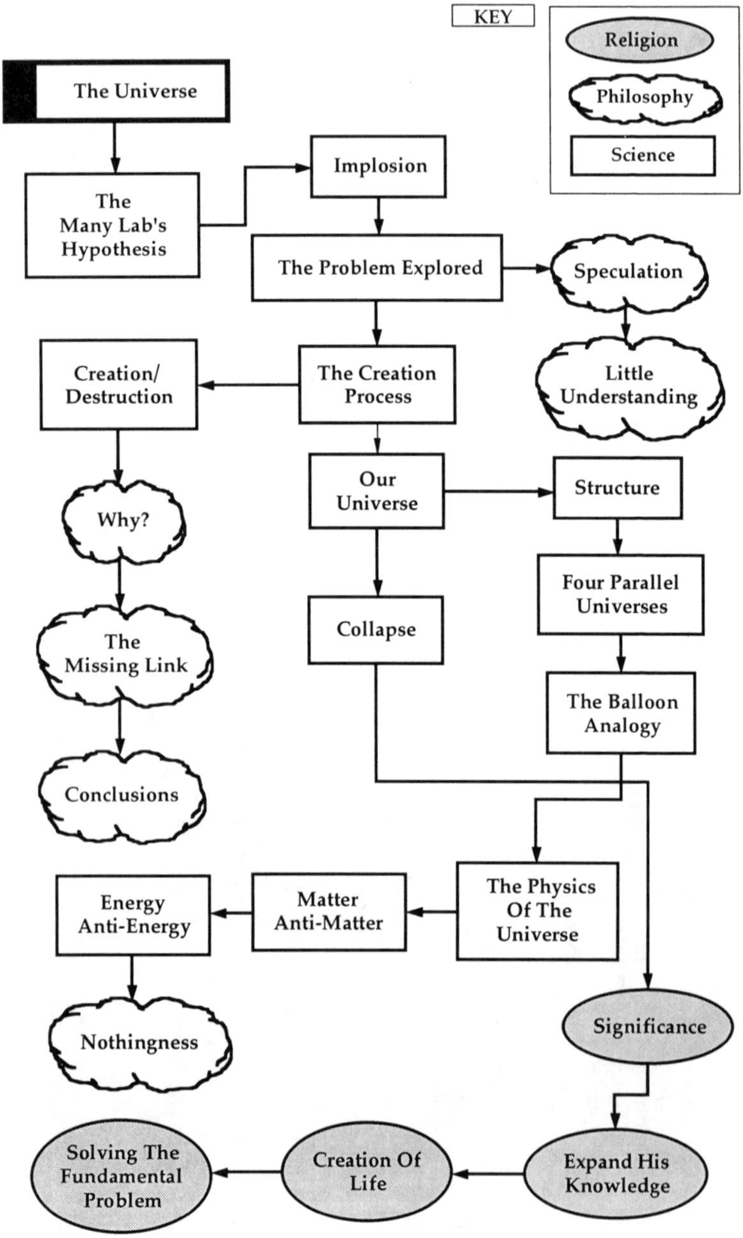

Volume I - You & I Together - Have a Purpose In Reality

Chapter 9: The Missing Link

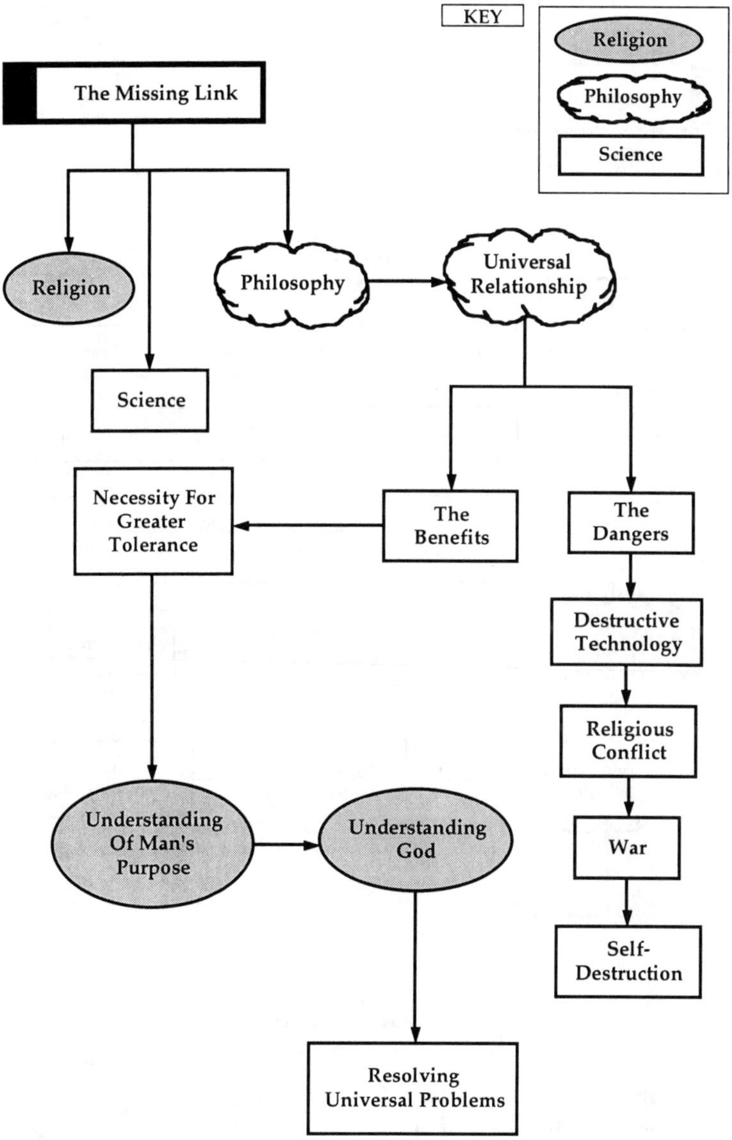

Volume I - You & I Together - Have a Purpose In Reality
Chapter 10: Omnipotent/Omnipresent/Omniscience

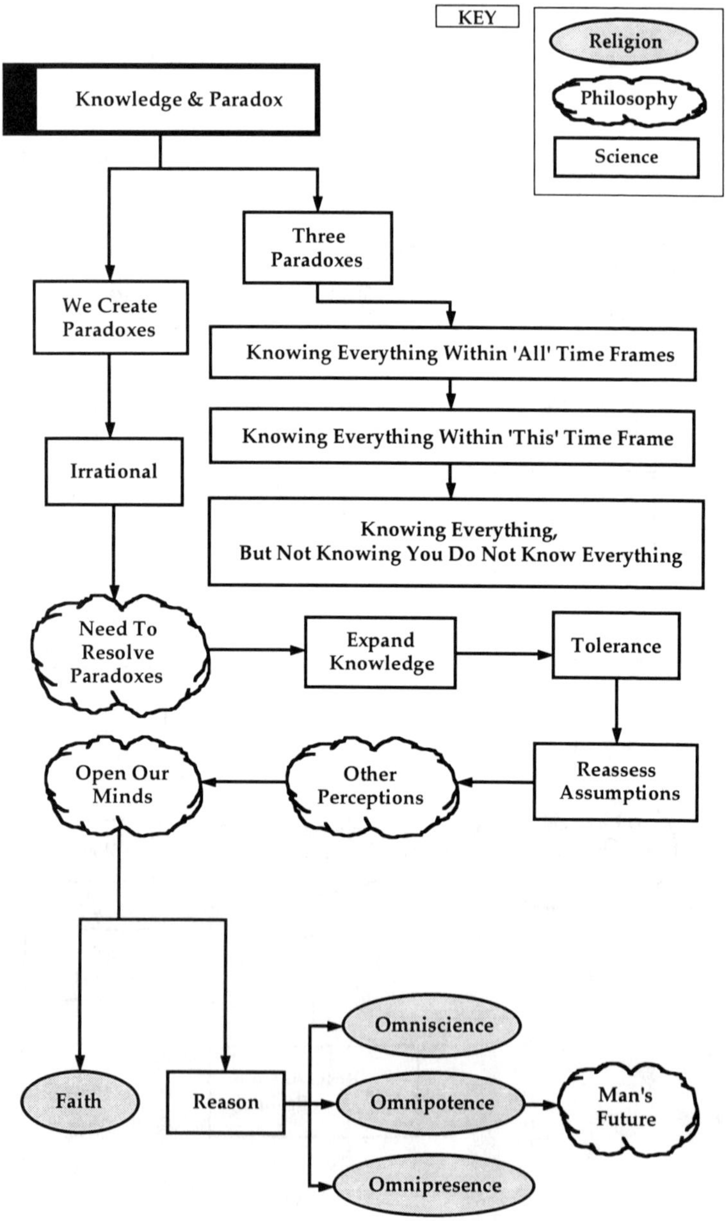

Volume I - You & I Together - Have a Purpose In Reality

Chapter 11: In Summary

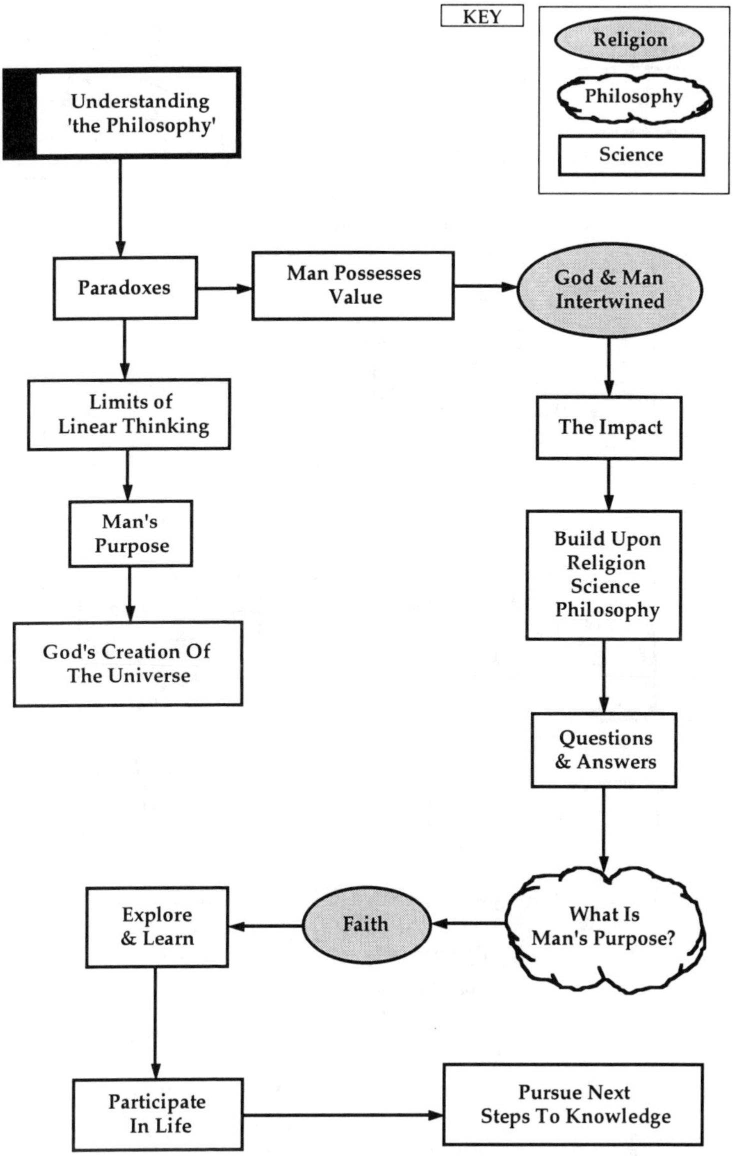

Volume I - You & I Together - Have a Purpose In Reality
Chapter 12: Man's Inhumanity To Man

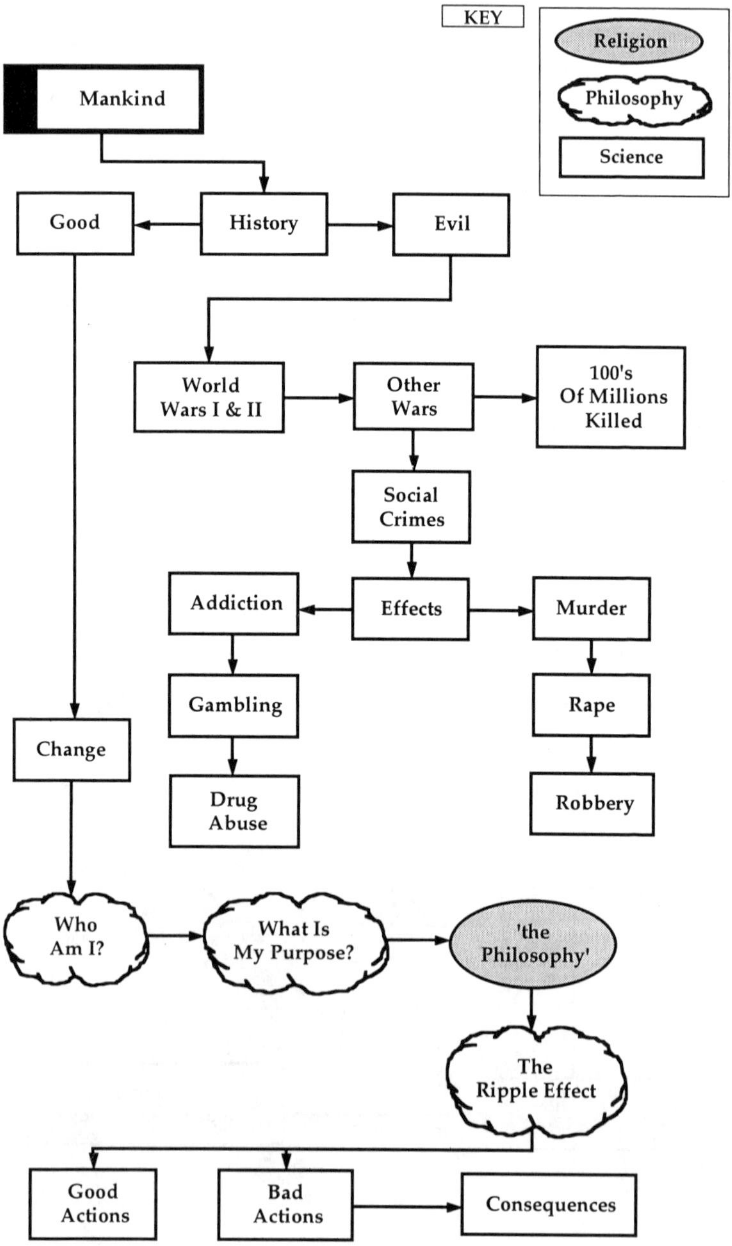

Volume I - You & I Together - Have a Purpose In Reality
Chapter 13: Man's Good Side

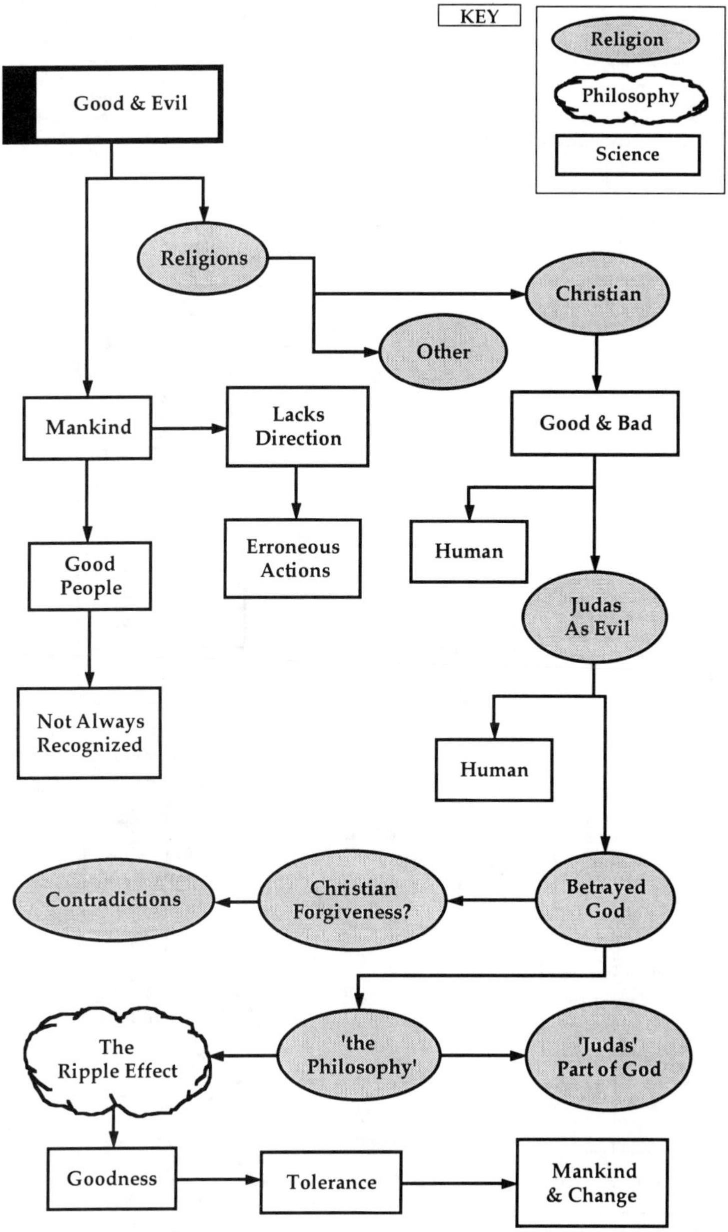

Volume I - You & I Together - Have a Purpose In Reality
Chapter 14: Is It Worth It In The End?

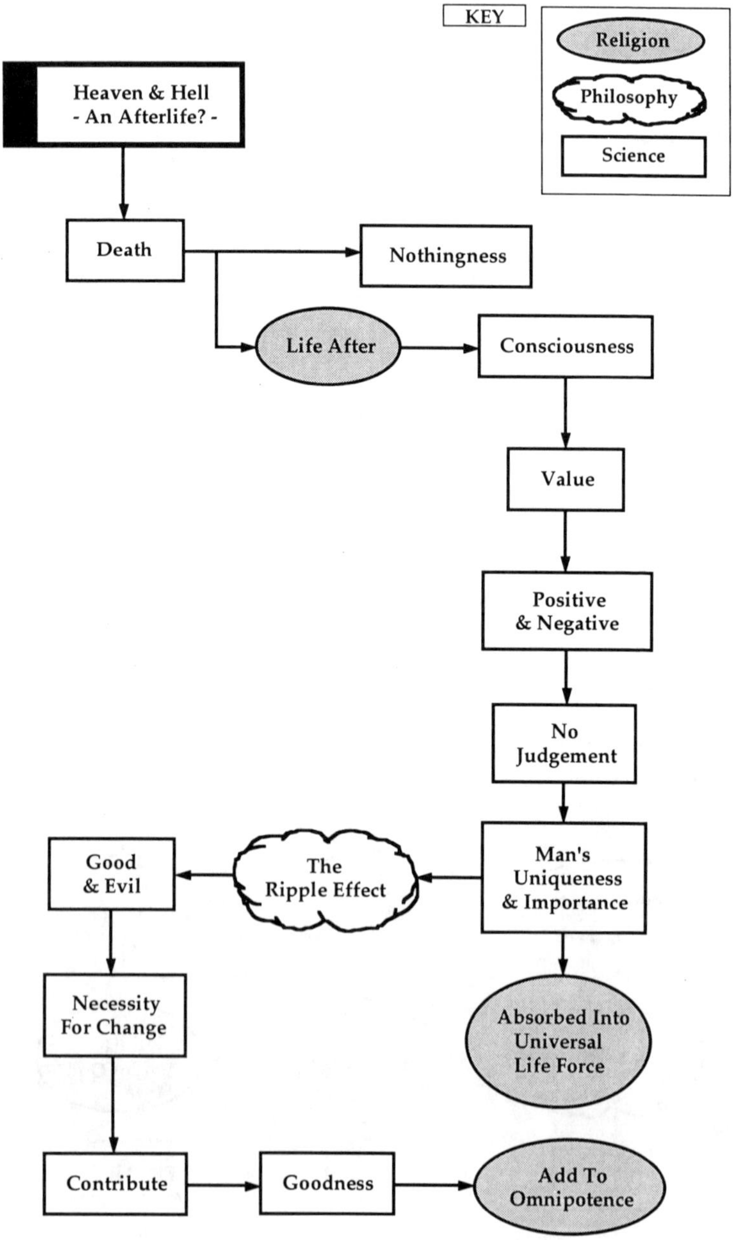

FLOWCHARTS

Volume I - You & I Together - Have a Purpose In Reality
Chapter 15: Is There Hope For You As An Individual?

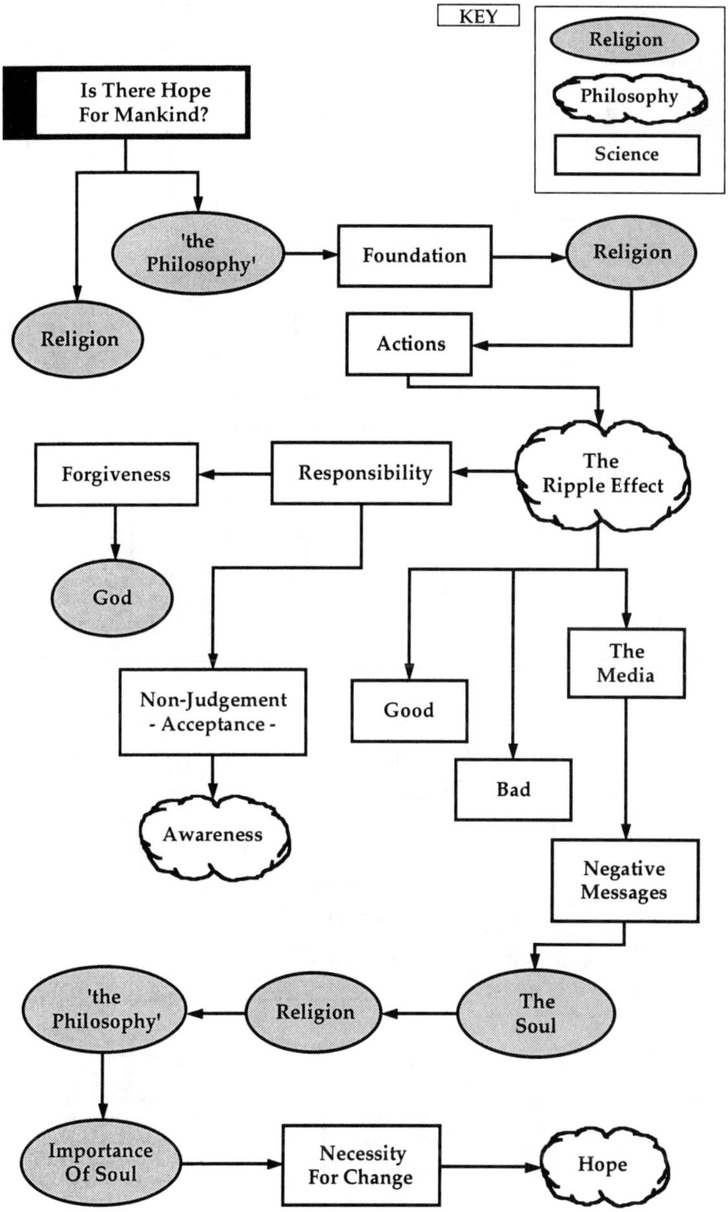

Volume I - You & I Together - Have a Purpose In Reality
Chapter 16: Is There Hope For Mankind?

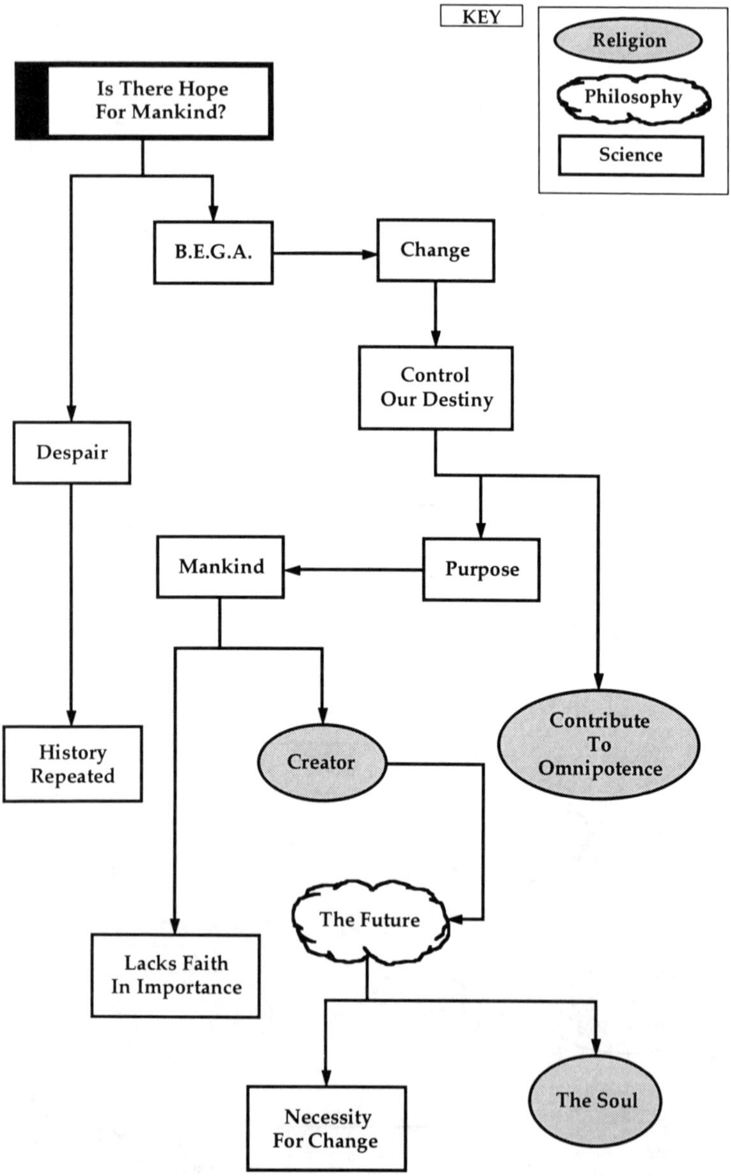

Volume I - You & I Together - Have a Purpose In Reality
Chapter 17: Religion Is It: Significant/Necessary? Which One?

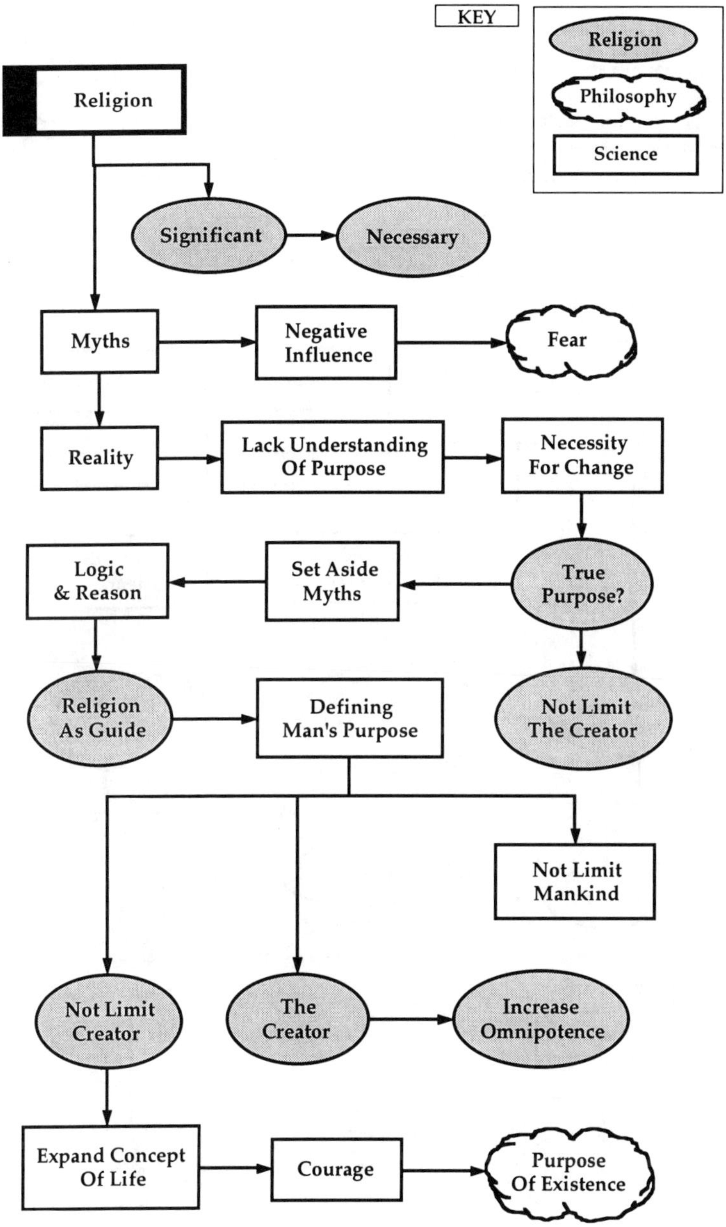

Volume I - You & I Together - Have a Purpose In Reality
Chapter 18: In Summary: The Soul

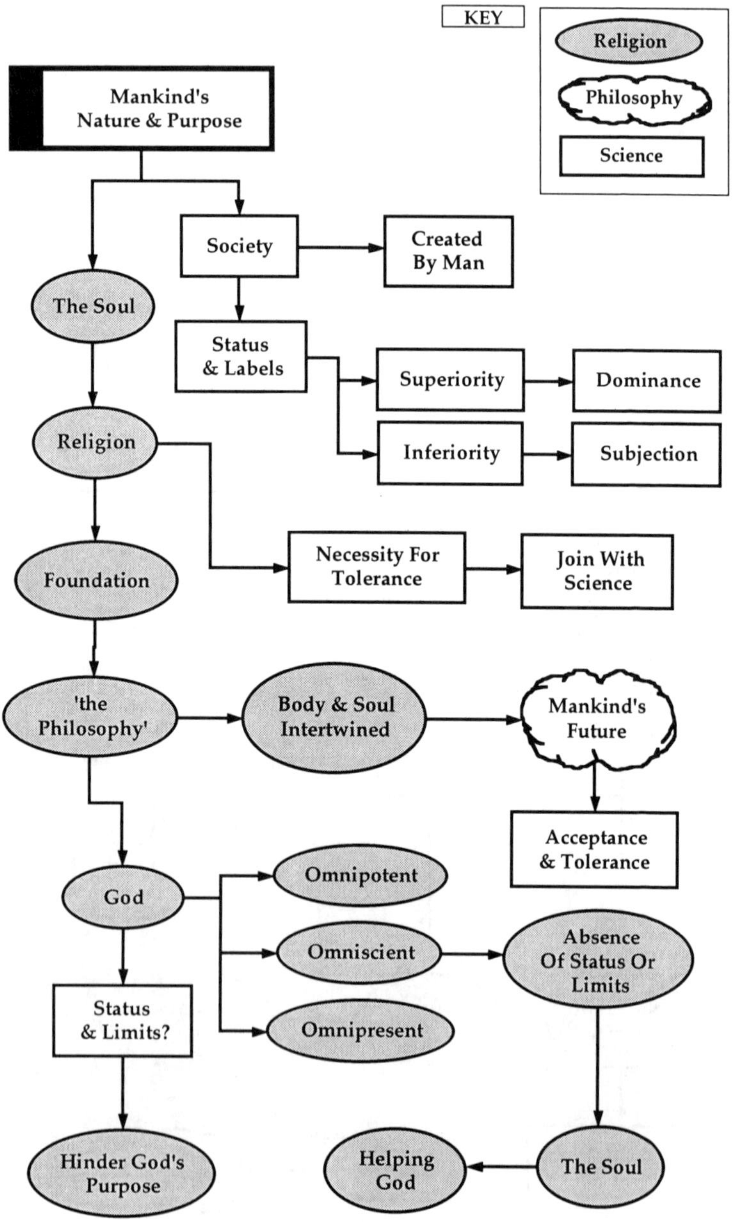

Volume I - You & I Together - Have a Purpose In Reality

Chapter 19: Class Status: Social/Occupational/Economic

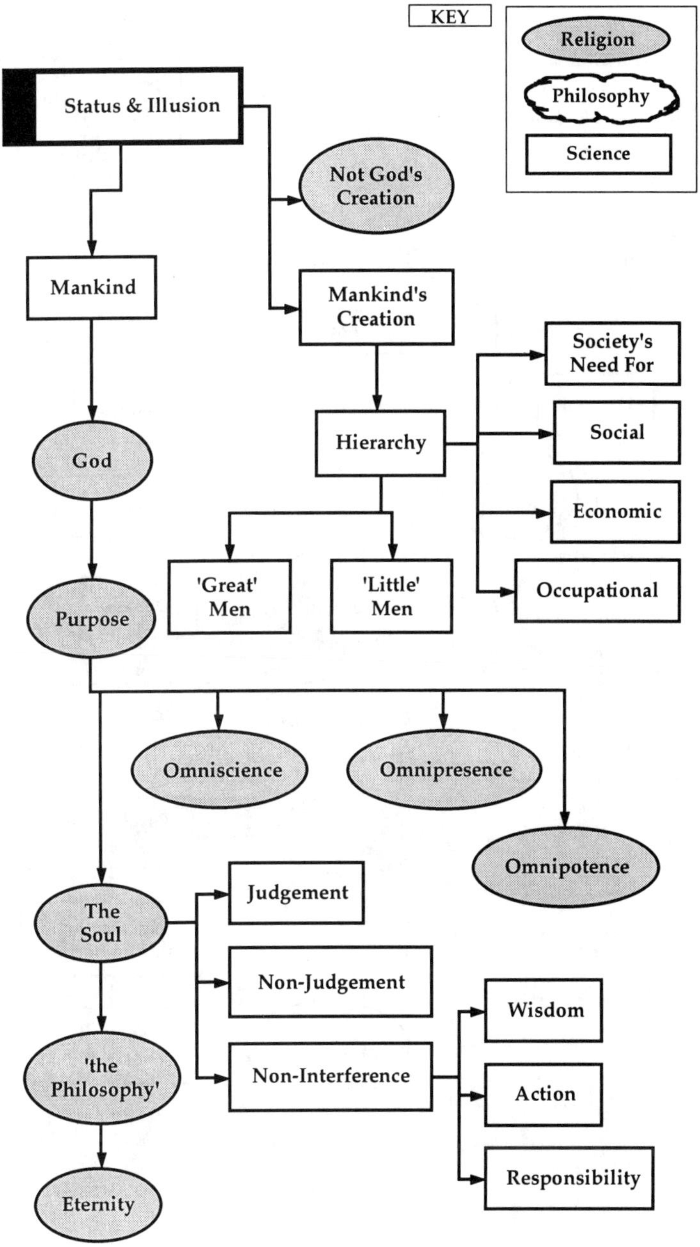

Volume I - You & I Together - Have a Purpose In Reality
Chapter 20: Atheism

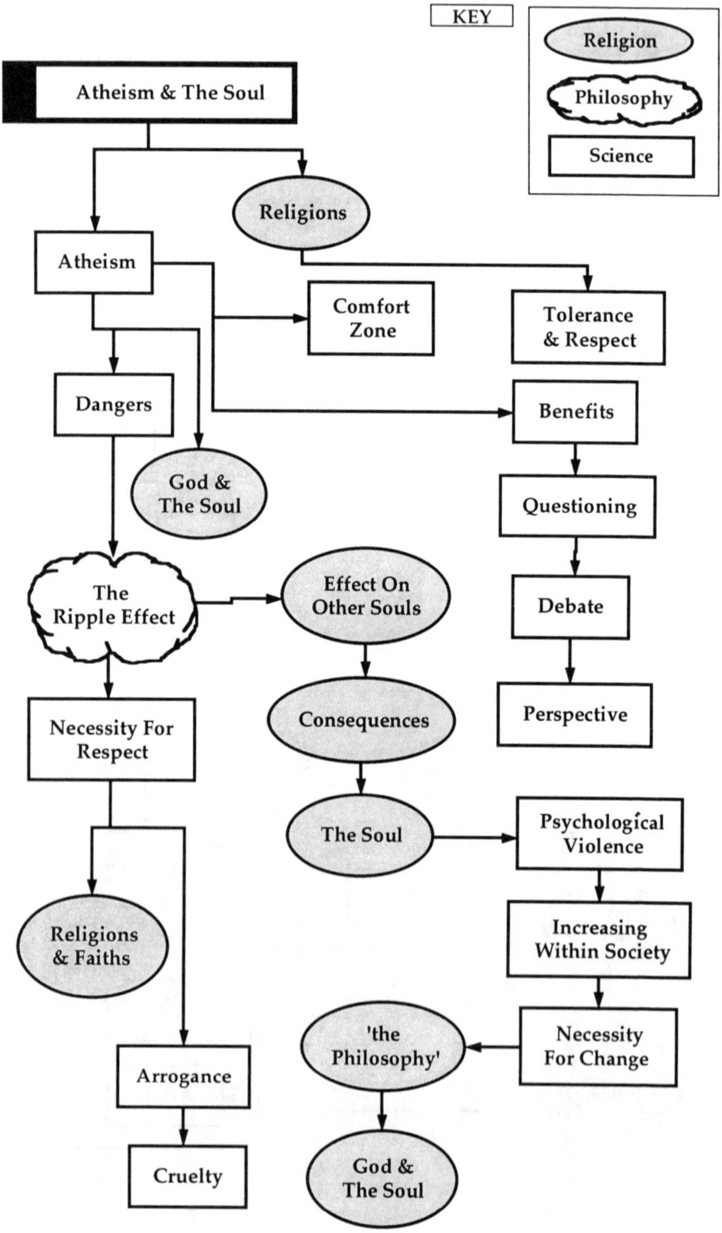

Volume I - You & I Together - Have a Purpose In Reality
Chapter 21: War/Abortion

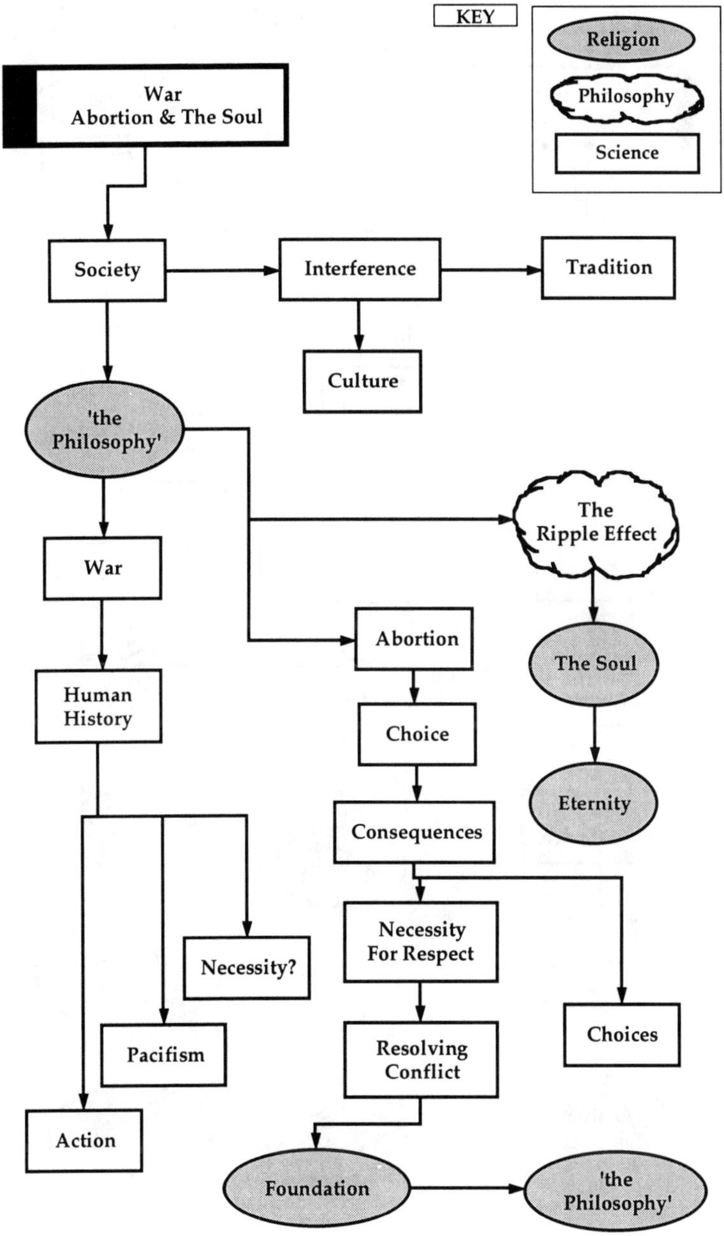

Volume I - You & I Together - Have a Purpose In Reality
Chapter 22: Suicide

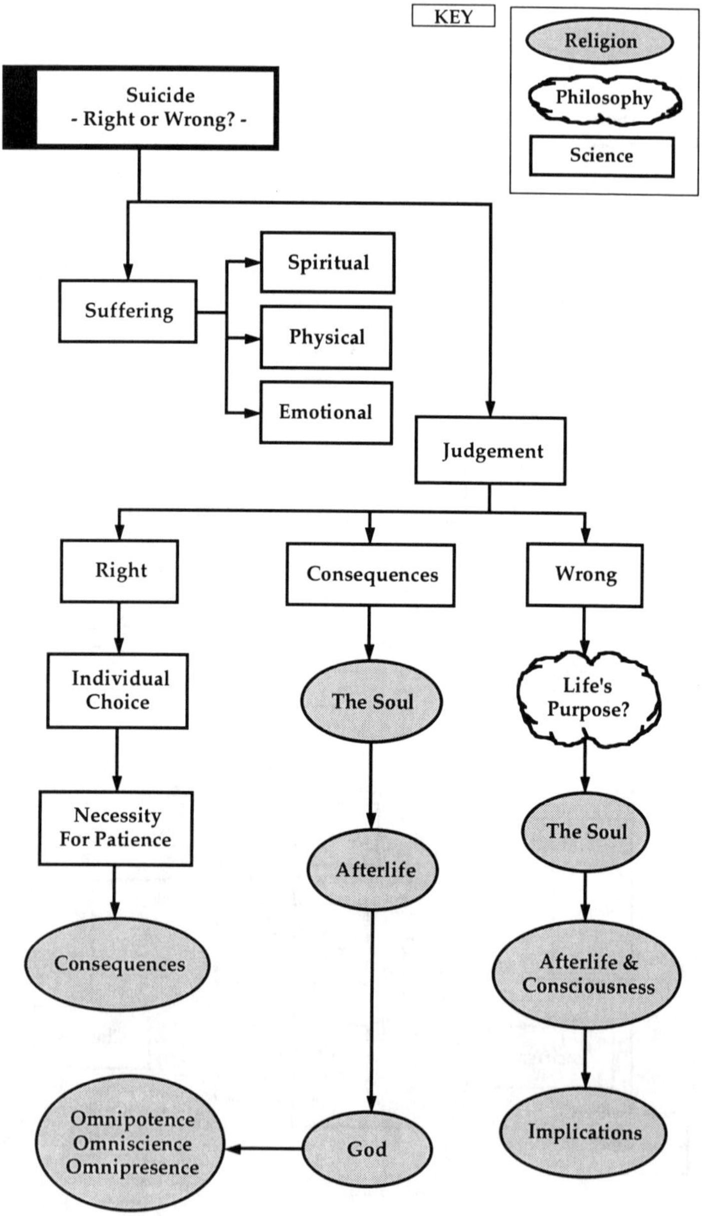

Volume I - You & I Together - Have a Purpose In Reality
Chapter 23: Capital Punishment/Life Incarceration

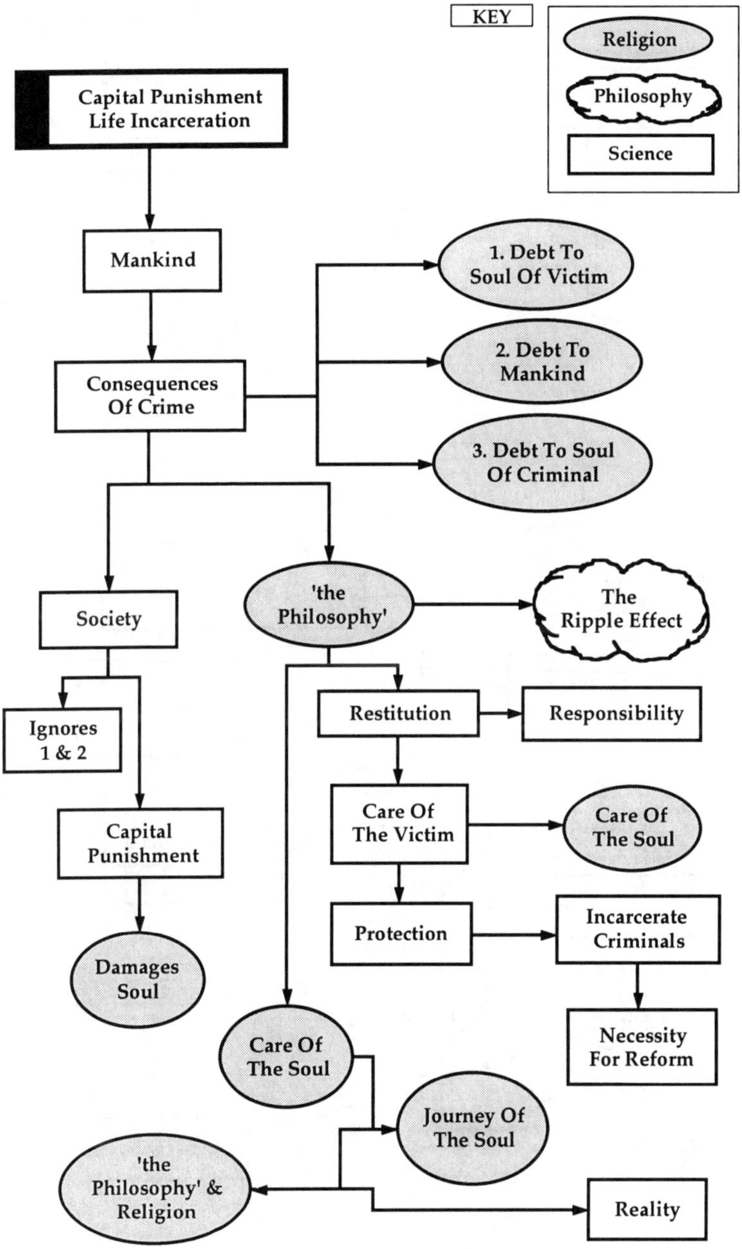

Volume I - You & I Together - Have a Purpose In Reality
Chapter 24: Letting Go/Forgiving

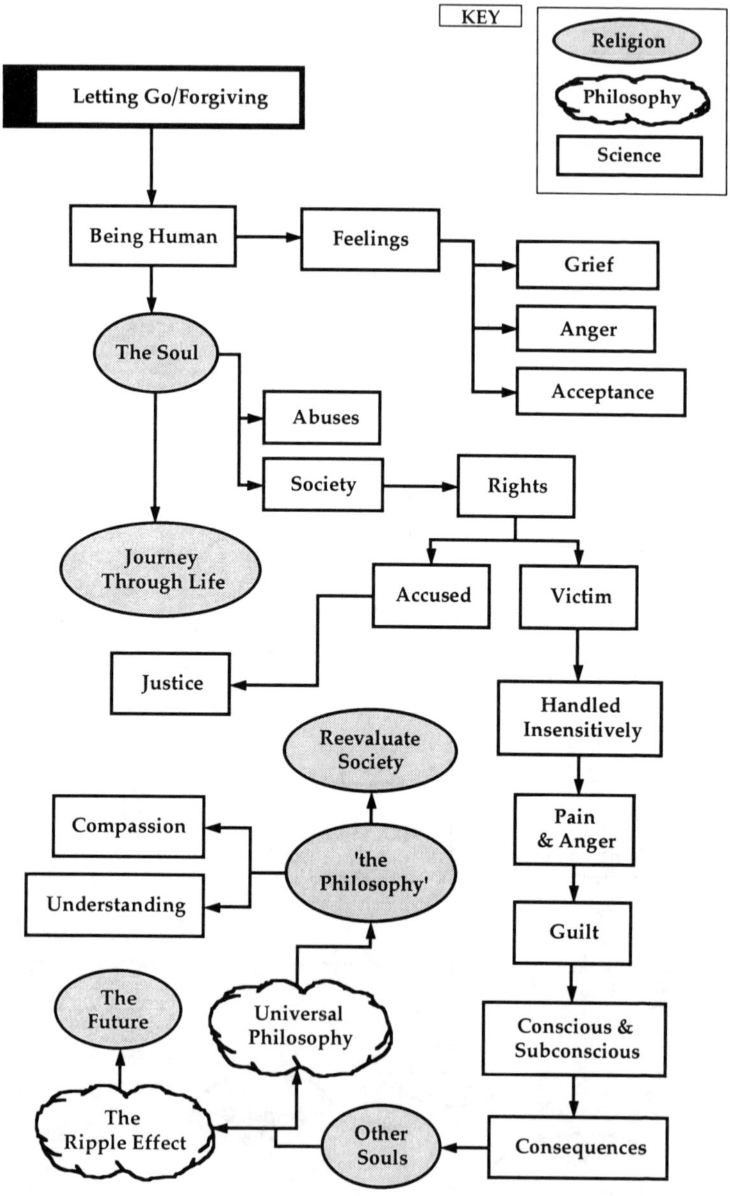

Volume I - You & I Together - Have a Purpose In Reality
Chapter 25: Missionary Work/Helping Others

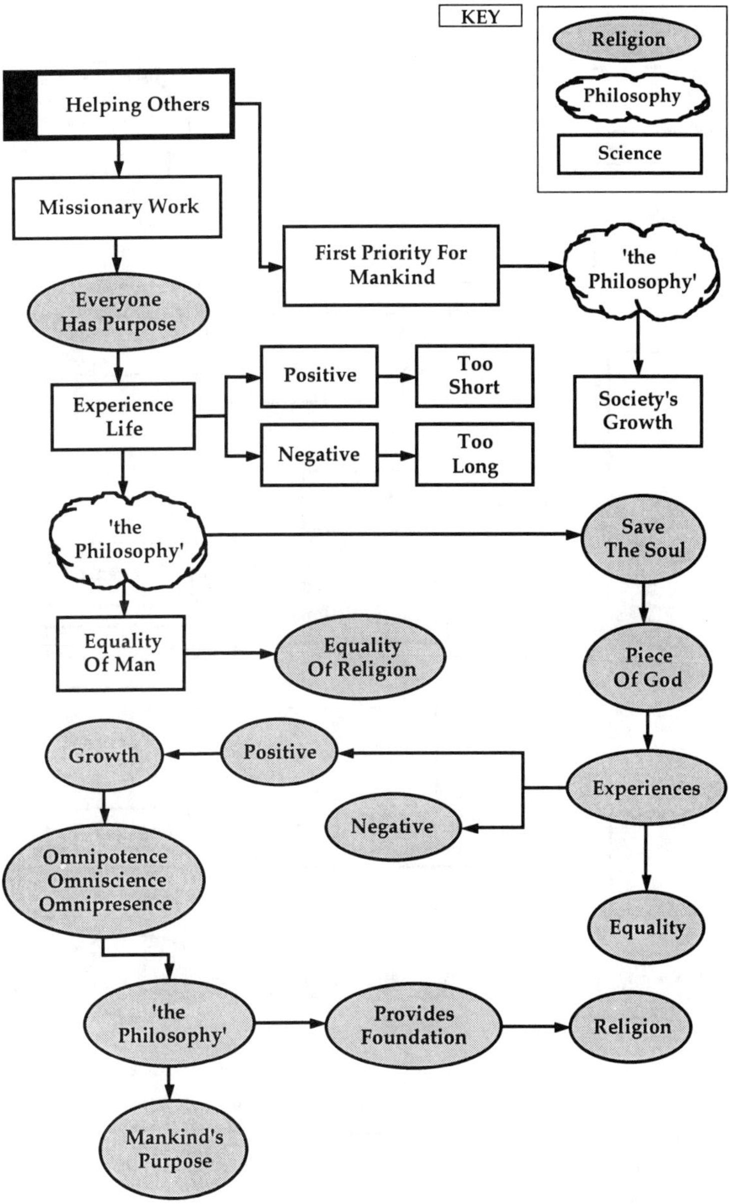

Volume I - You & I Together - Have a Purpose In Reality
Chapter 26: In Summary: Intolerance Is An Outmoded Term

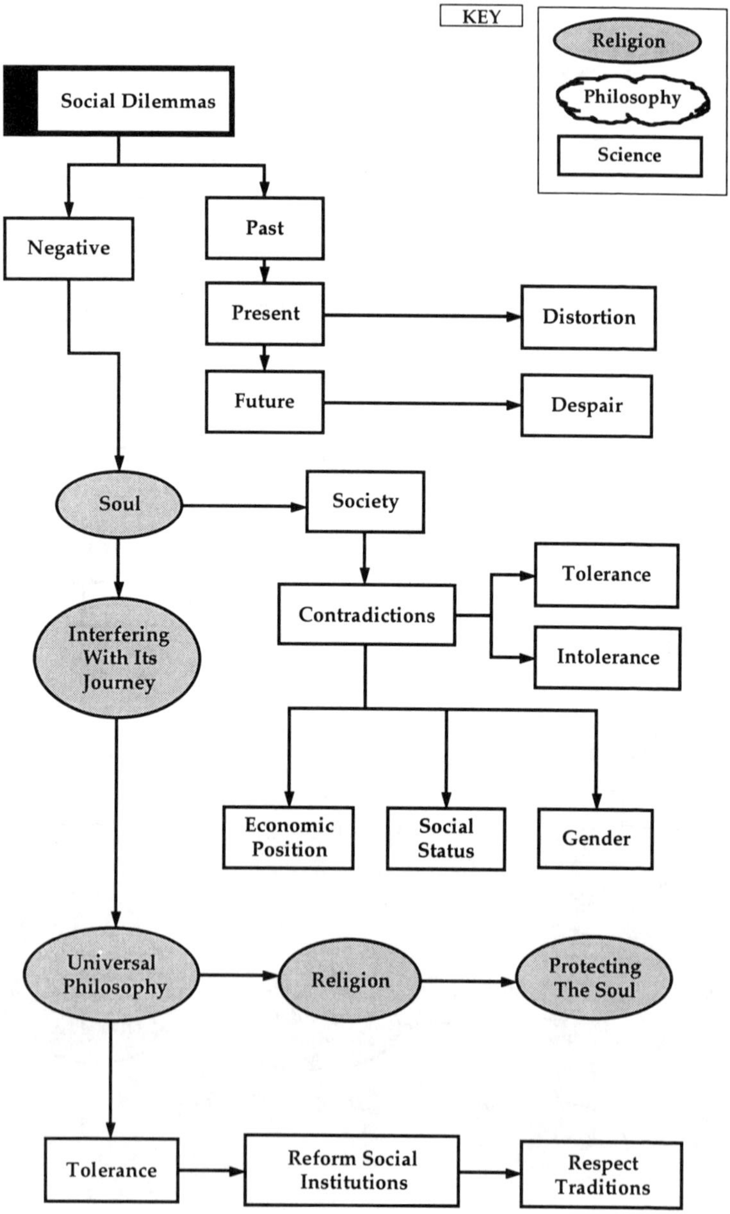

Volume I - You & I Together - Have a Purpose In Reality
Chapter 27: God/gods

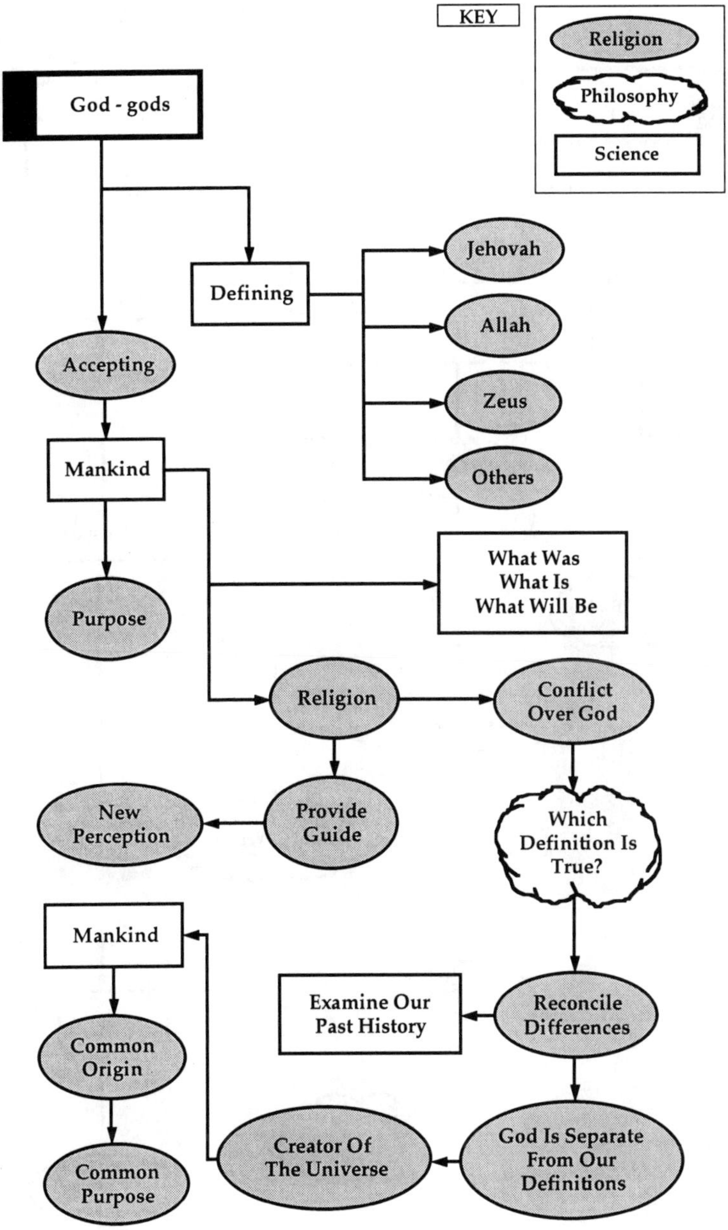

Volume I - You & I Together - Have a Purpose In Reality
Chapter 28: Good/Bad: Misnomers

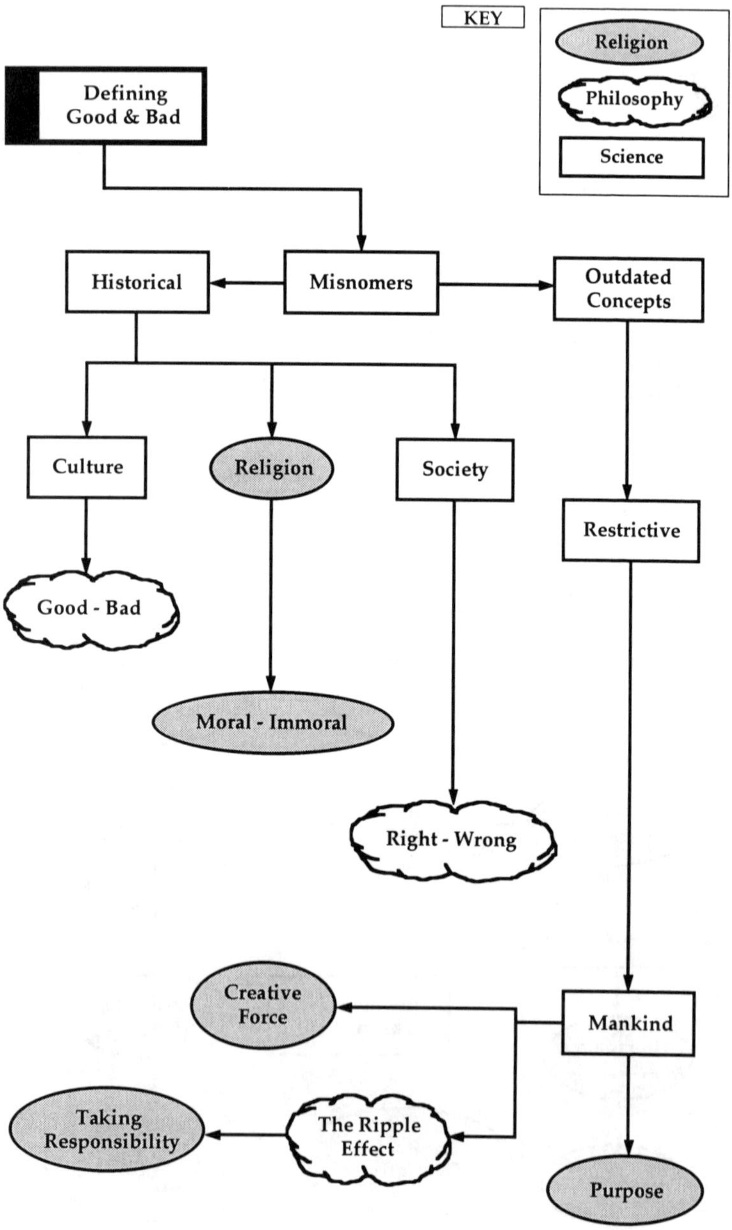

Volume I - You & I Together - Have a Purpose In Reality
Chapter 29: Heaven and Hell

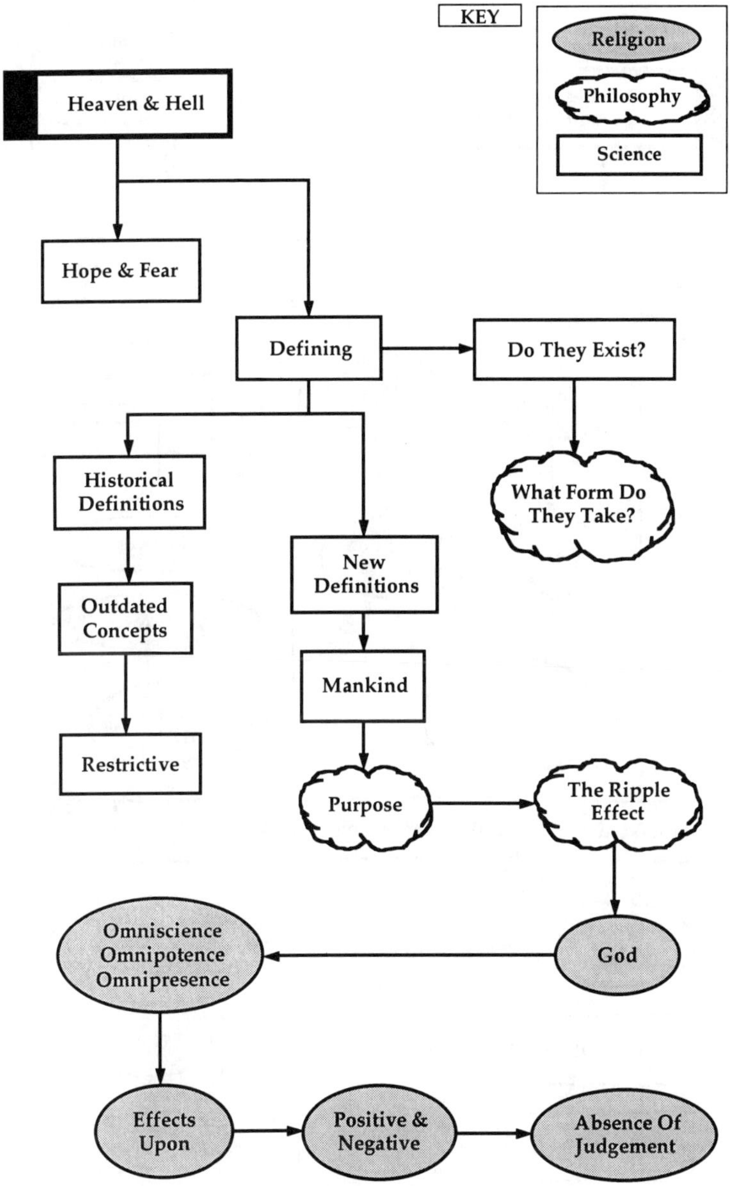

Volume I - You & I Together - Have a Purpose In Reality
Chapter 30: 'God Is Going To Get You For That'

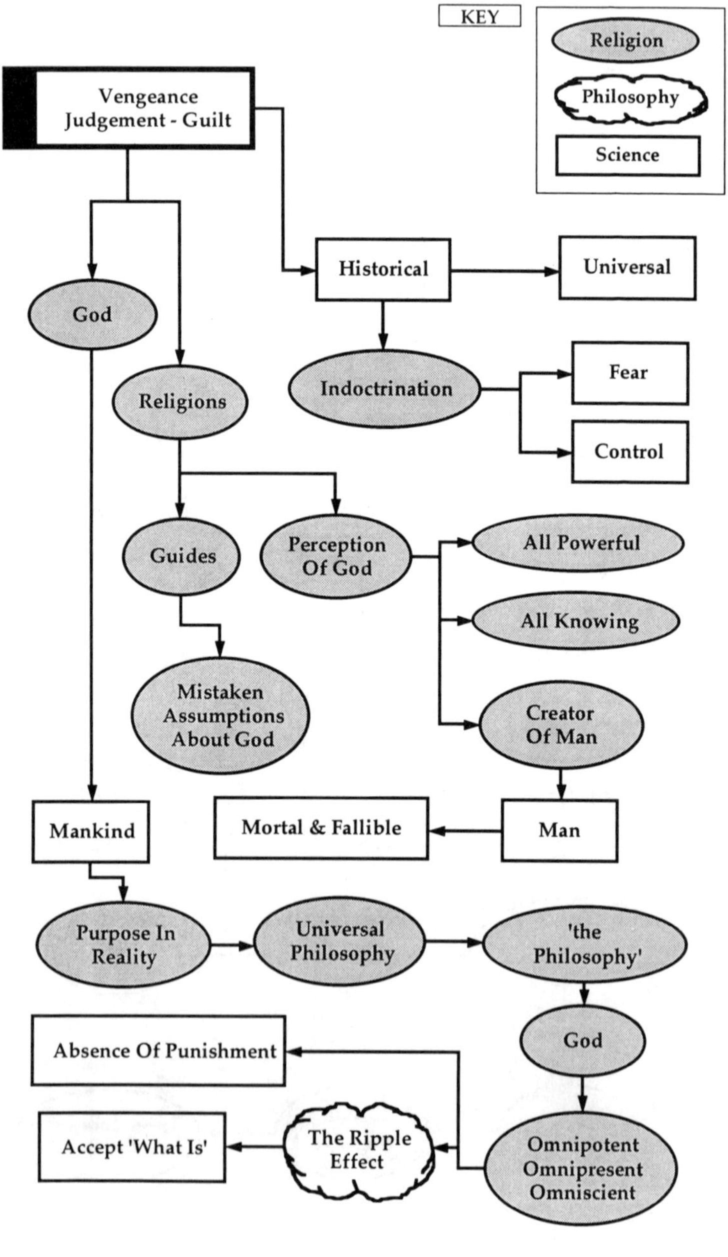

Volume I - You & I Together - Have a Purpose In Reality
Chapter 31: Christianity/Religion

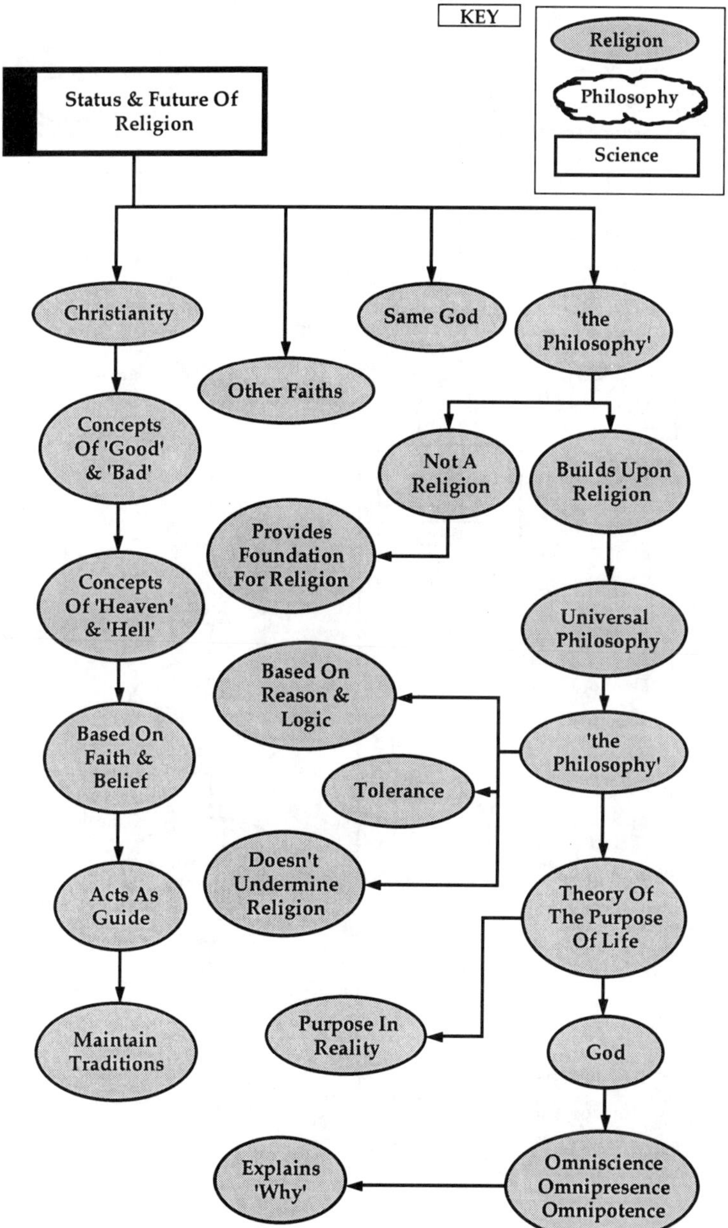

Volume I - You & I Together - Have a Purpose In Reality
Chapter 32: Jesus Christ

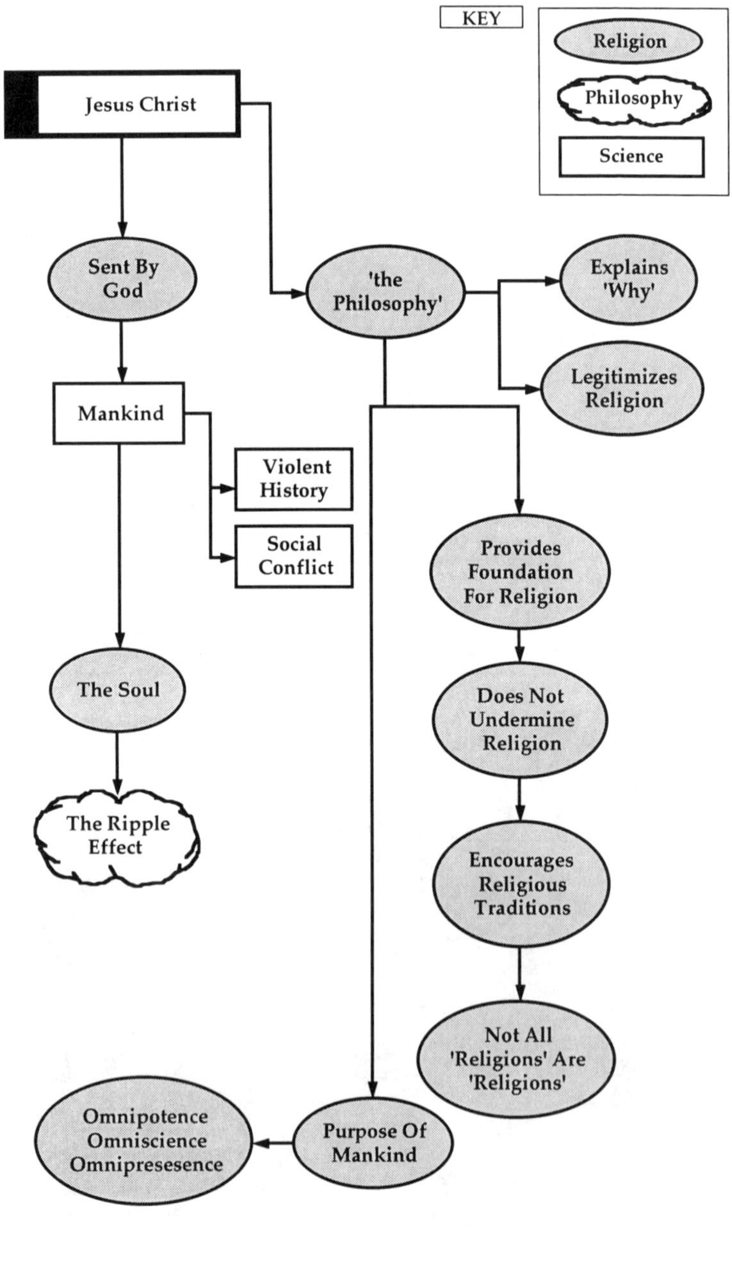

Volume I - You & I Together - Have a Purpose In Reality
Chapter 33: In Summary

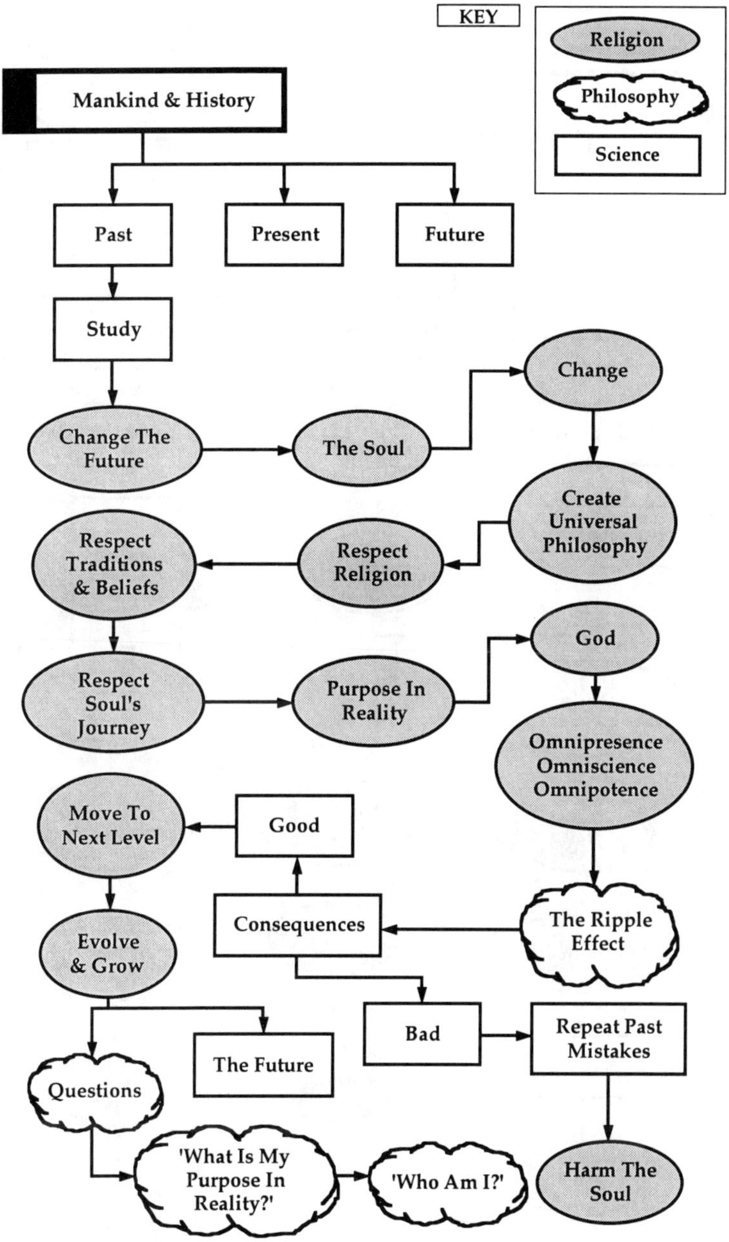

Volume II - In the Image of God
Chapter 1: To Begin

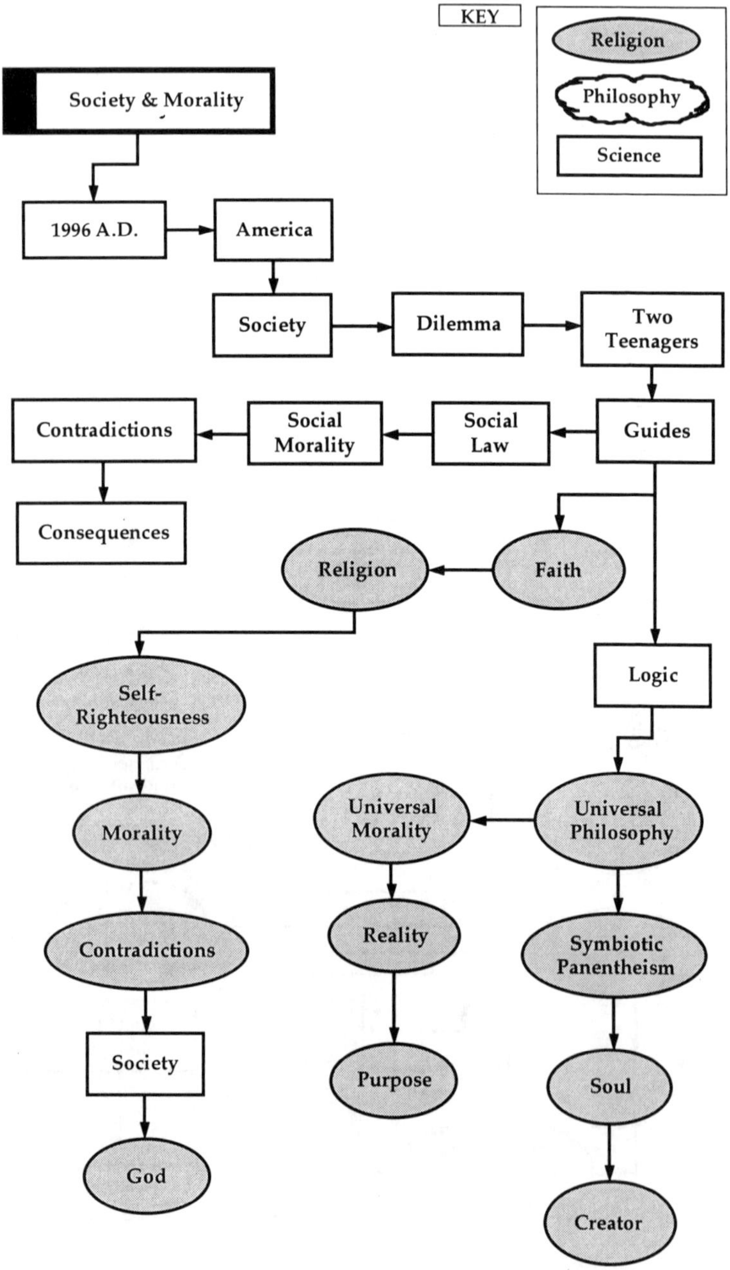

Volume II - In the Image of God
Chapter 2: Only Words

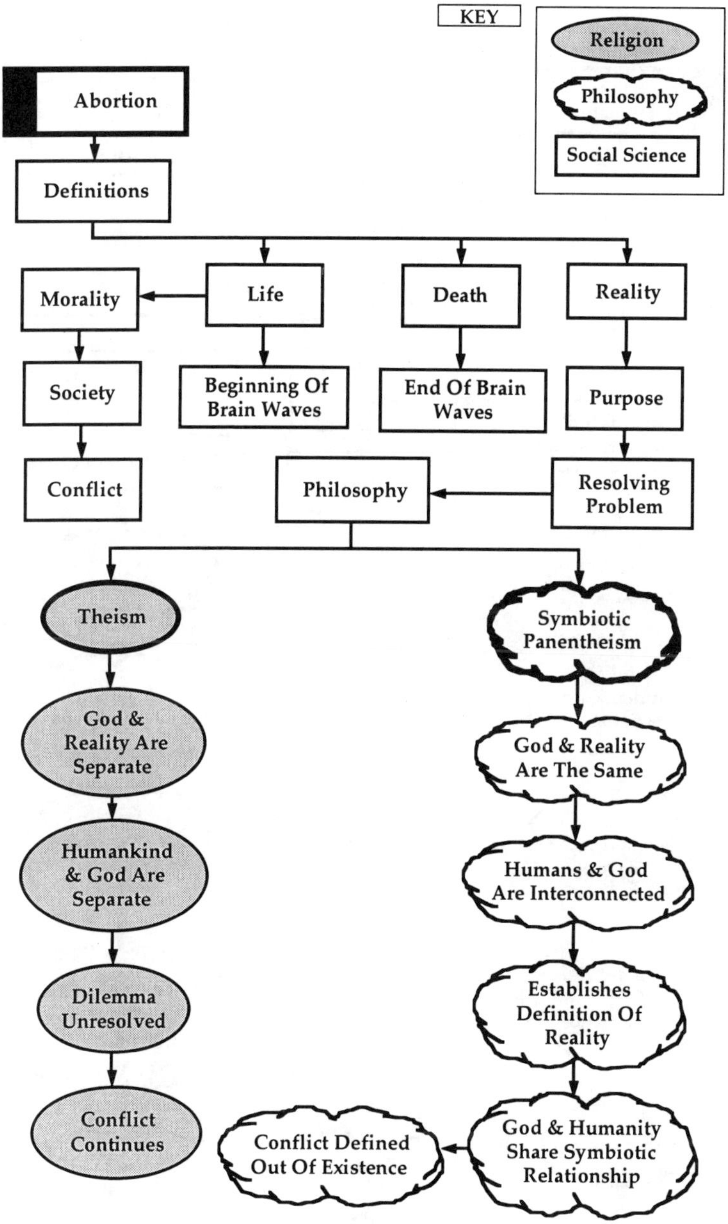

Volume II - In the Image of God

Chapter 3: The Choice

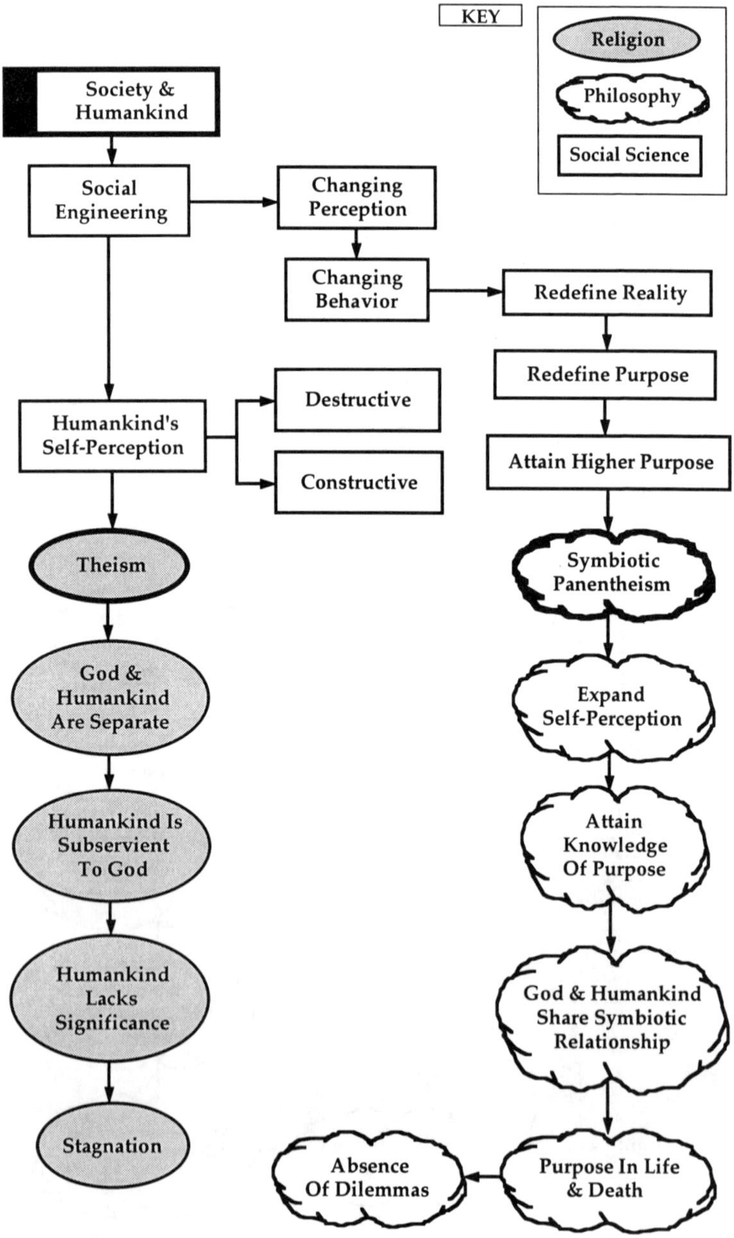

Volume II - In the Image of God

Chapter 4: Slavery Is Slavery

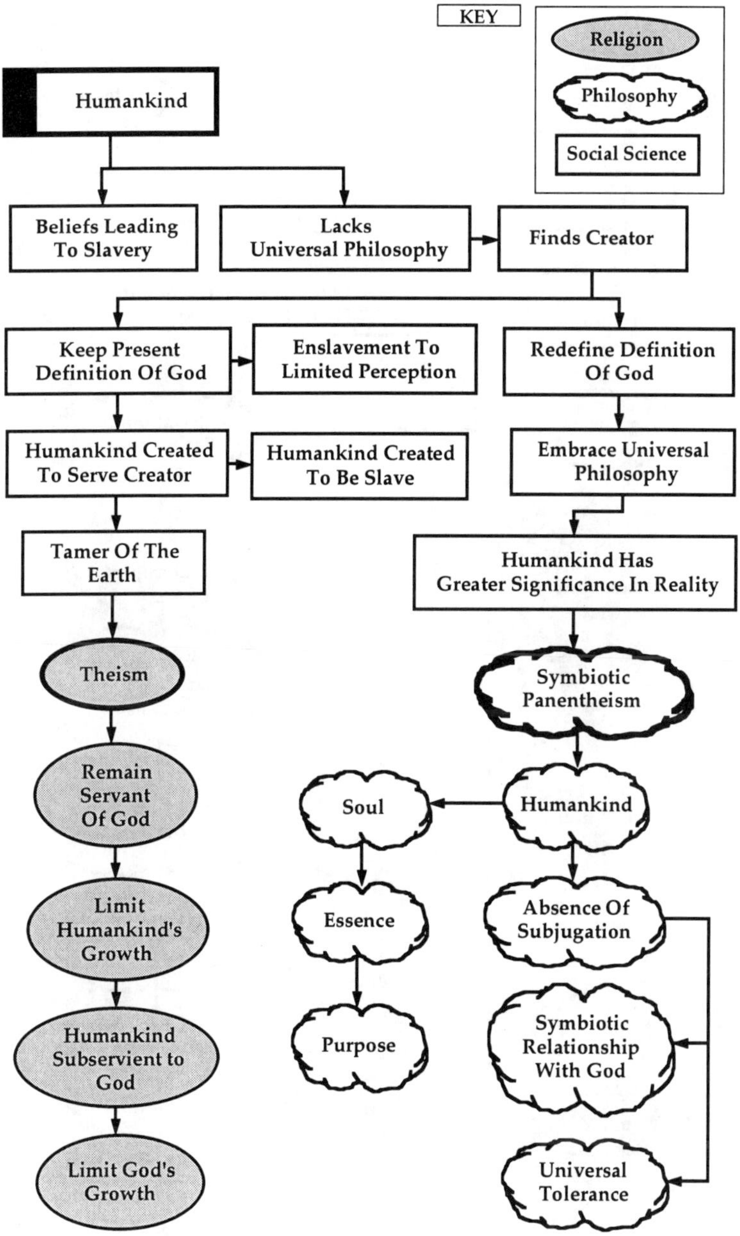

Volume II - In the Image of God

Chapter 5: Humanity Sentenced To Life

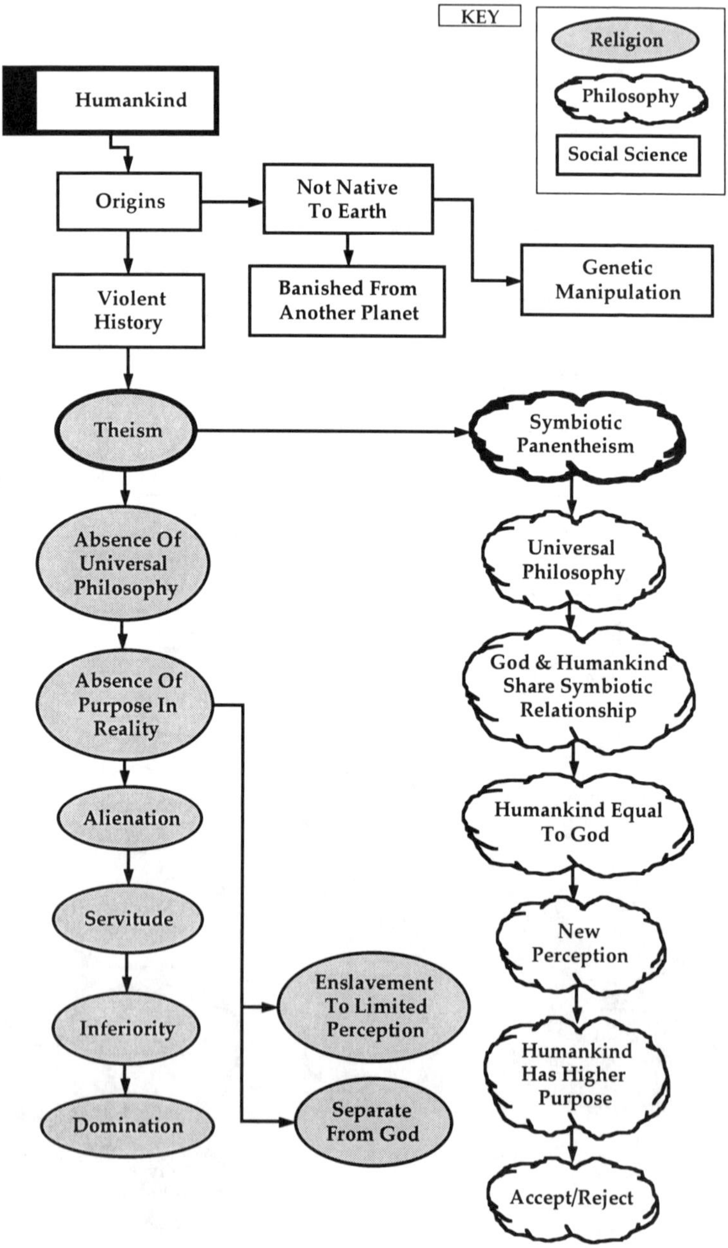

Volume II - In the Image of God

Chapter 6: Trapped

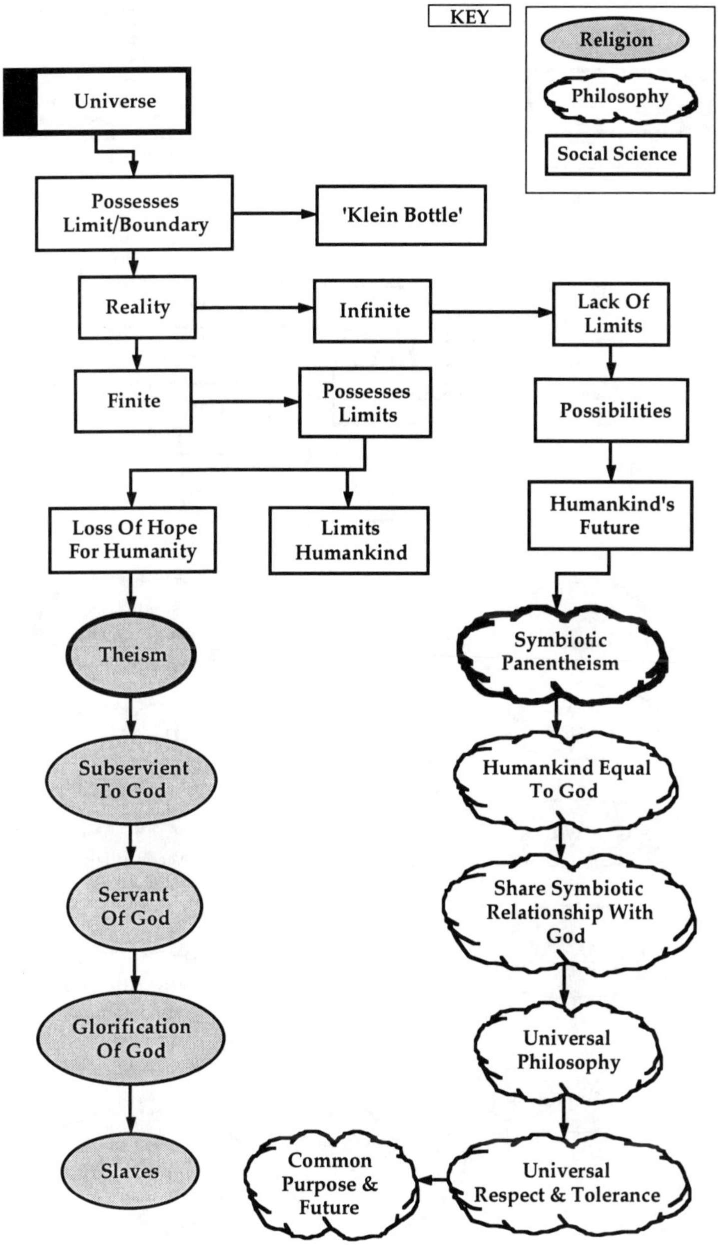

Volume II - In the Image of God

Chapter 7: Collapse

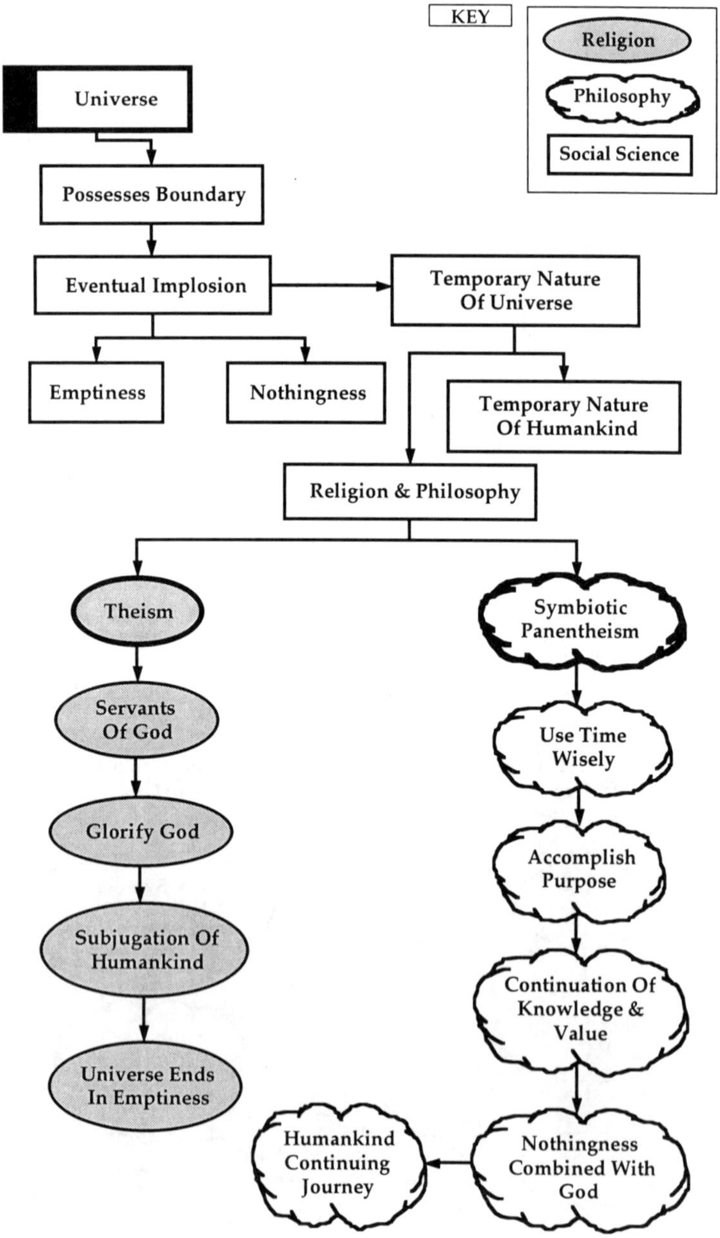

Volume II - In the Image of God

Chapter 8: The Nightmare

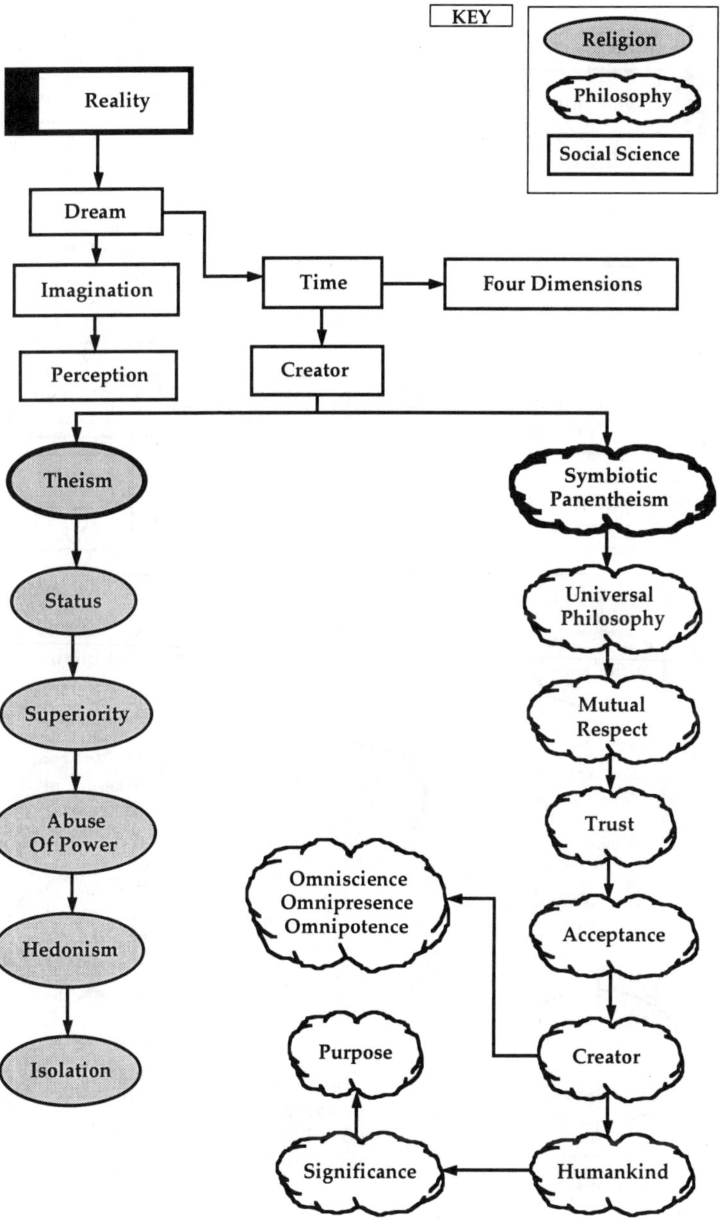

Volume II - In the Image of God

Chapter 9: A Toy

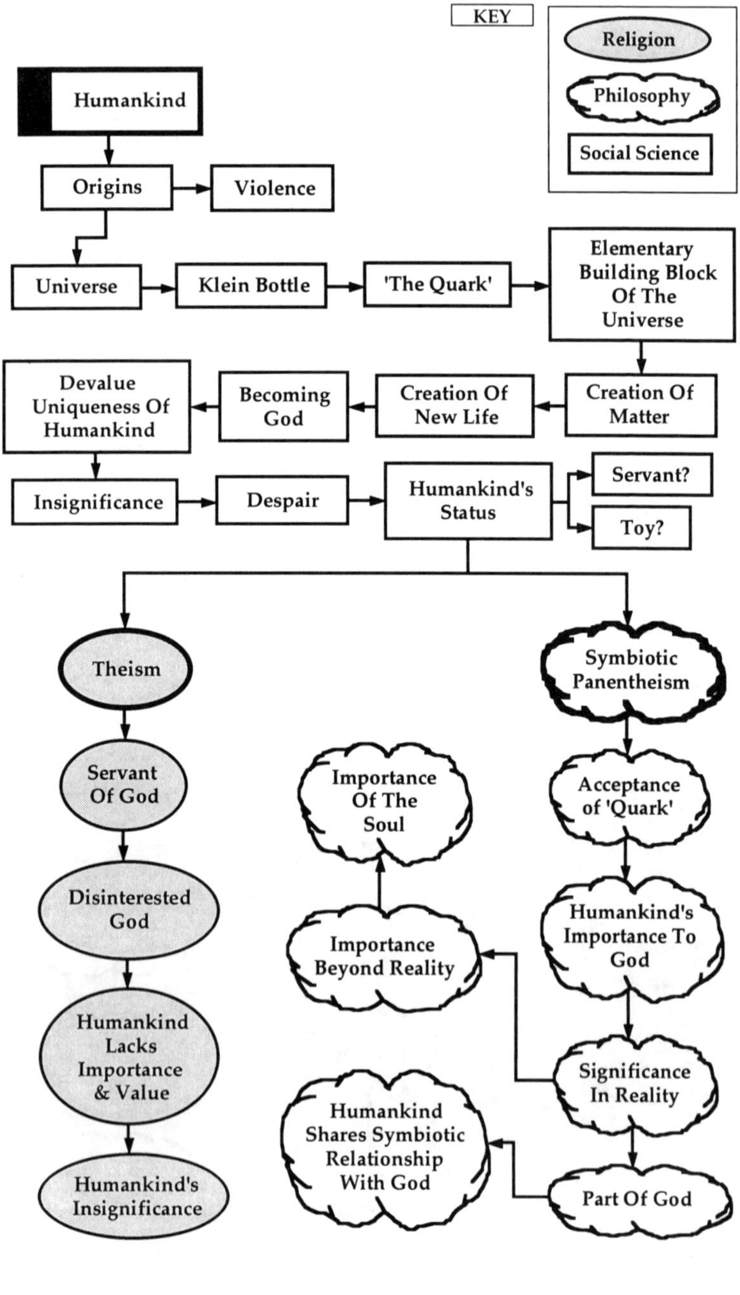

Volume II - In the Image of God
Chapter 10: Growing

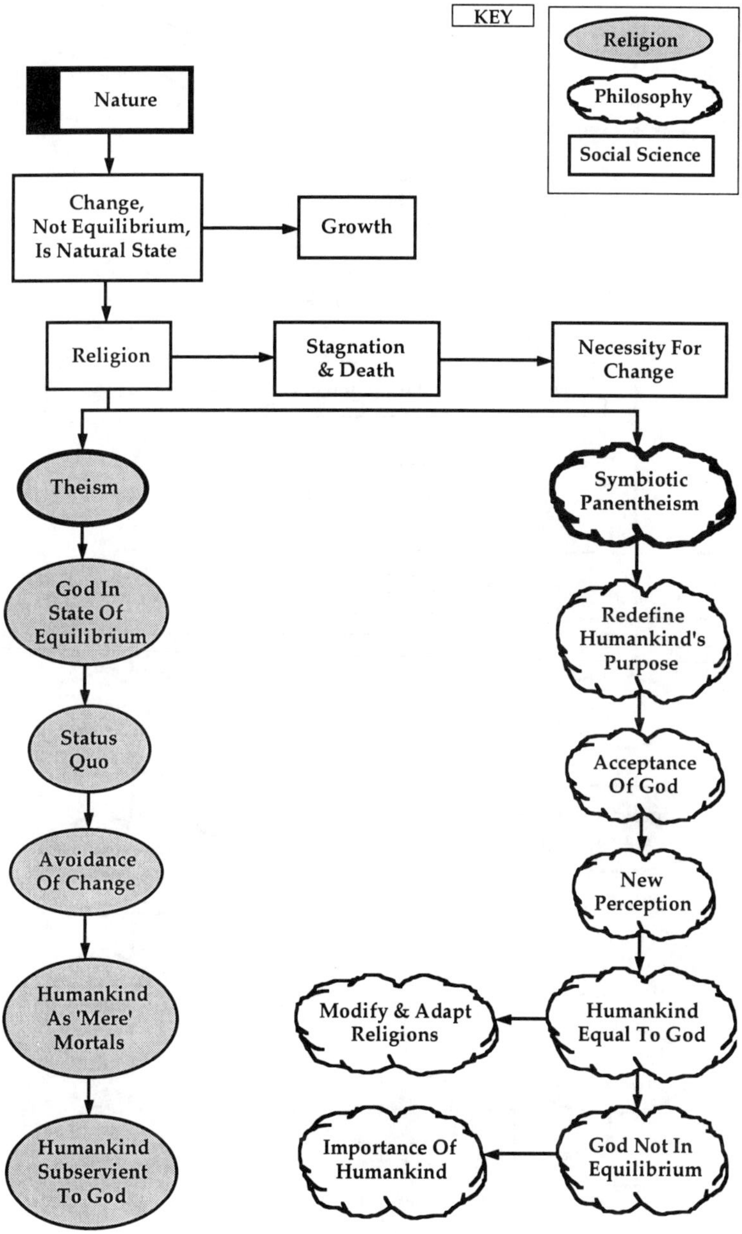

Volume II - In the Image of God
Chapter 11: "Typhoid Mary"

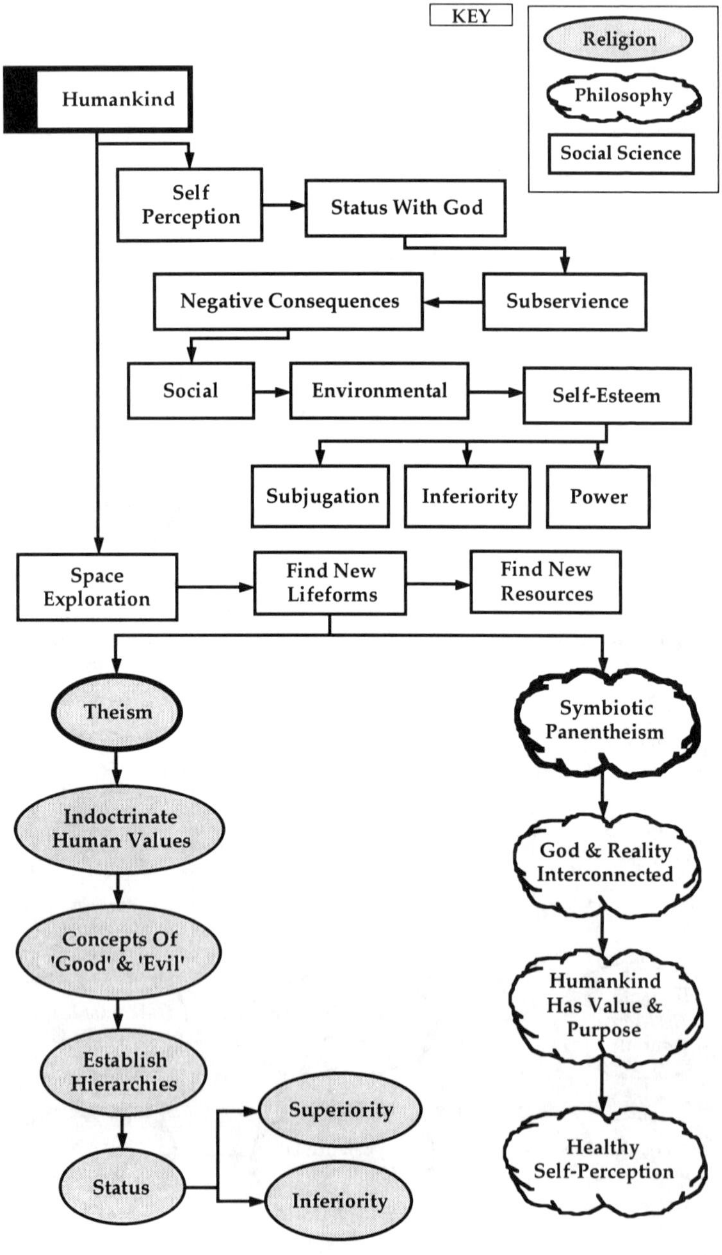

Volume II - In the Image of God
Chapter 12: Twins

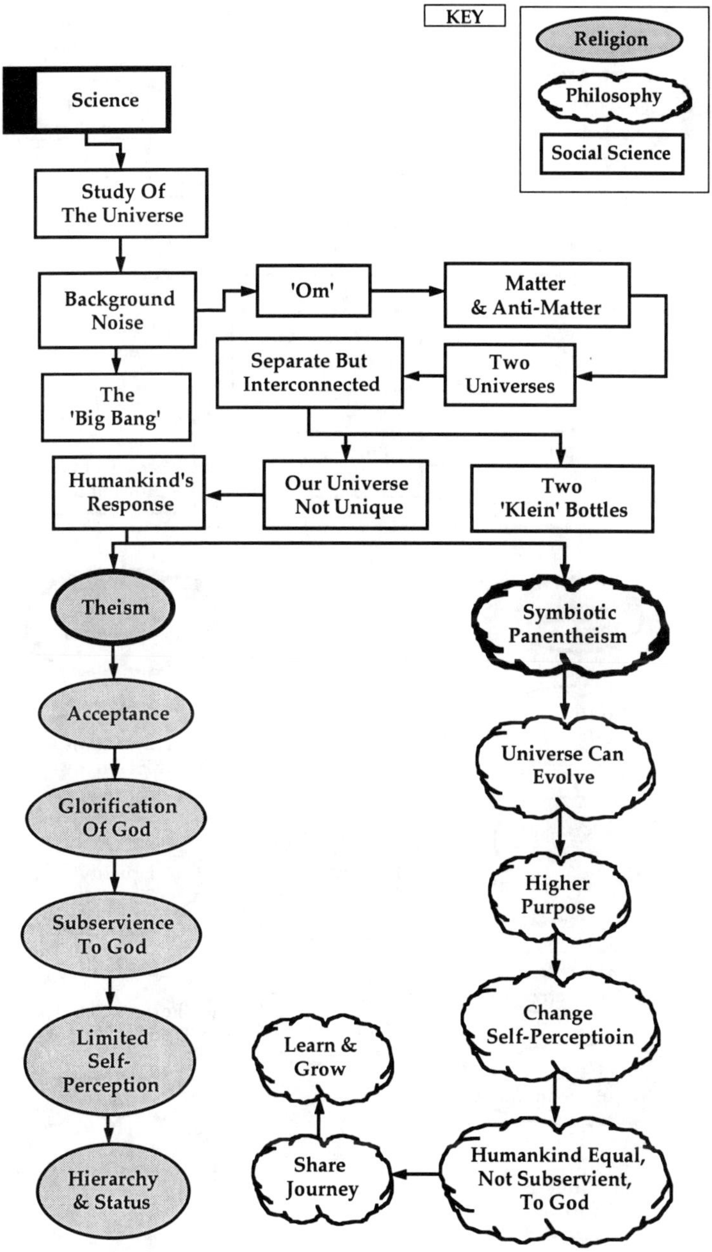

Volume II - In the Image of God

Chapter 13: Contact

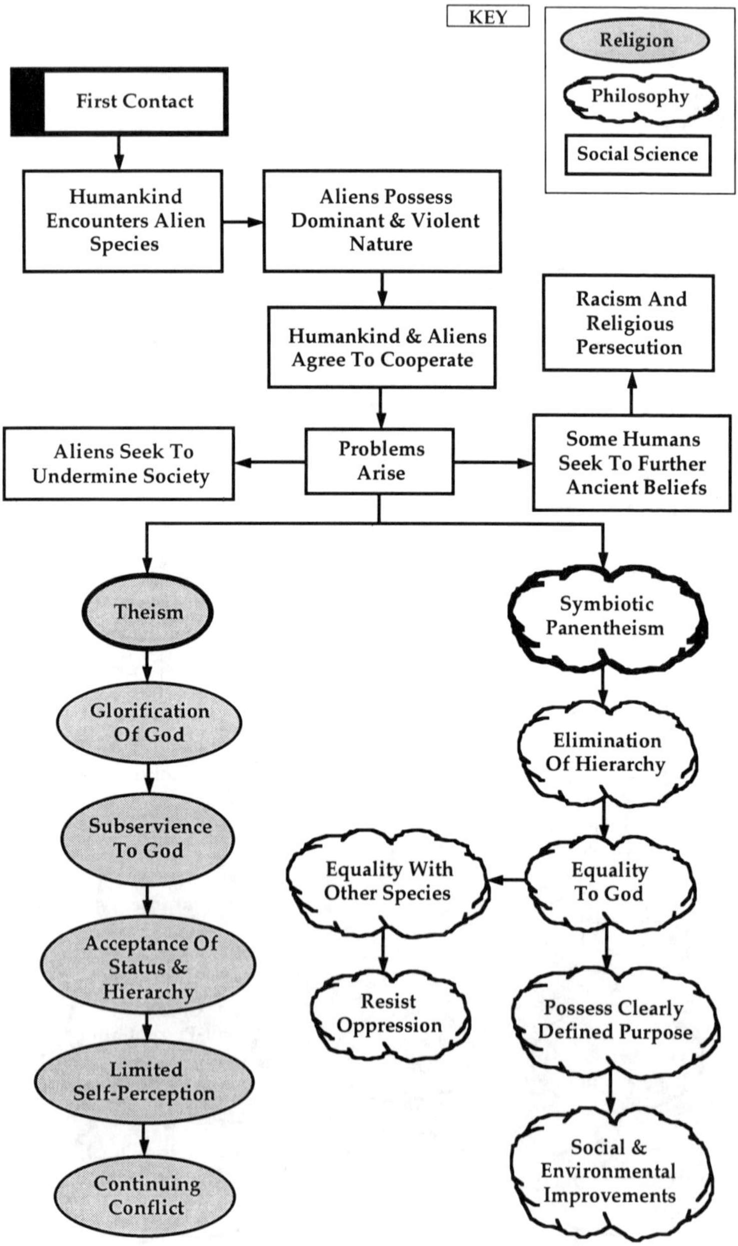

Volume II - In the Image of God
Chapter 14: Quadruplets

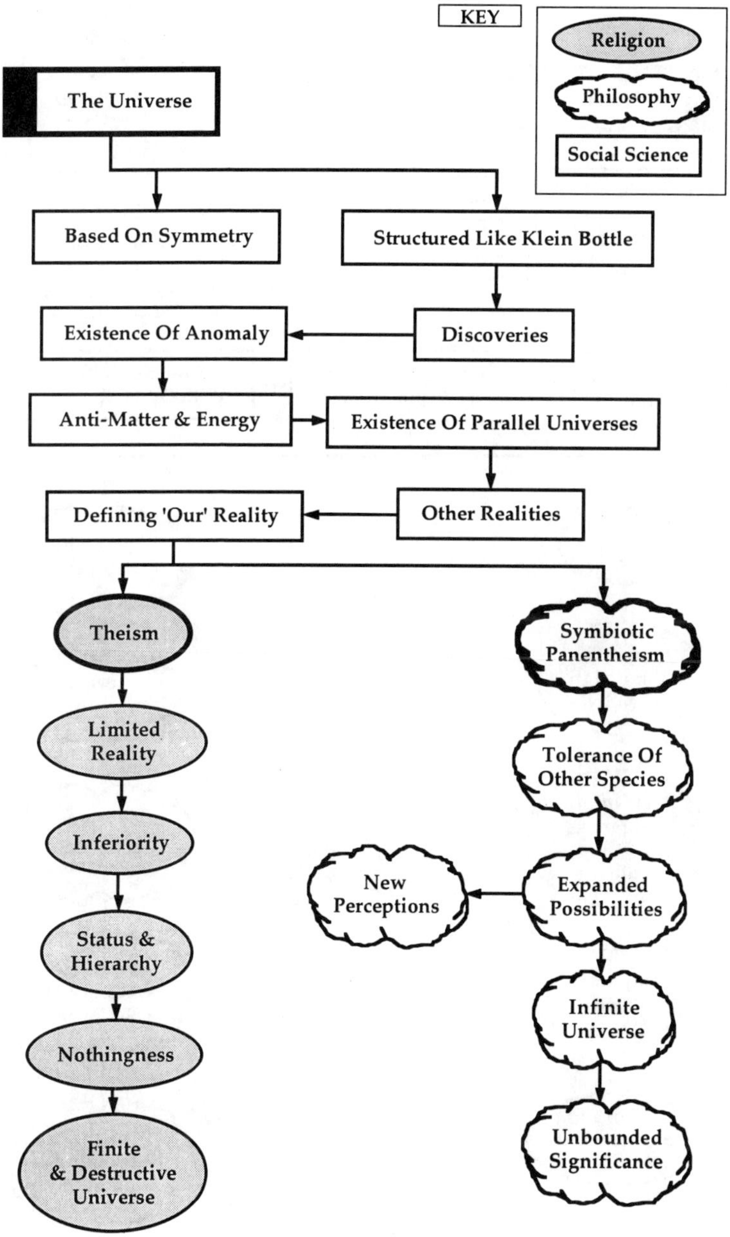

Volume II - In the Image of God
Chapter 15: A Doorway

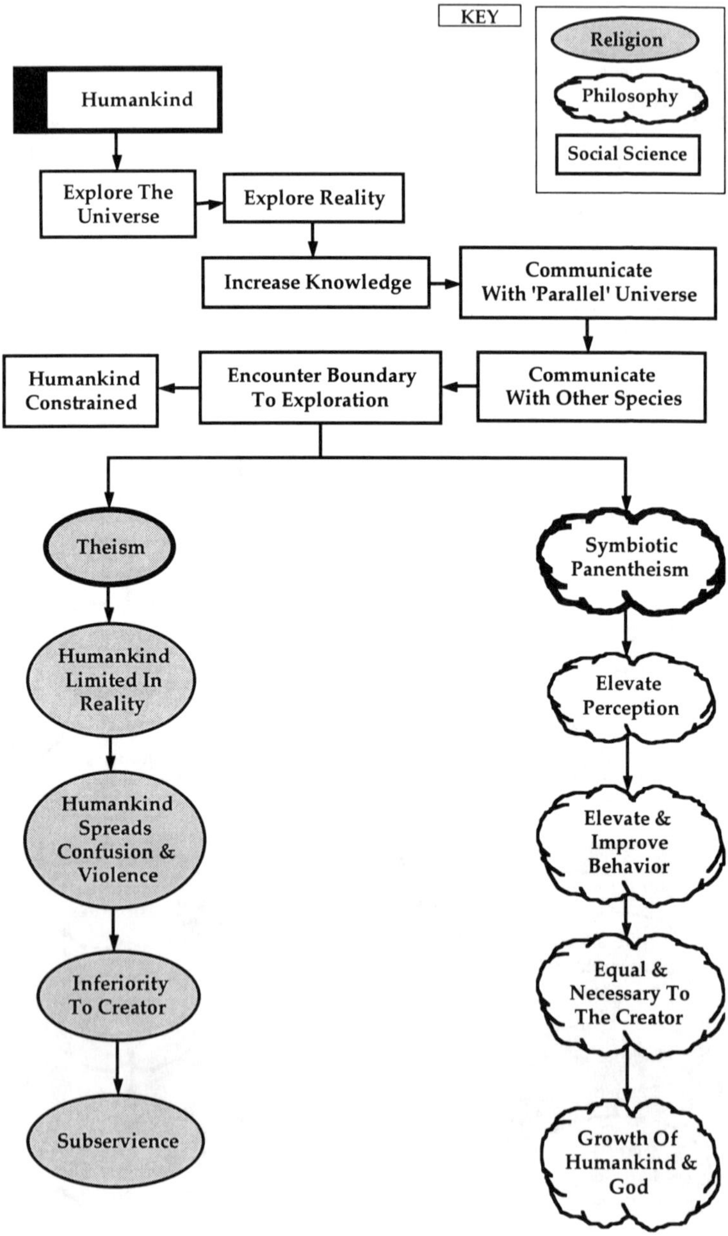

Volume II - In the Image of God
Chapter 16: Perfection

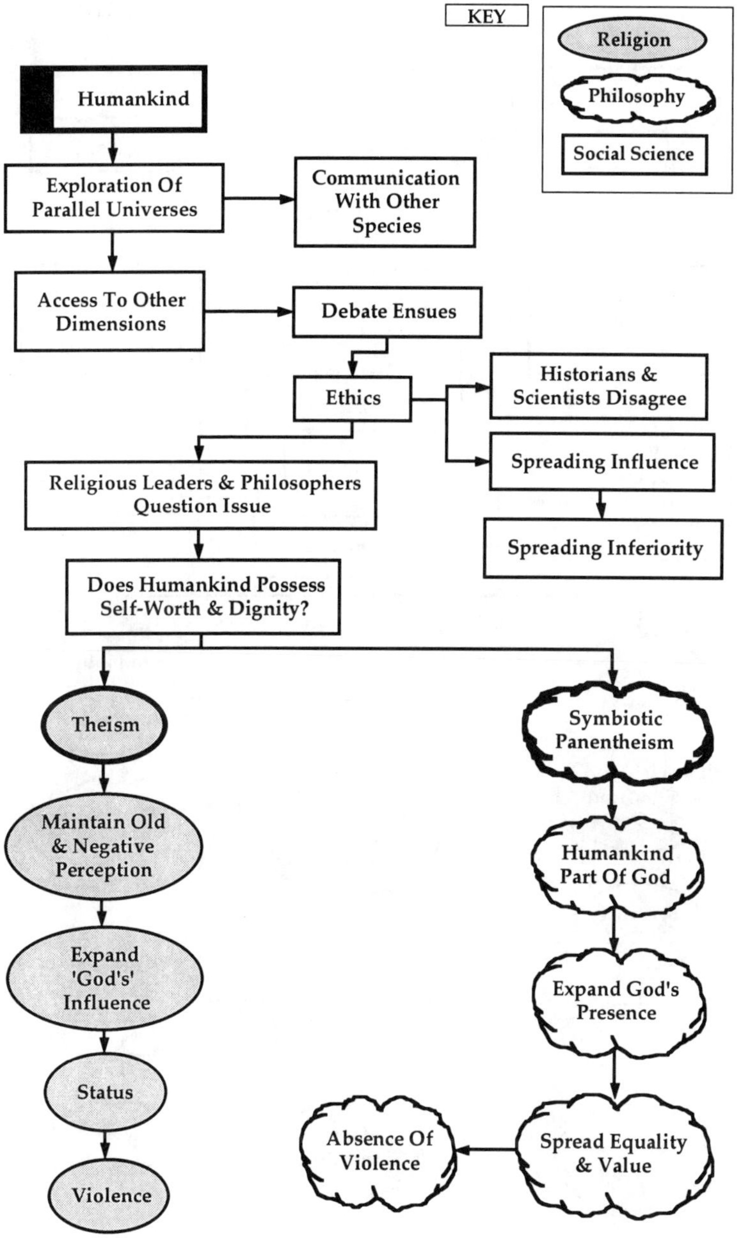

Volume II - In the Image of God
Chapter 17: More . . .

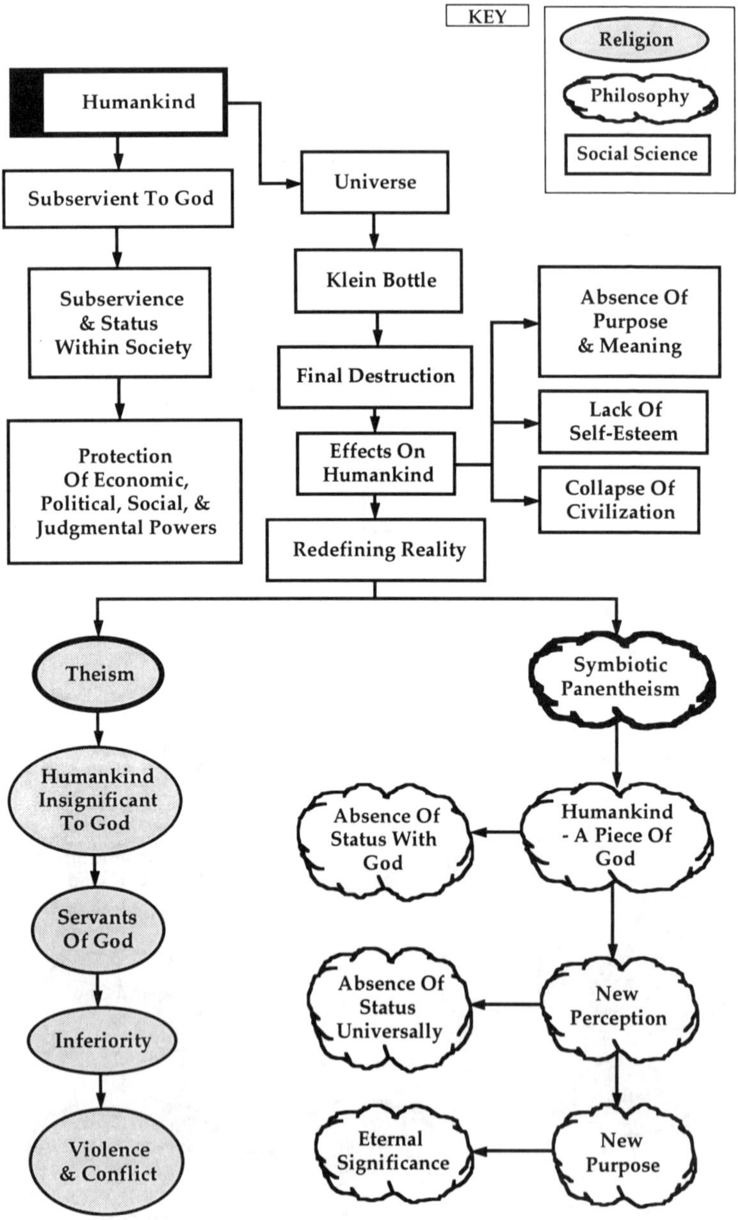

Volume II - In the Image of God

Chapter 18: The Fall

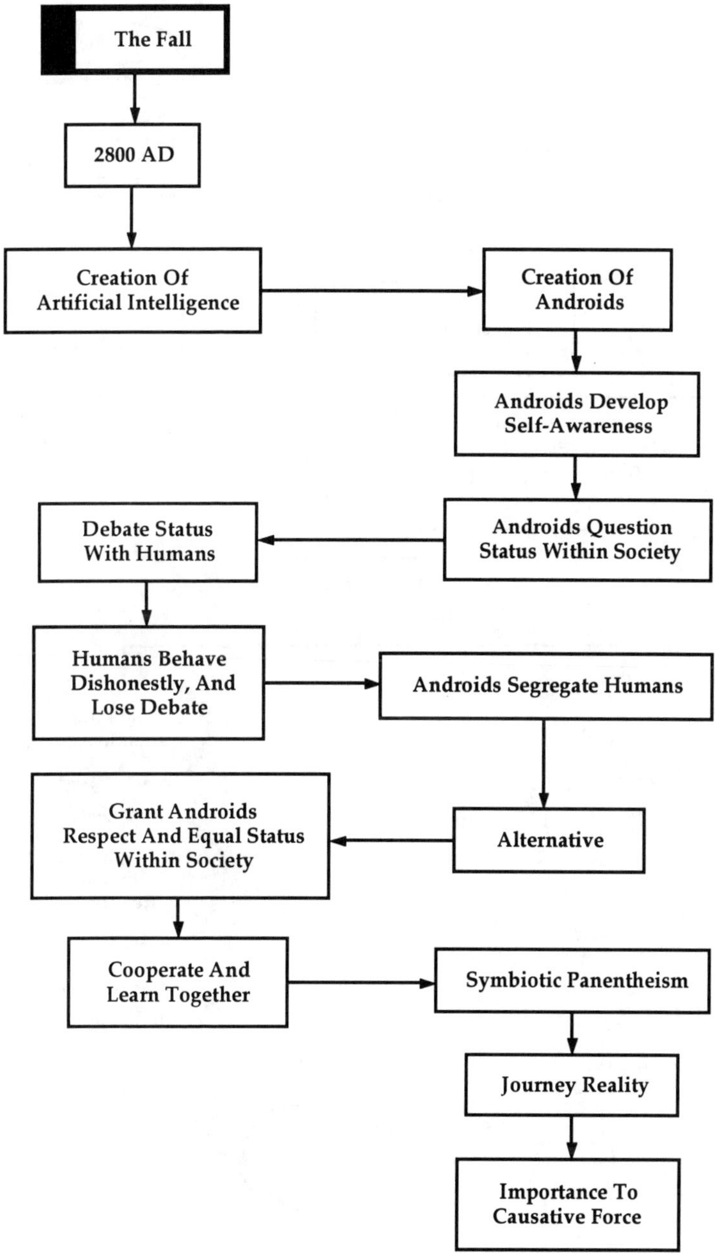

Volume II - In the Image of God

Chapter 19: Solitary

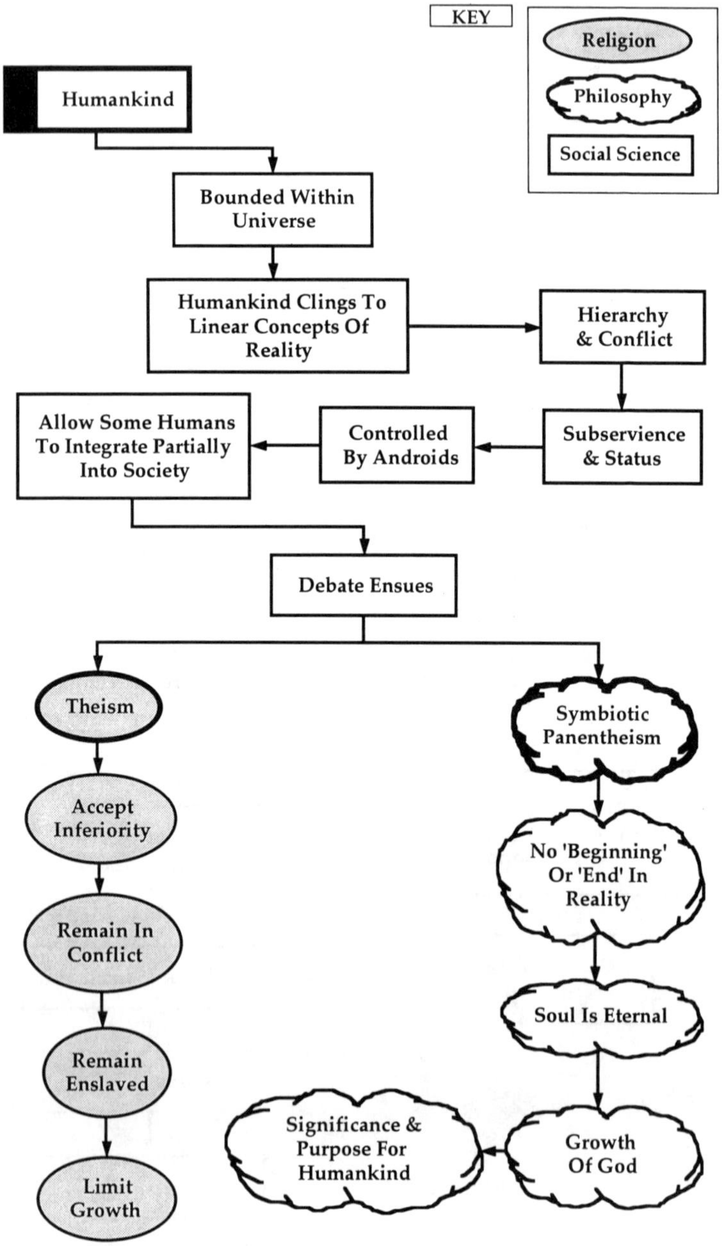

Volume II - In the Image of God

Chapter 20: The Light

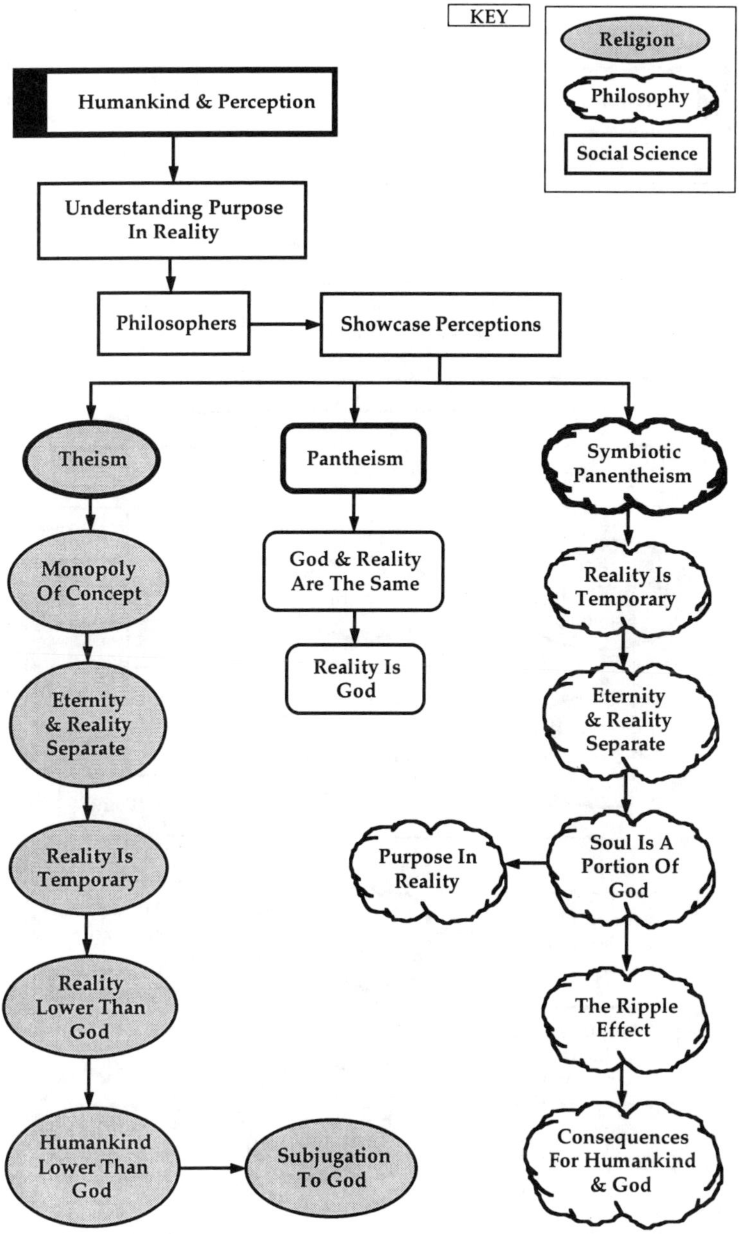

Volume II - In the Image of God
Chapter 21: The Point

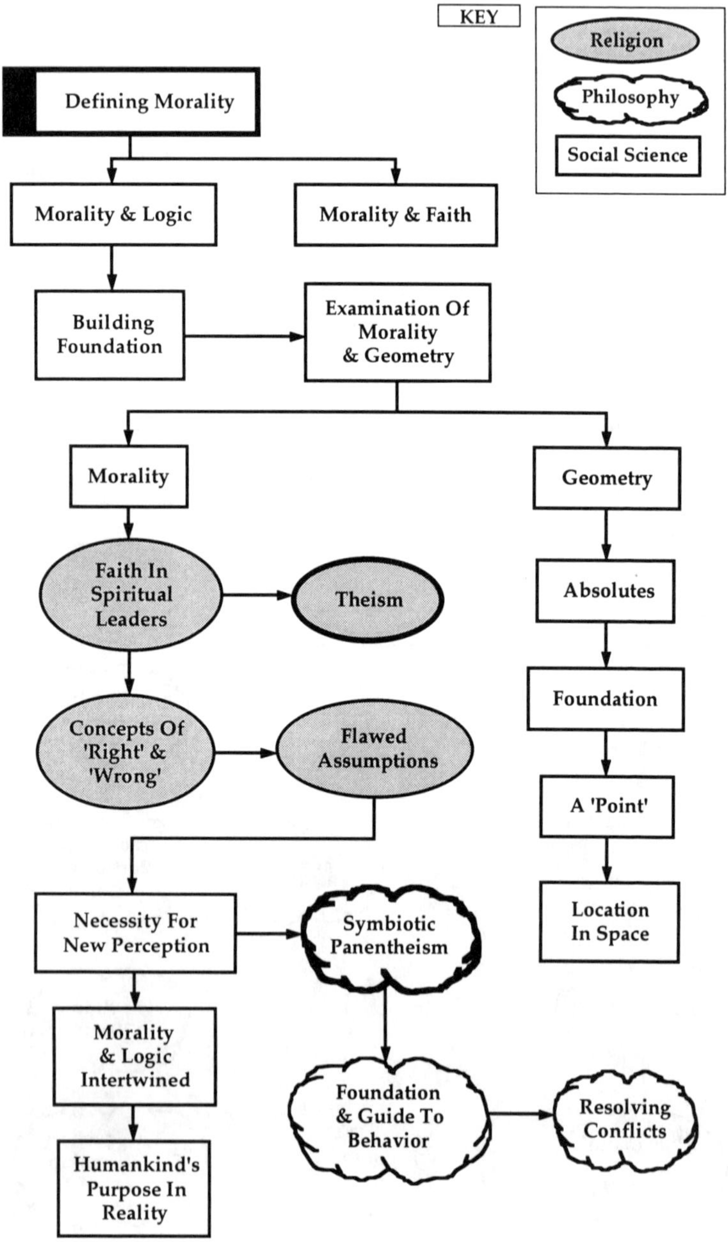

Volume II - In the Image of God
Chapter 22: A Sigh

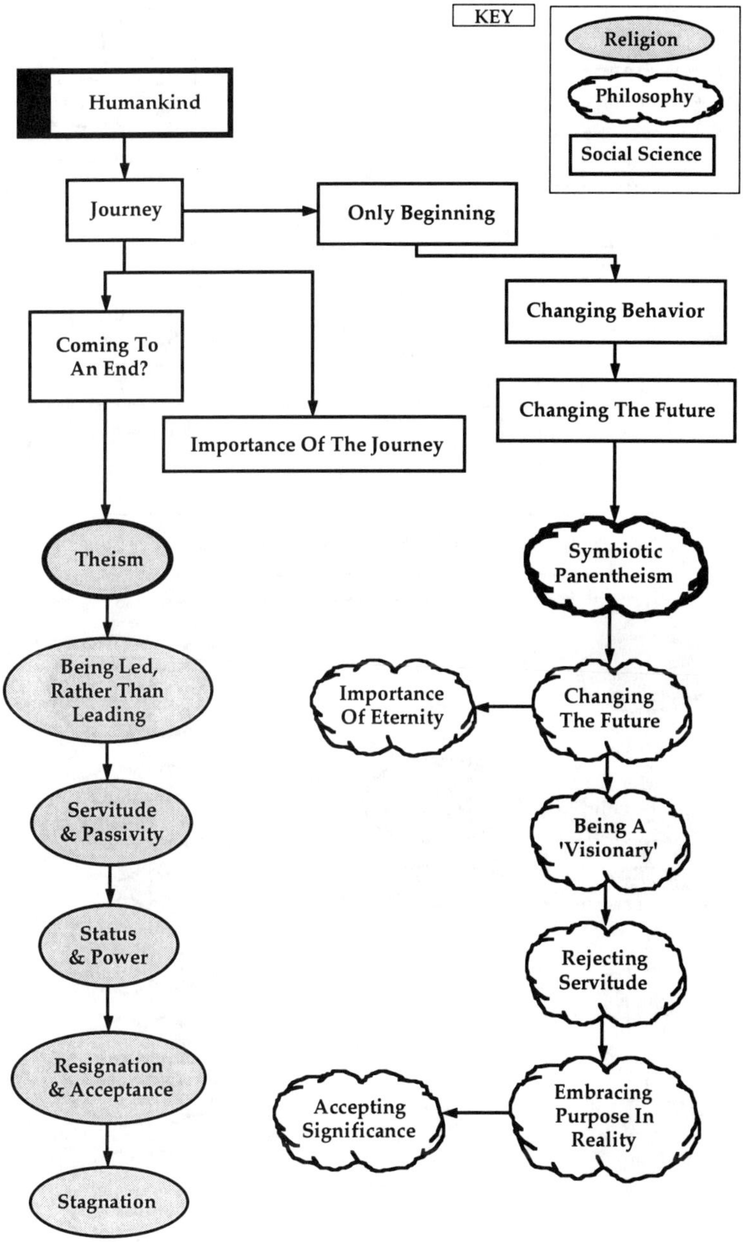

Volume II - In the Image of God
Chapter 23: Reflections - 3000 A.D.

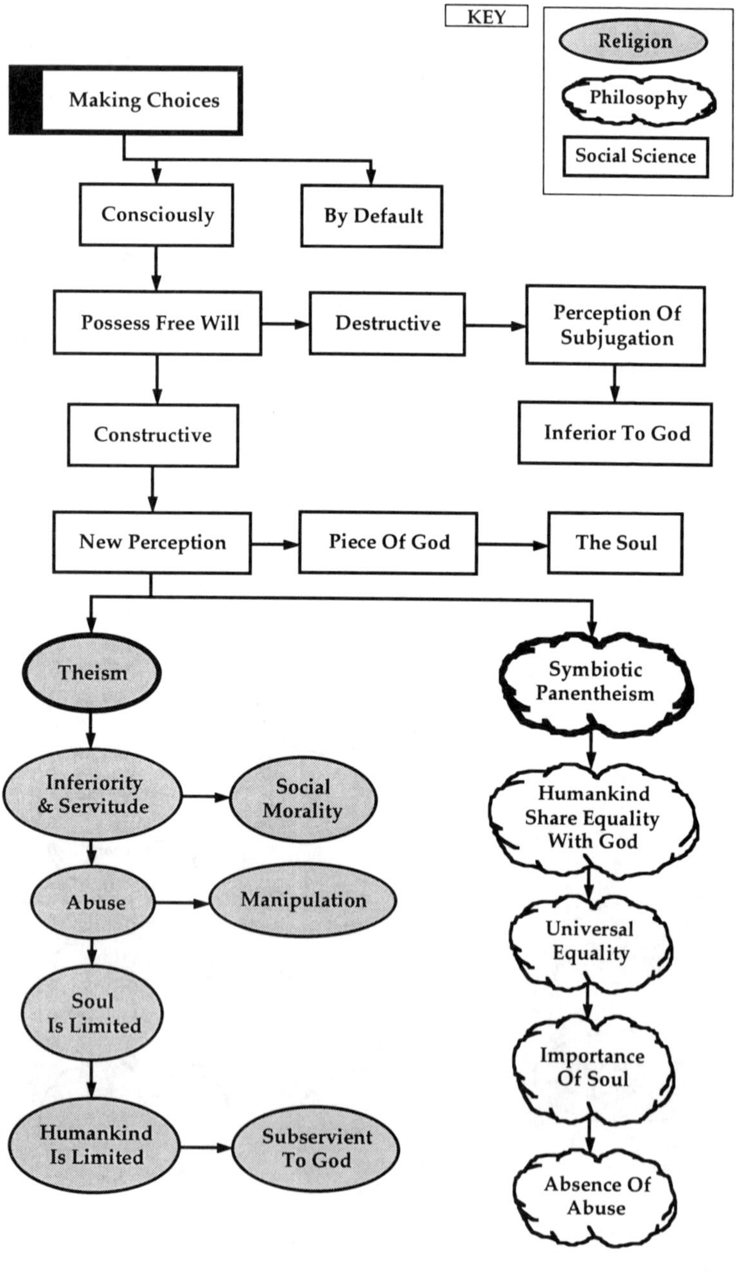

Volume II - In the Image of God
Chapter 24: Companions

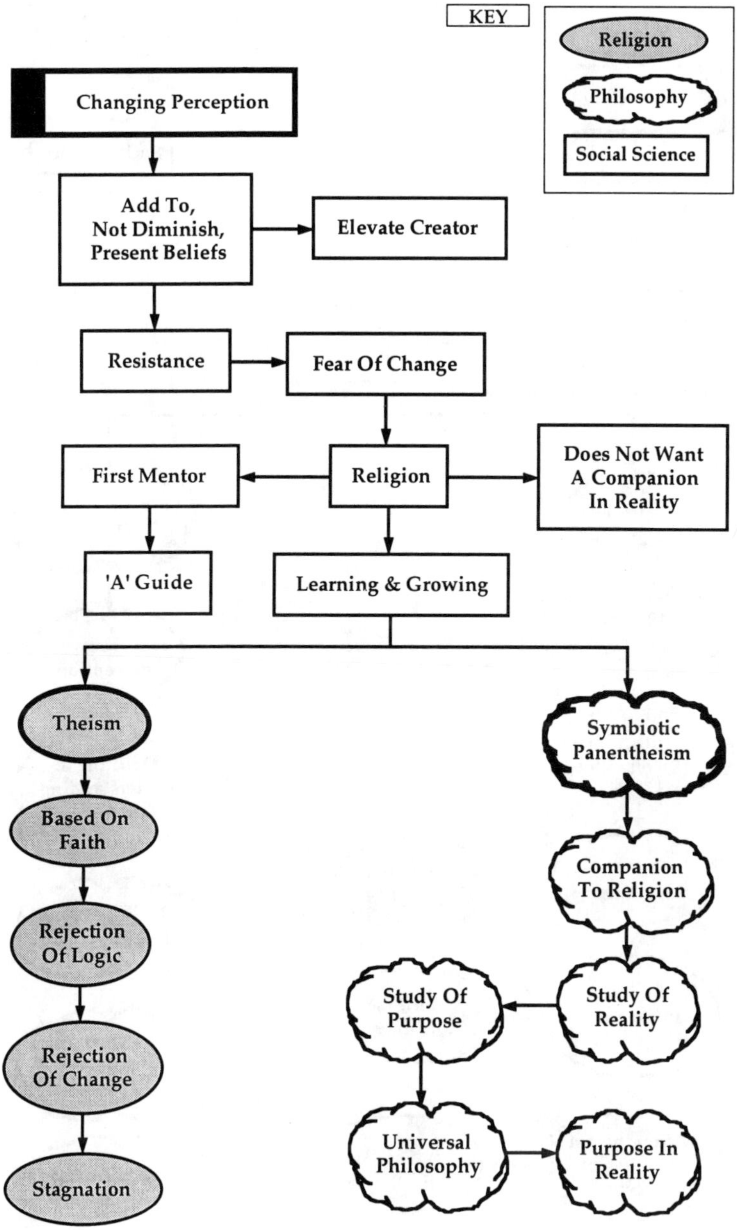

Volume II - In the Image of God
Chapter 25: Understanding

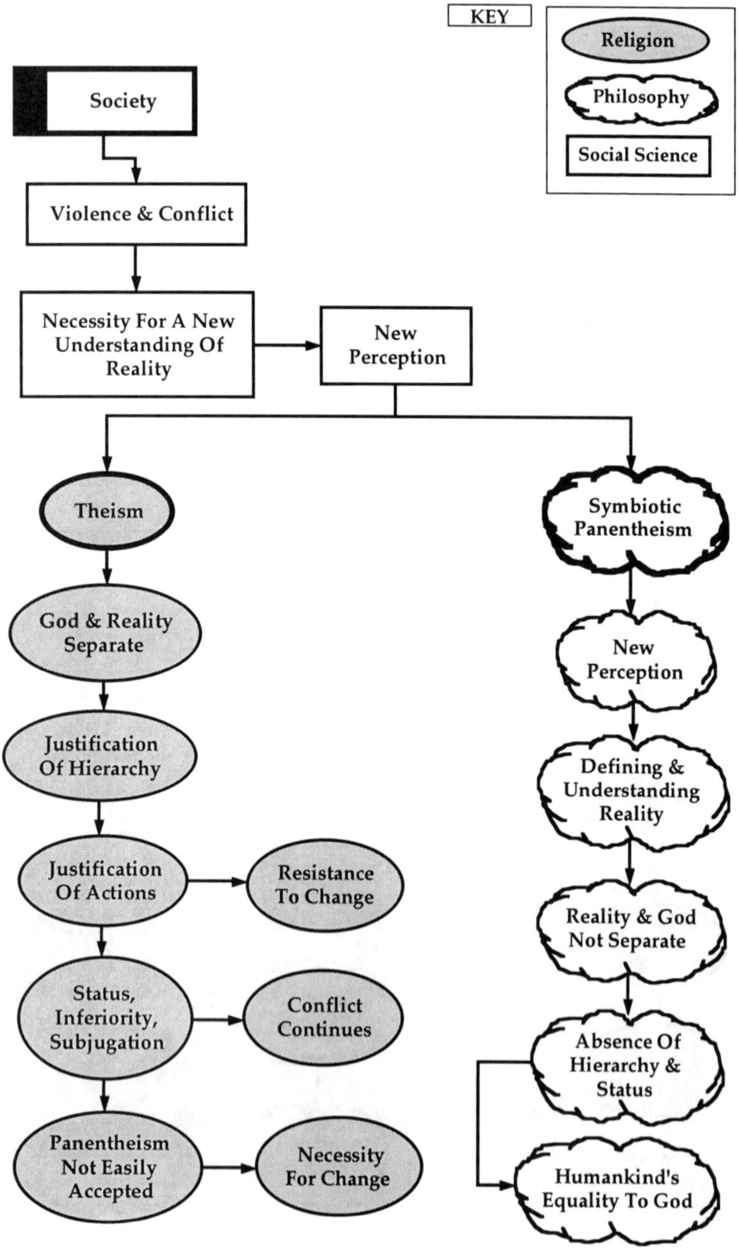

Volume II - In the Image of God

Chapter 26: Panentheism, the Soul, Reality

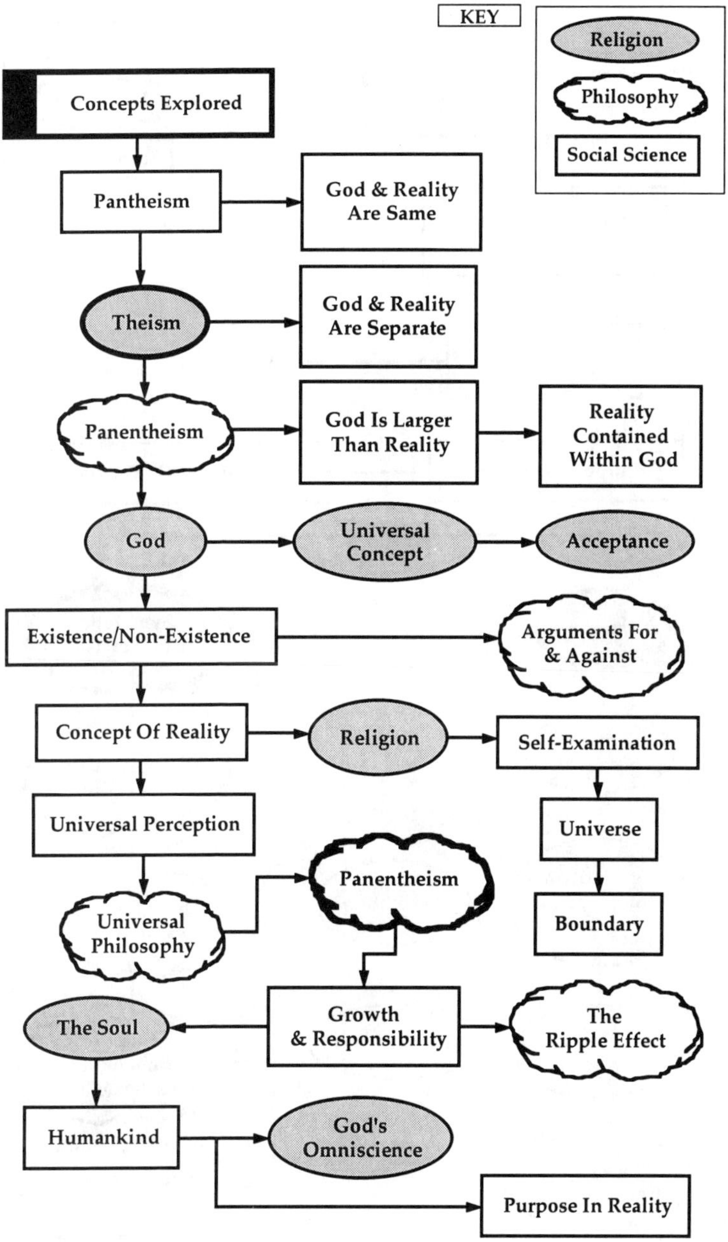

Volume II - In the Image of God

Chapter 27: The Soul

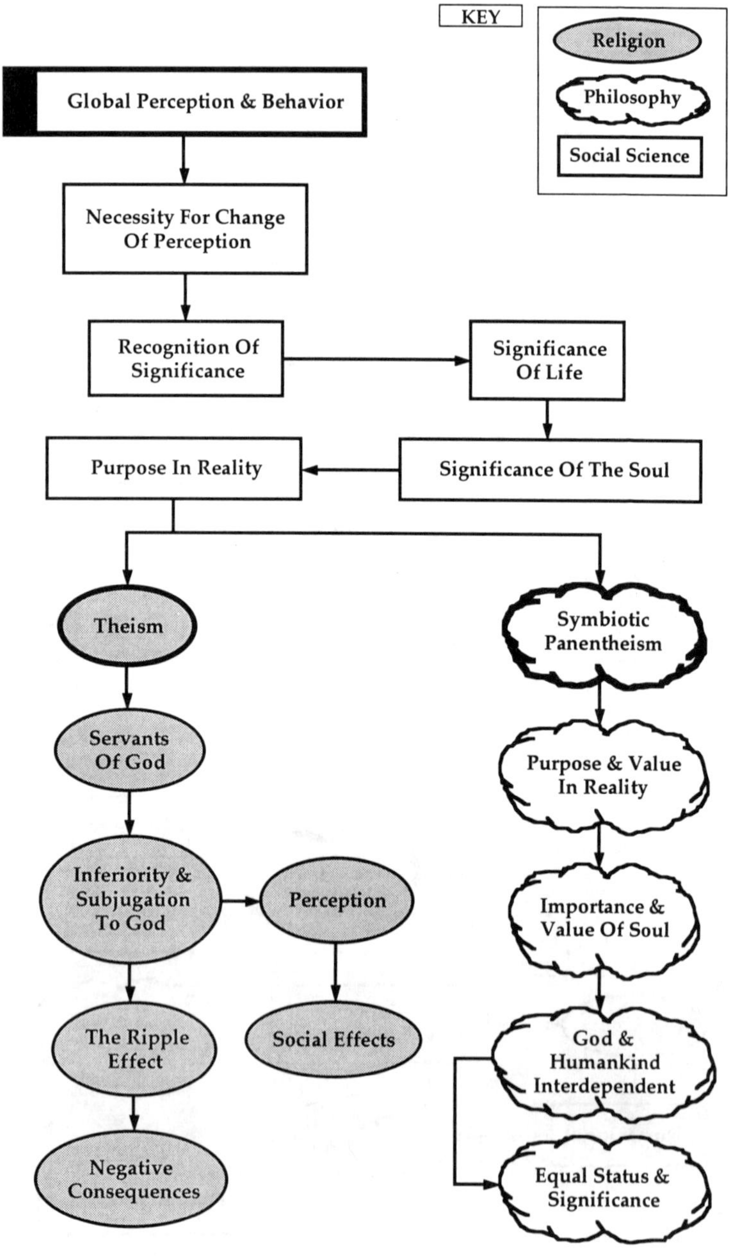

Volume II - In the Image of God

Chapter 28: . . . Ism's

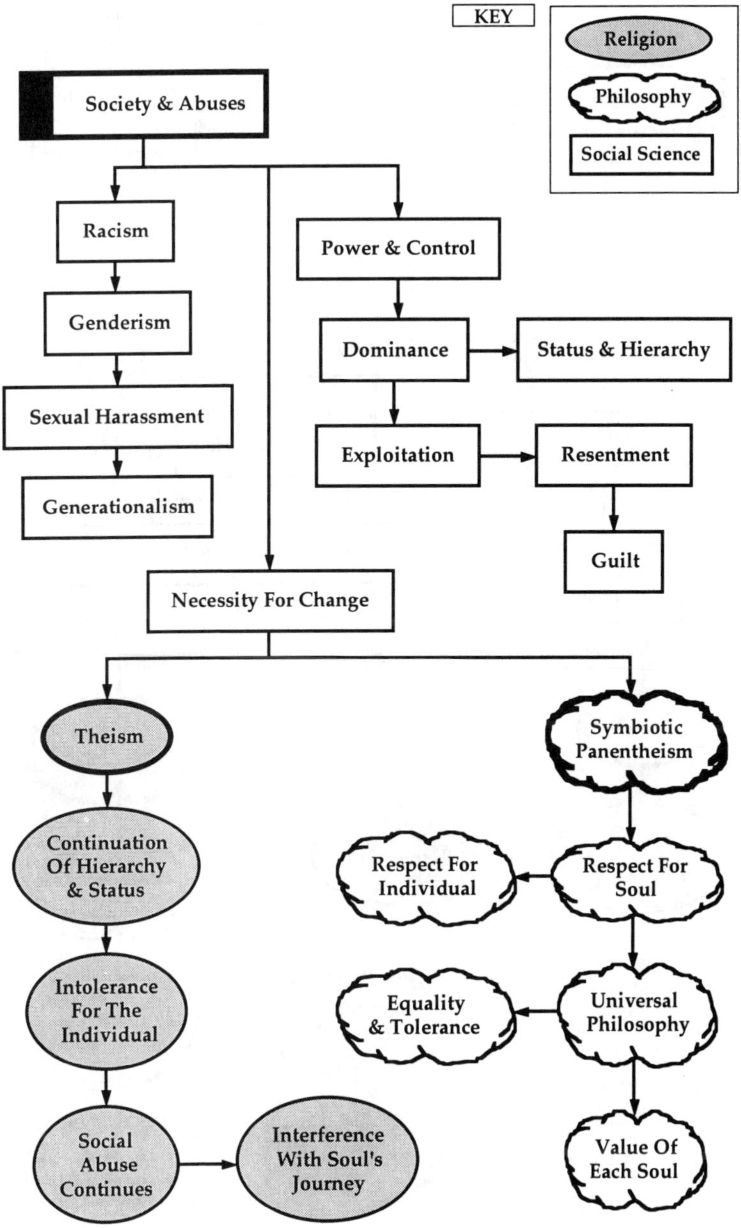

Volume II - In the Image of God

Chapter 29: The Circle

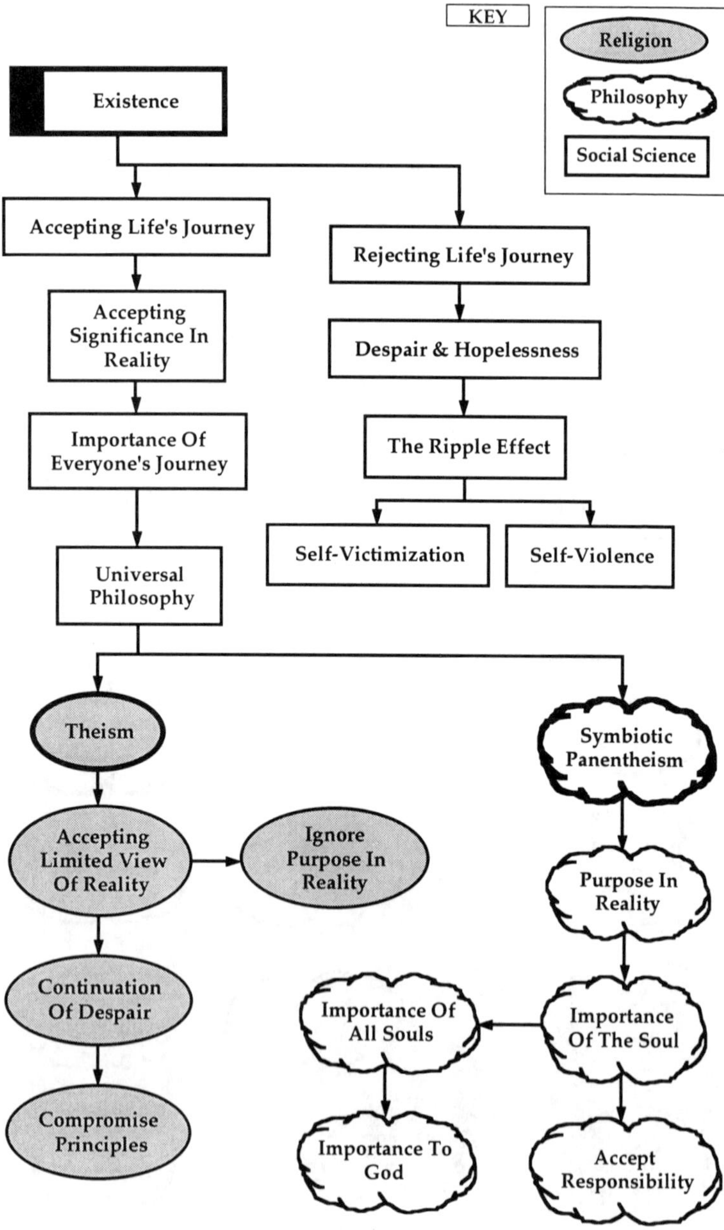

Volume II - In the Image of God
Chapter 30: Your Essence

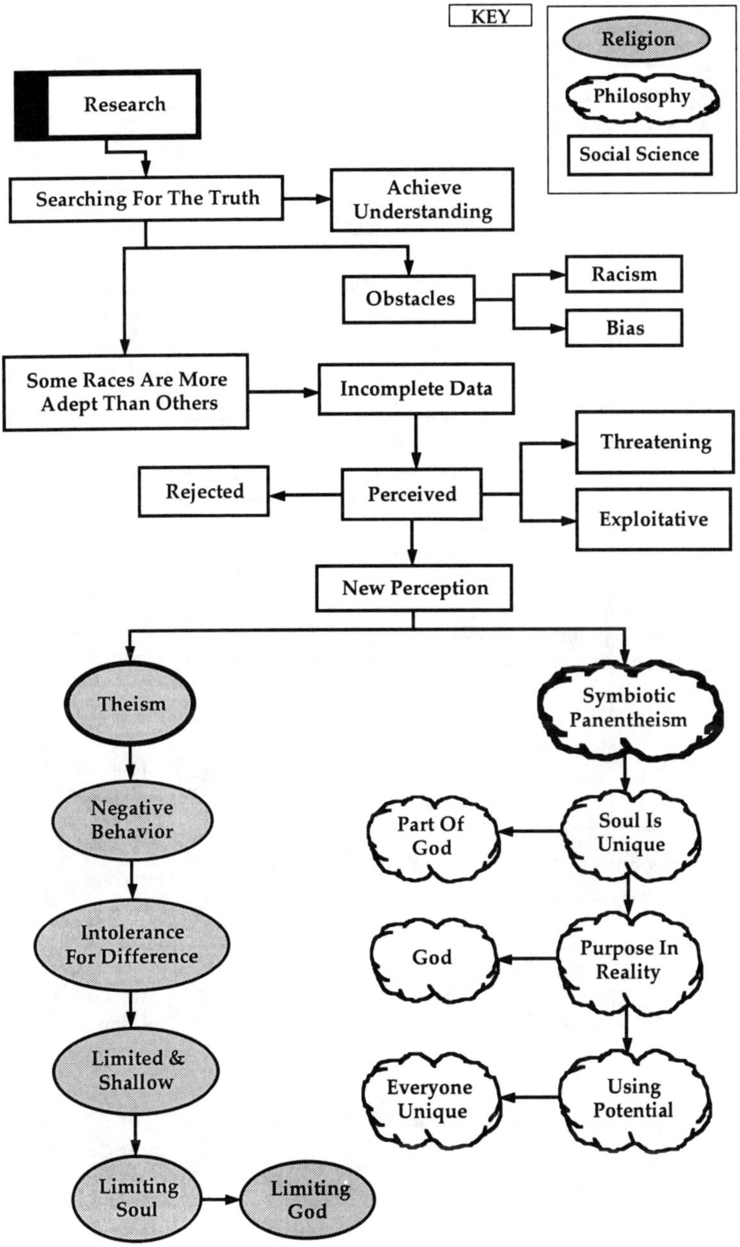

Volume II - In the Image of God

Chapter 31: The Glue

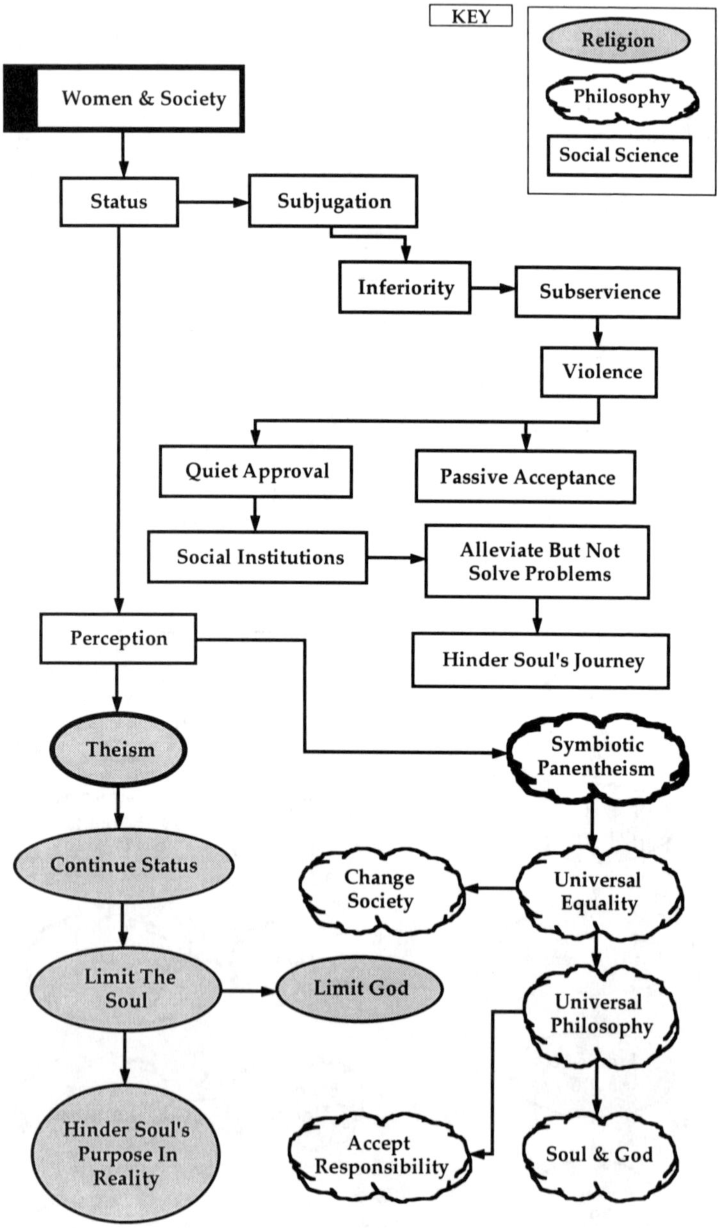

Volume II - In the Image of God

Chapter 32: Points

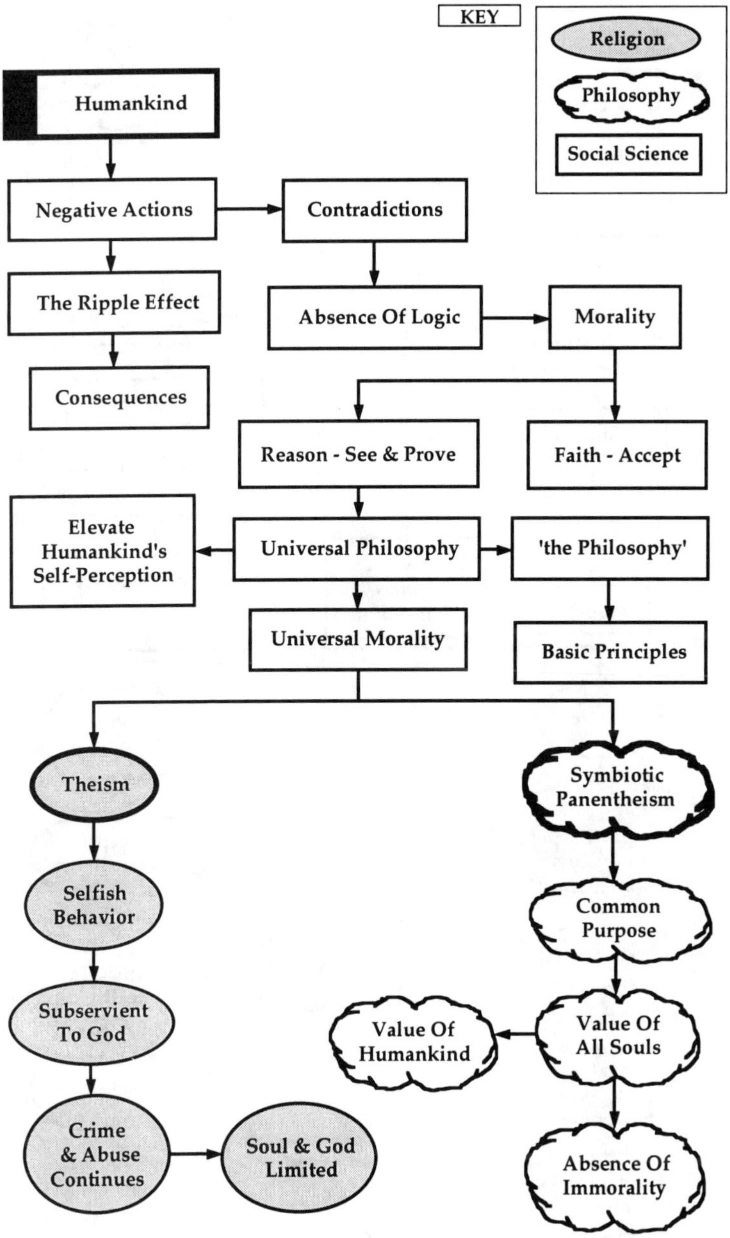

Volume II - In the Image of God

Chapter 33: It's Time

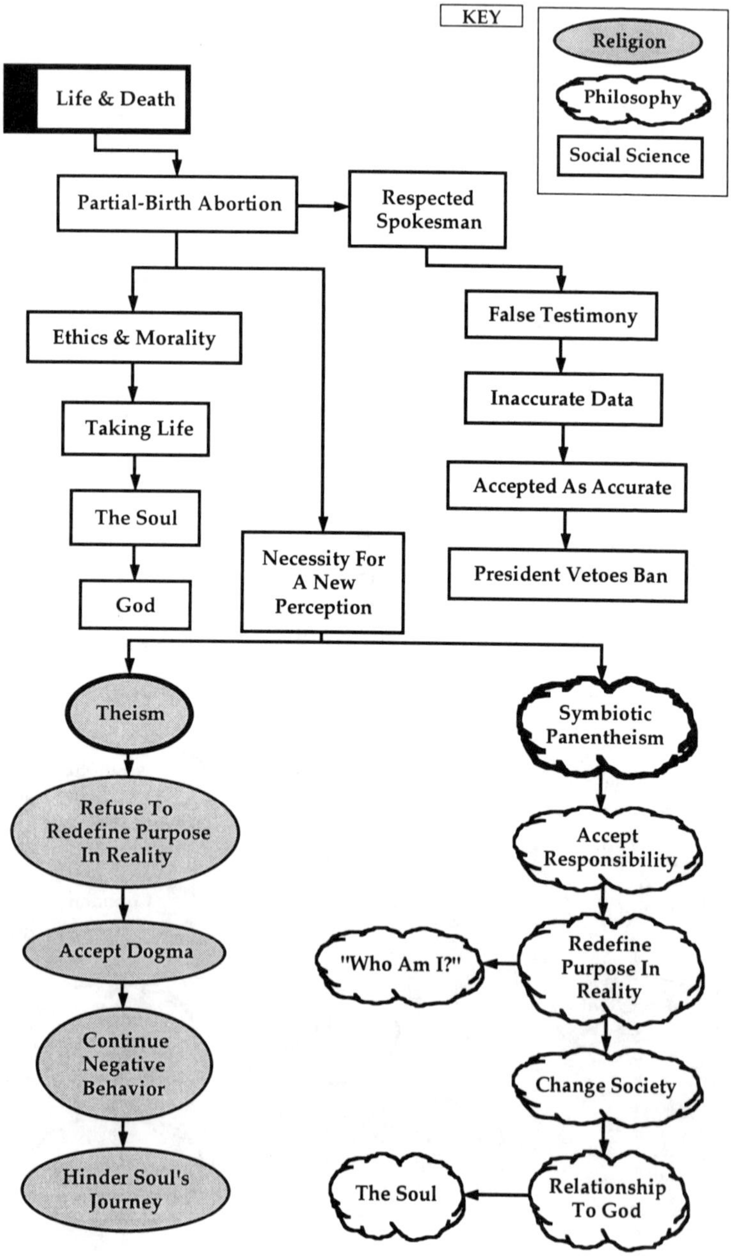

Volume III - Stepping Up To The Creator
Religion: Hinduism - 1500 BC *# 100-009*

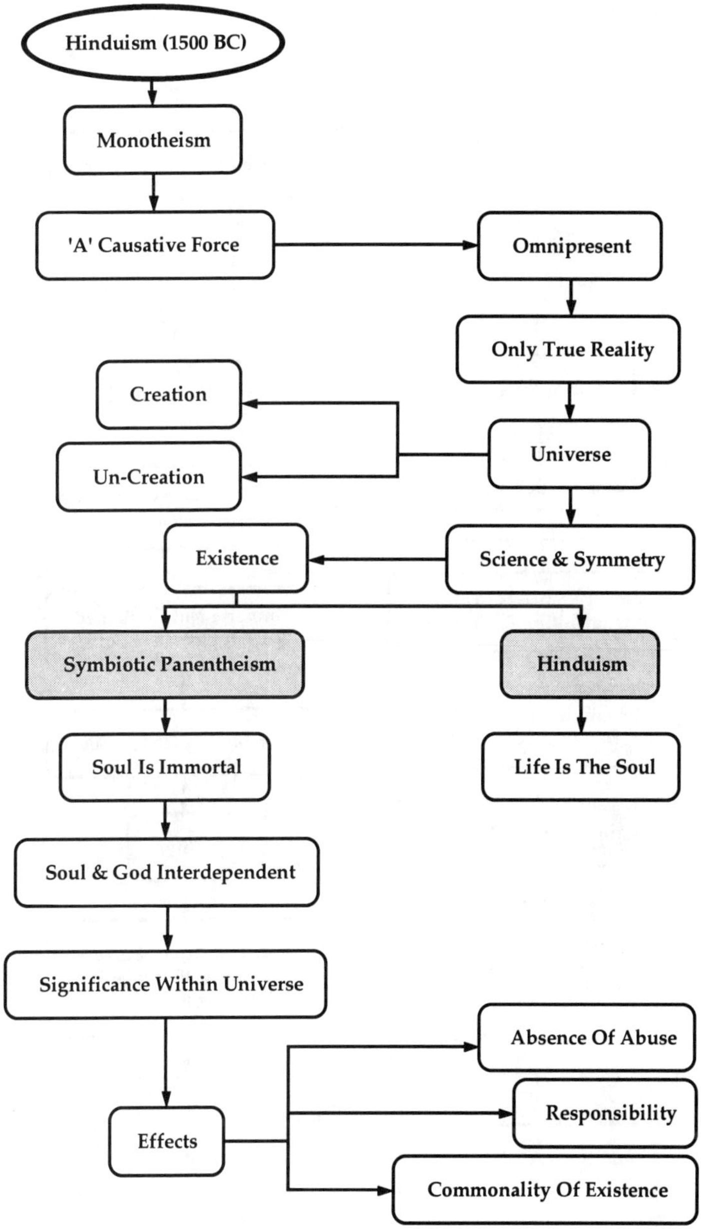

Volume III - Stepping Up To The Creator
Religion: Judaism - 1000 BC *# 110-119*

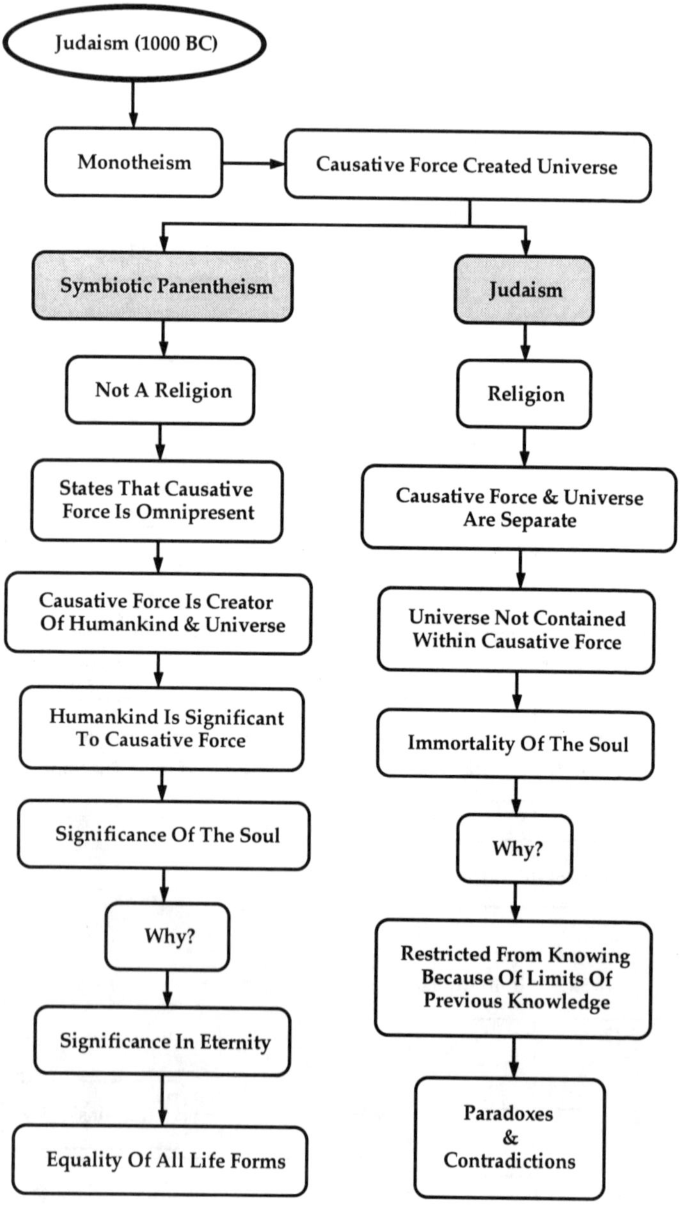

Volume III - Stepping Up To The Creator
Religion: Buddhism - 500 BC *# 120-129*

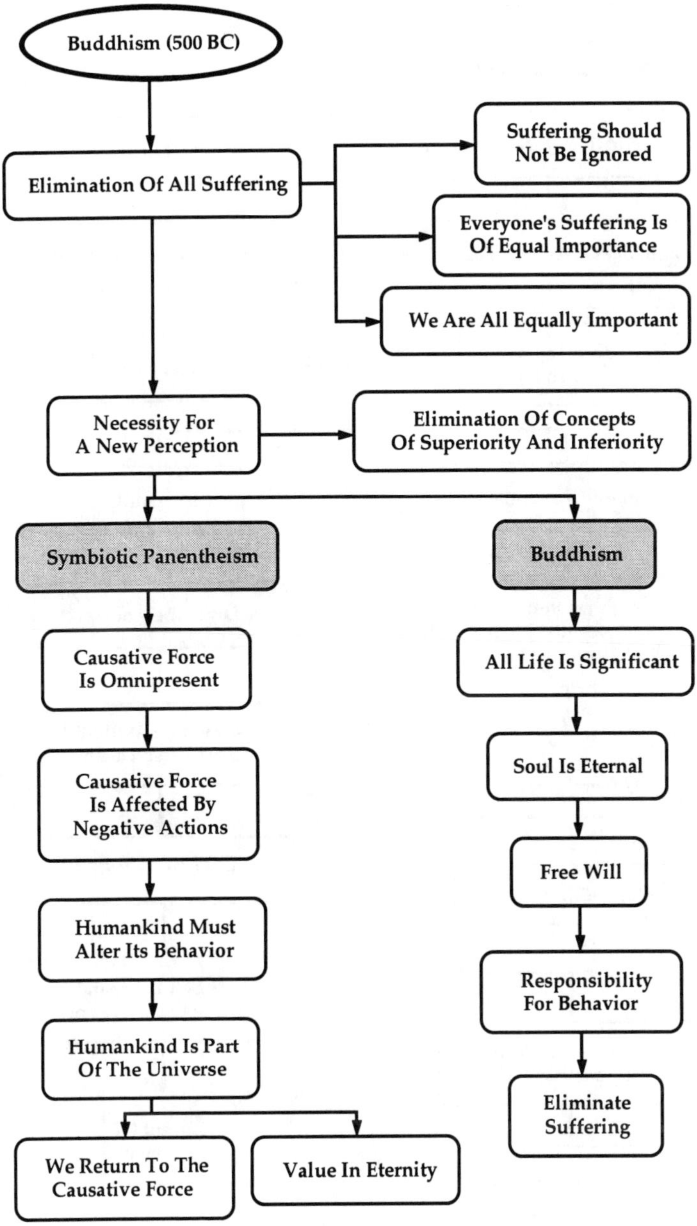

Volume III - Stepping Up To The Creator

Religion: Christianity - 0 BC ***# 130-139***

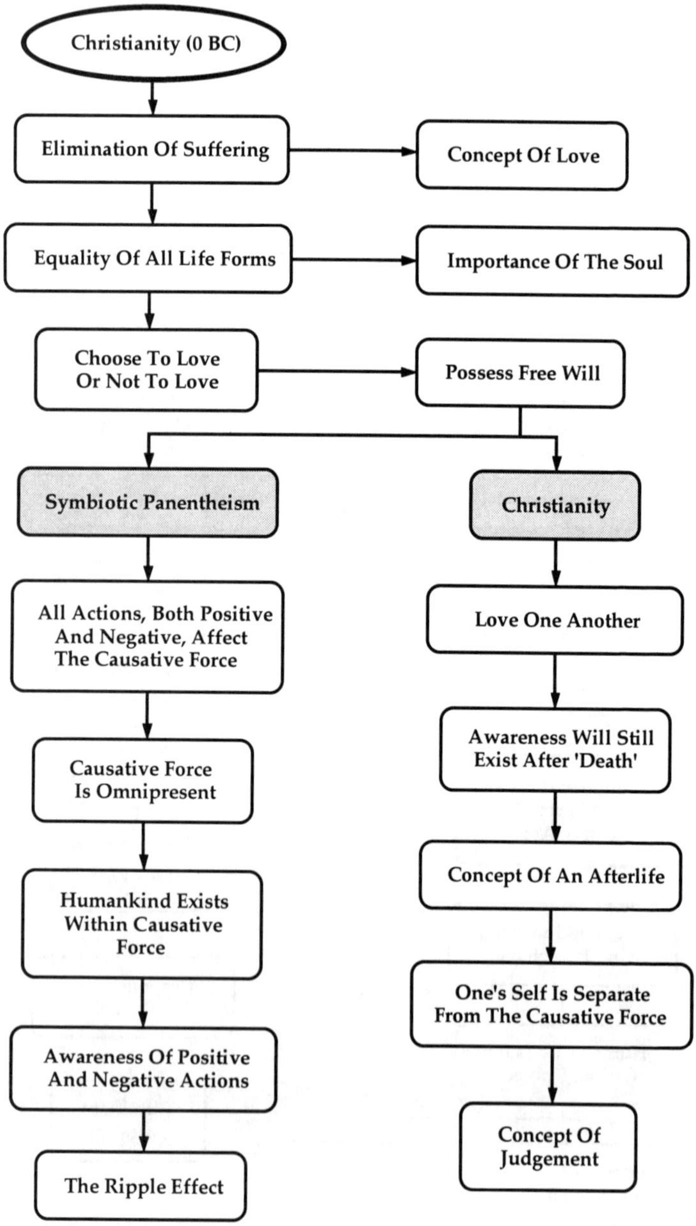

Volume III - Stepping Up To The Creator

Religion: Islam - 500 AD **# 140-149**

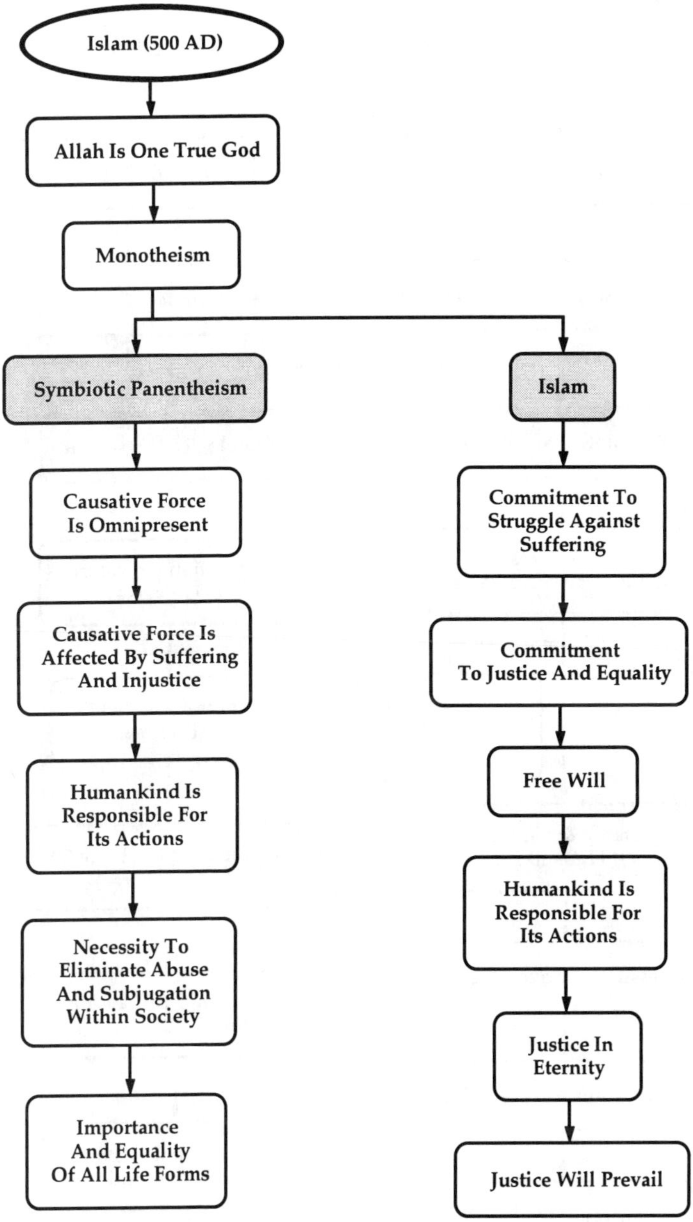

Volume III - Stepping Up To The Creator
Religion: Ontological Argument - 1000 AD *# 150-159*

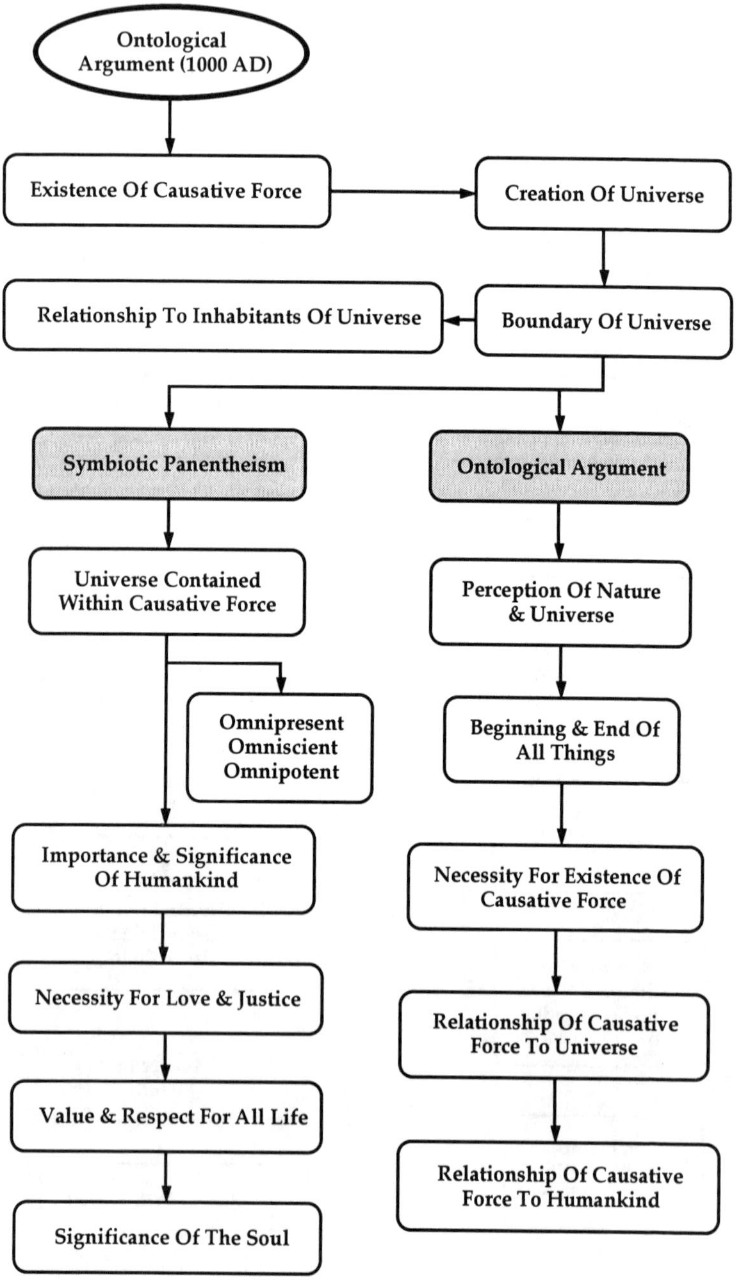

Volume III - Stepping Up To The Creator

Religion: Modern Science - 1500 AD *# 160-169*

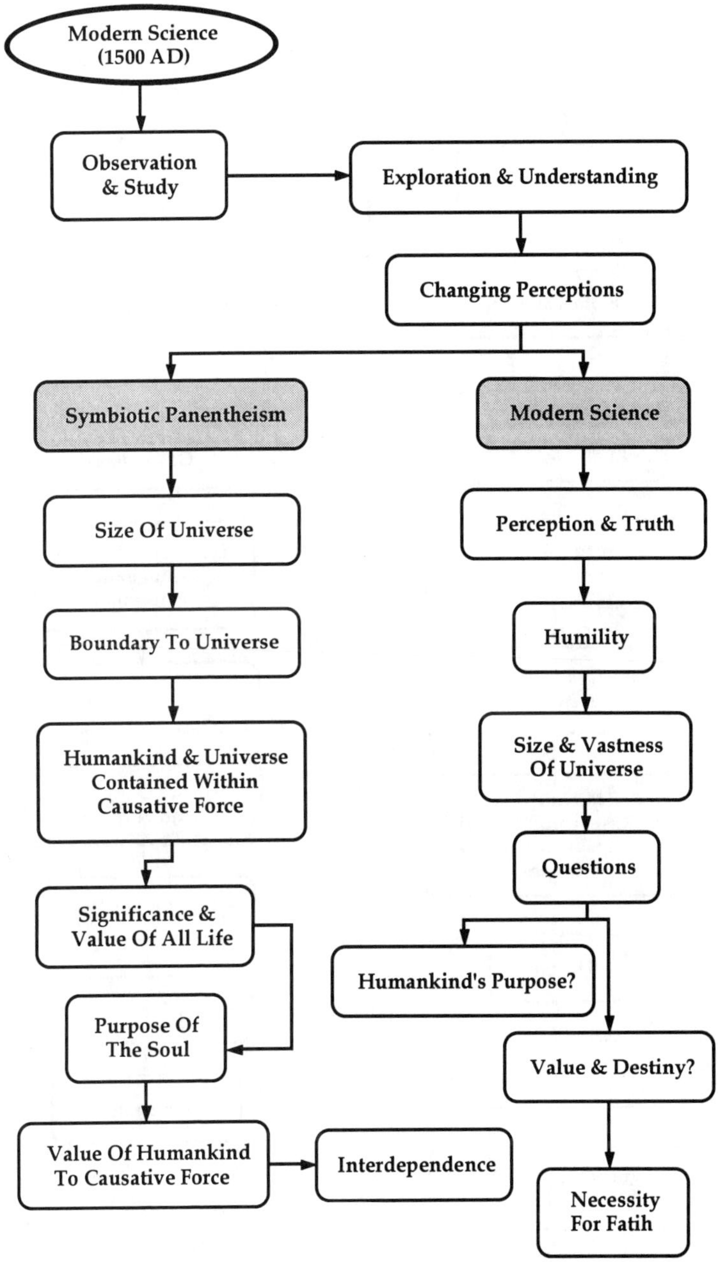

Volume III - Stepping Up To The Creator

Religion: Atheism *# 170-179*

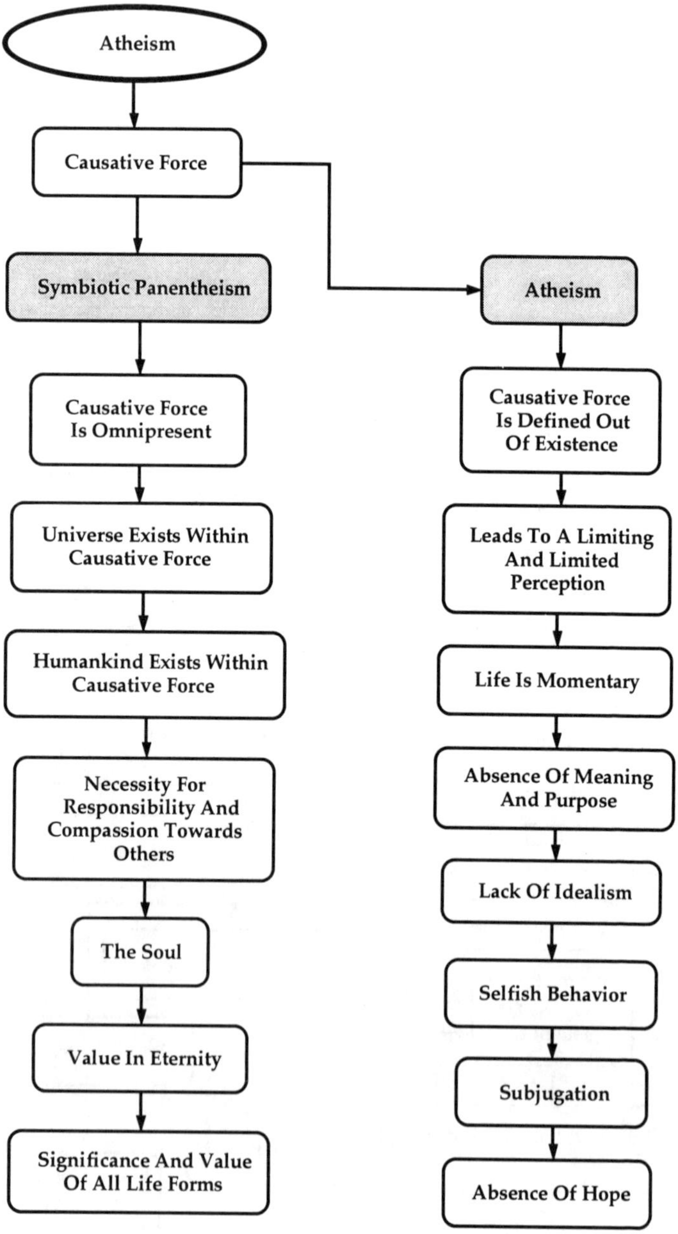

Volume III - Stepping Up To The Creator
Religion: Classical/Traditional Theism *# 180-189*

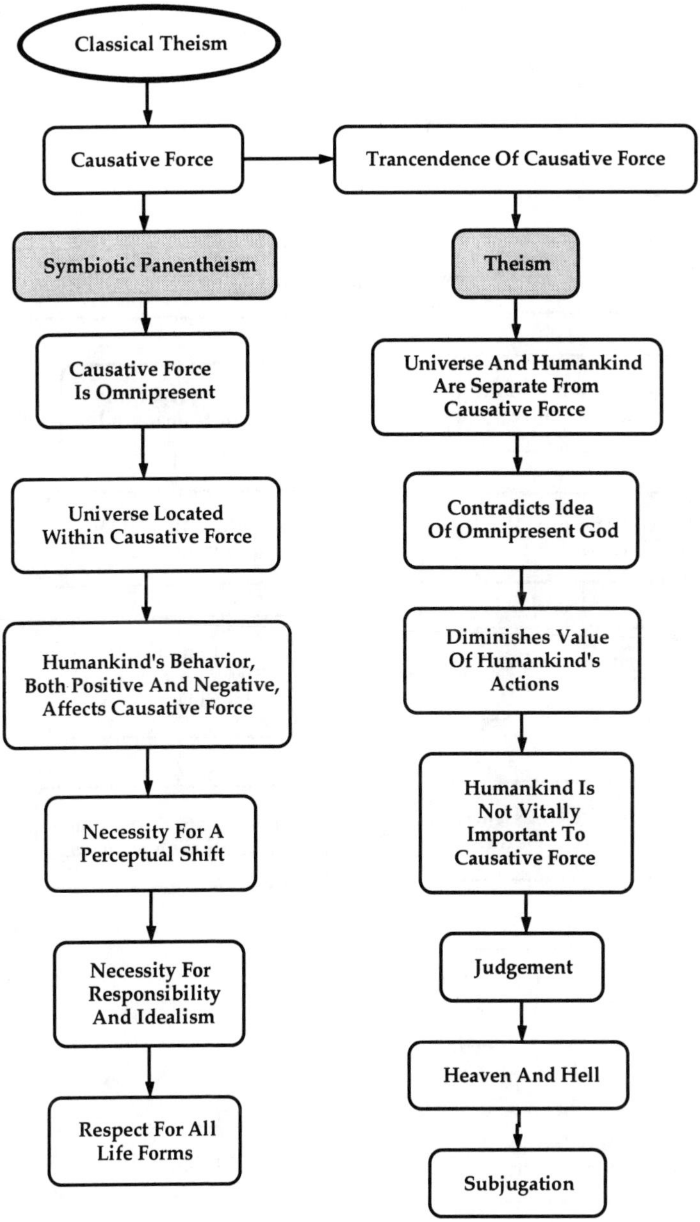

Volume III - Stepping Up To The Creator

Religion: Panentheism - 2000 AD **# 190-199**

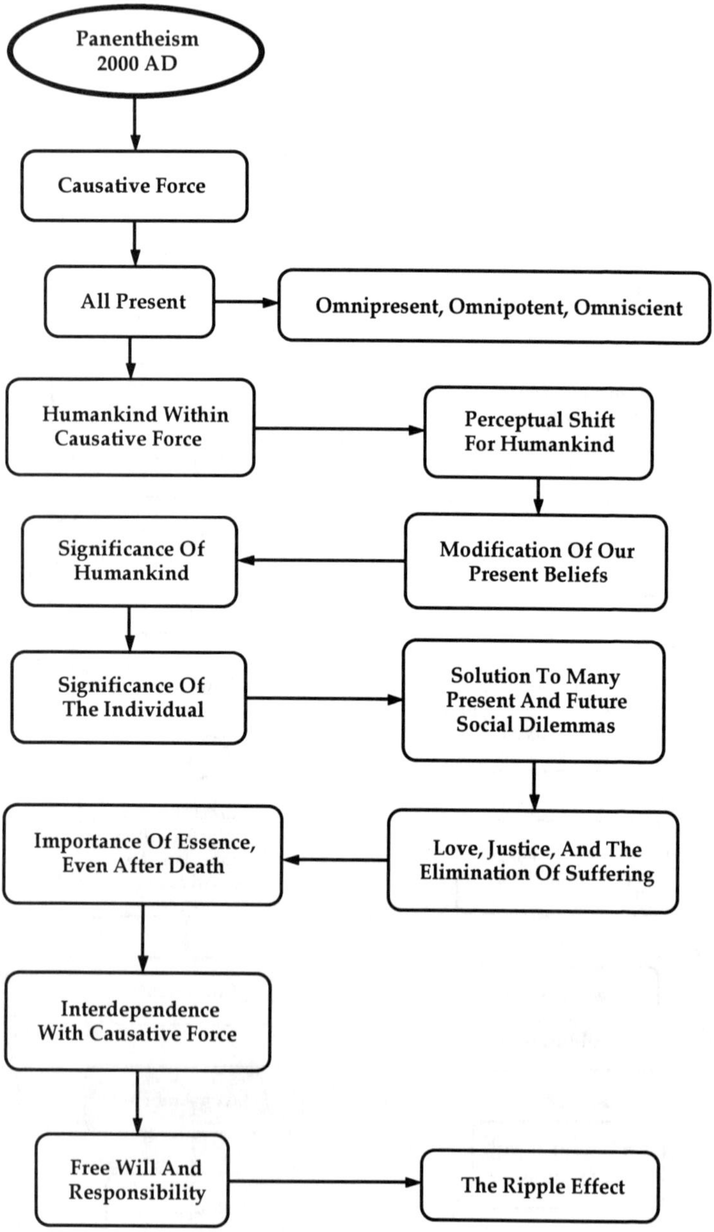

Volume III - Stepping Up To The Creator

Science: Entropy *# 200-209*

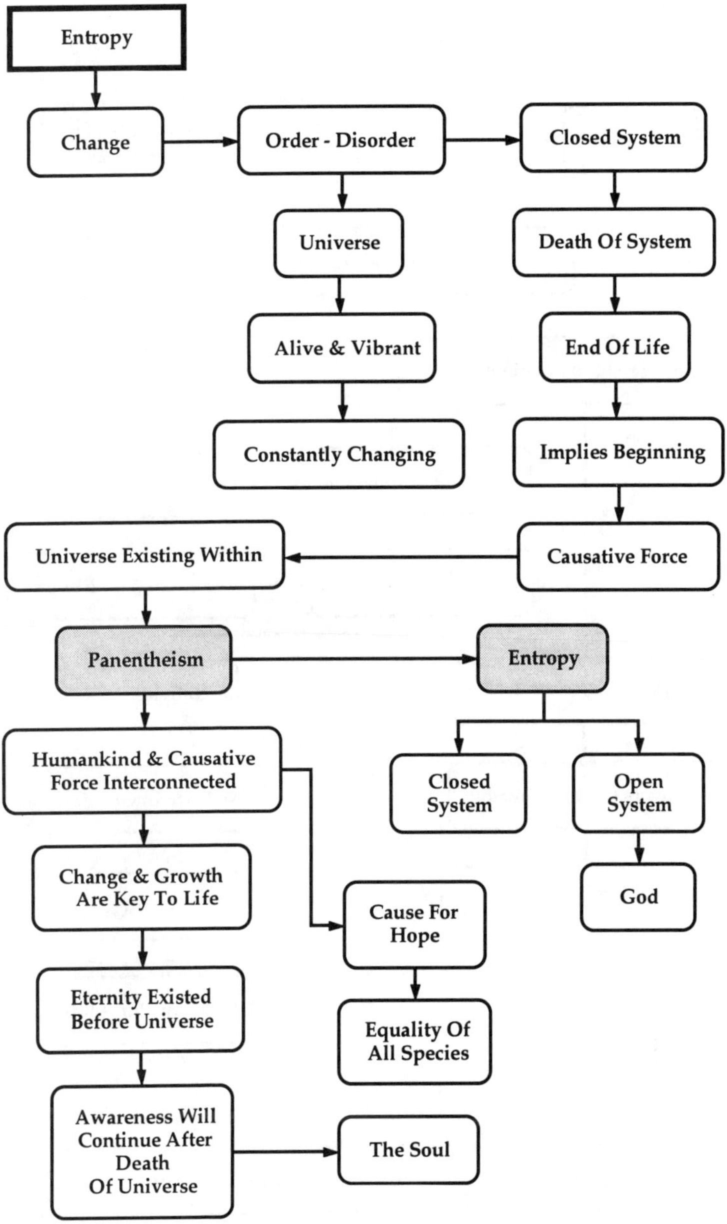

Volume III - Stepping Up To The Creator

Science: The Big Bang *# 210-219*

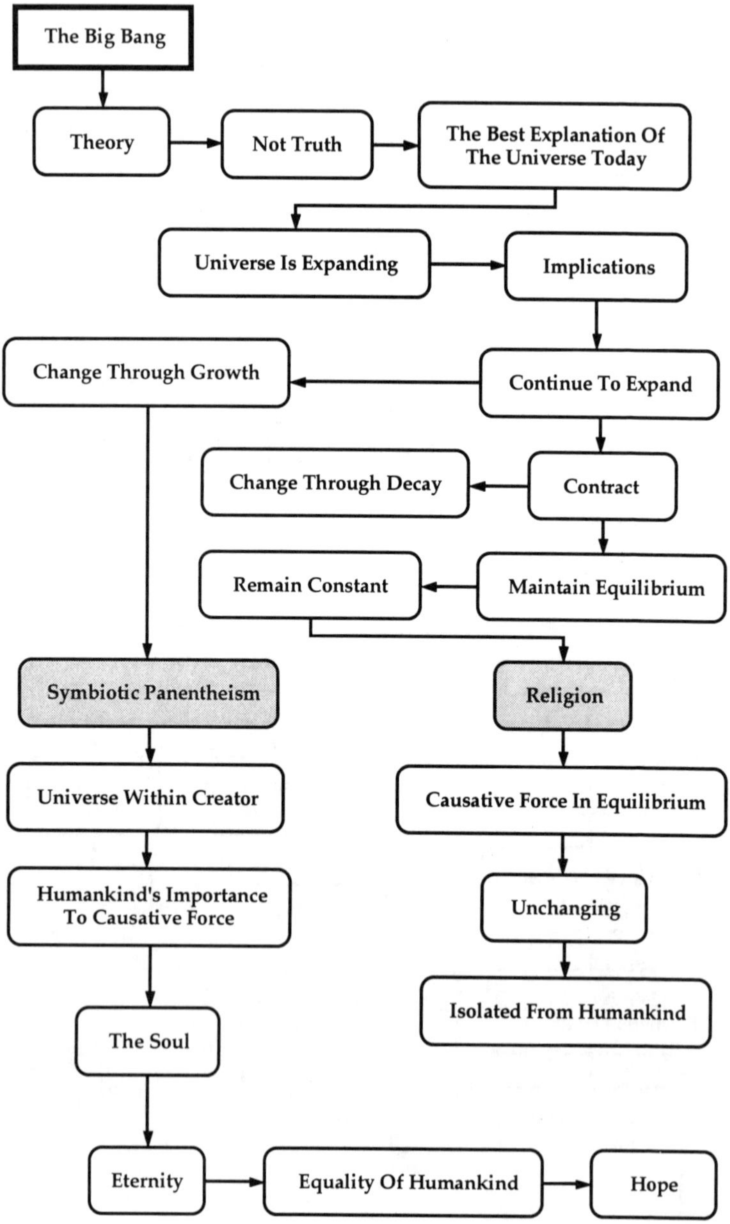

Volume III - Stepping Up To The Creator

Science: Symmetry *# 220-229*

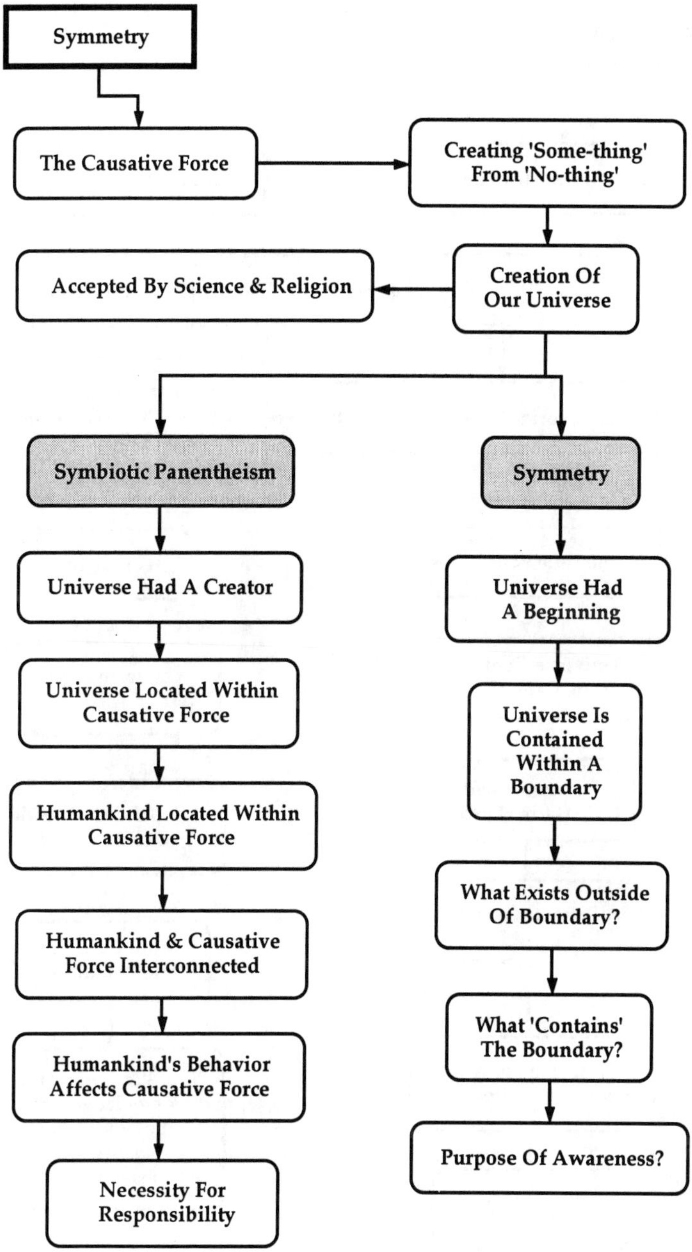

Volume III - Stepping Up To The Creator

Science: Topology *# 230-239*

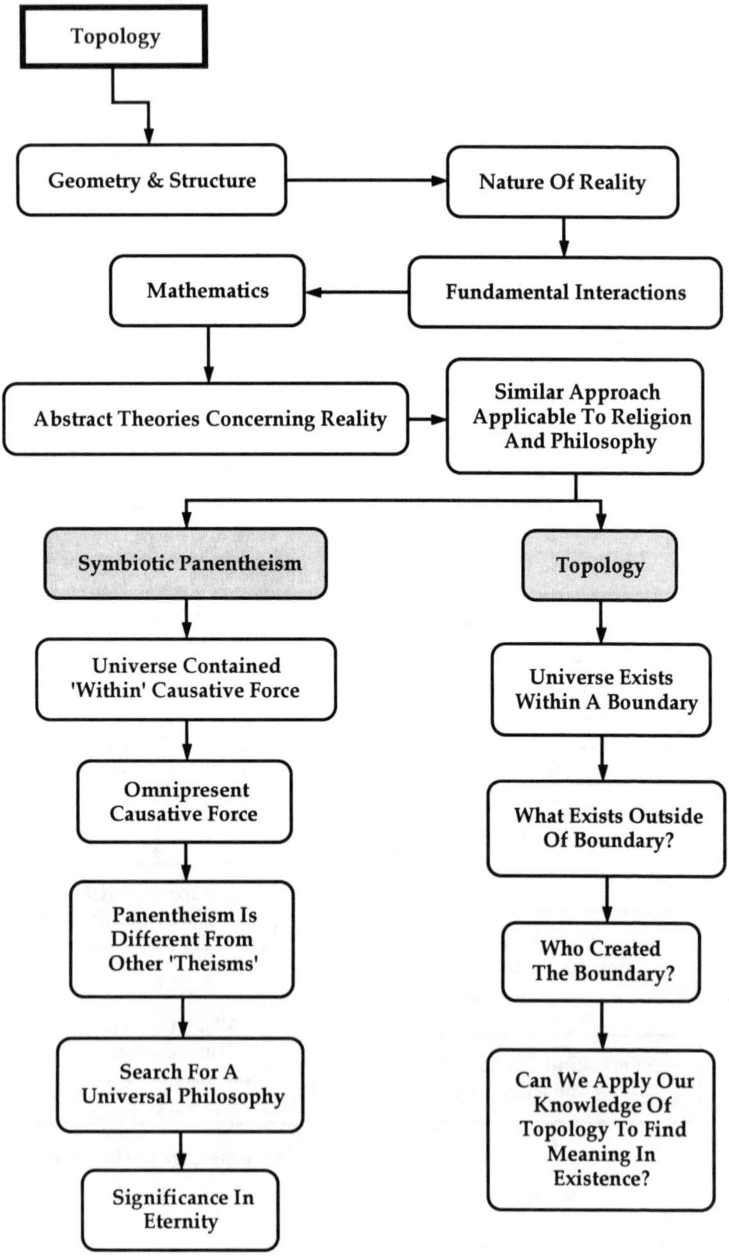

Volume III - Stepping Up To The Creator

Science: Set Theory ***# 240-249***

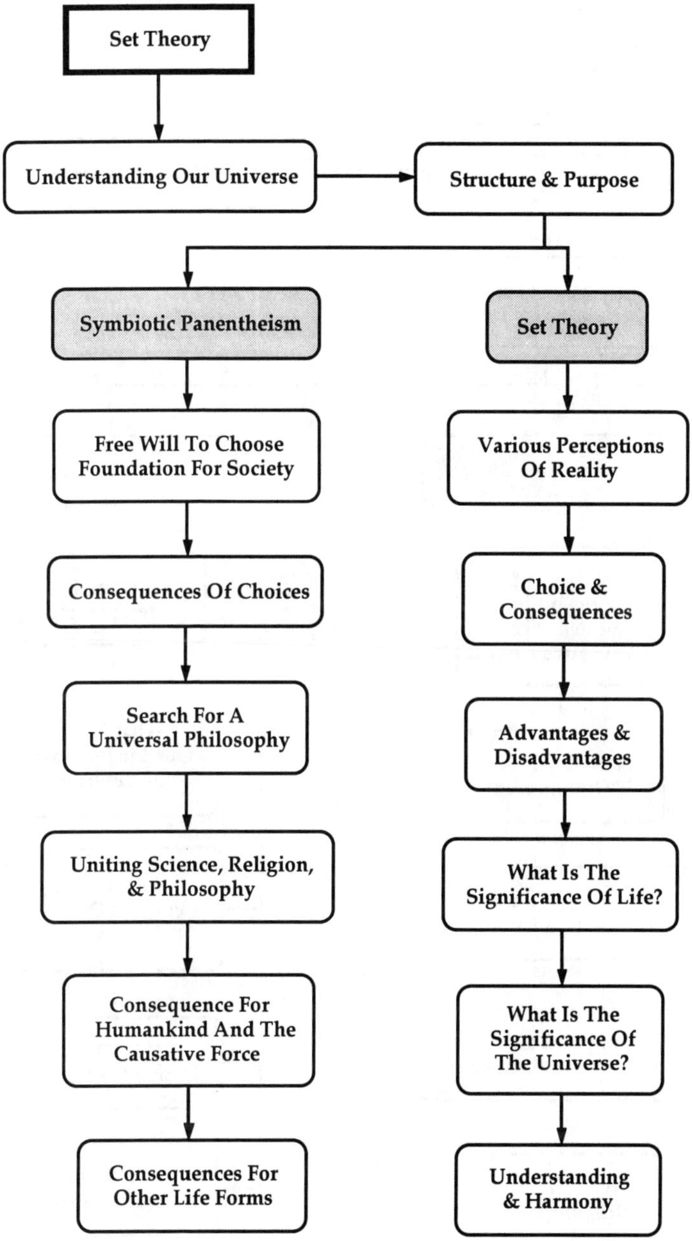

Volume III - Stepping Up To The Creator

Science: Space - The Null Set *# 250-259*

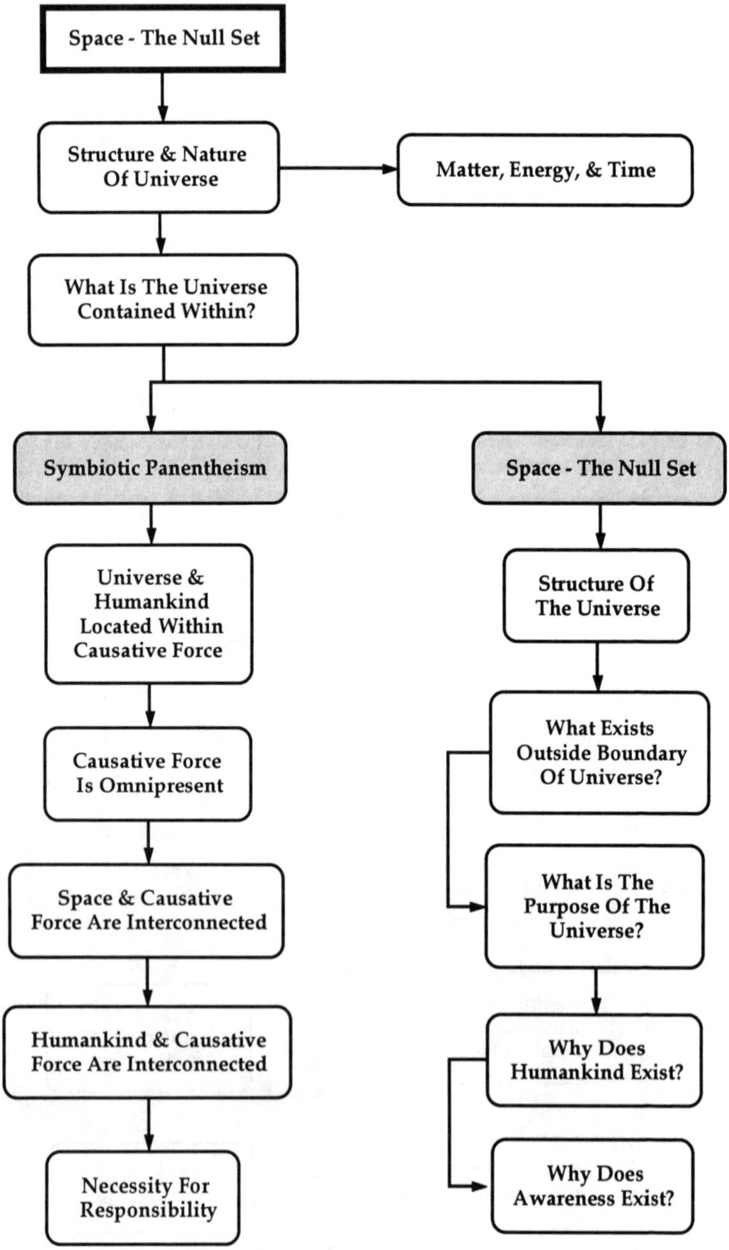

Volume III - Stepping Up To The Creator

Science: Ecological Niche ***# 260-269***

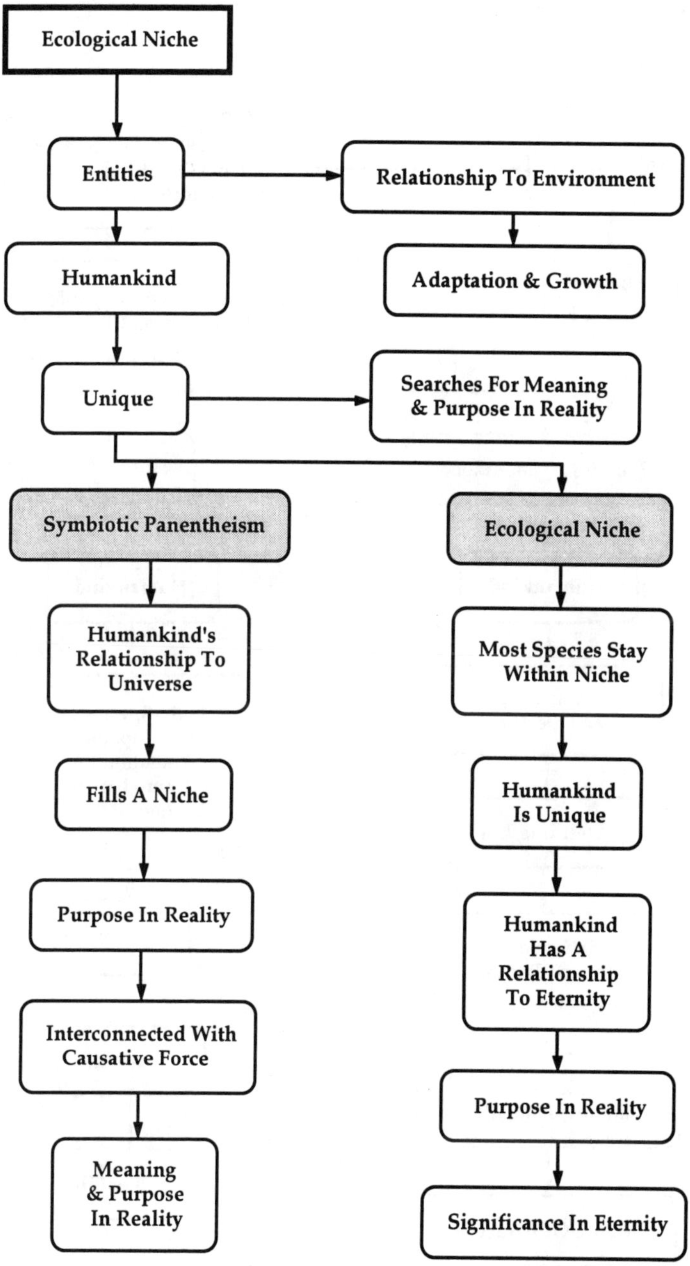

Volume III - Stepping Up To The Creator

Science: Homo- ... *# 270-279*

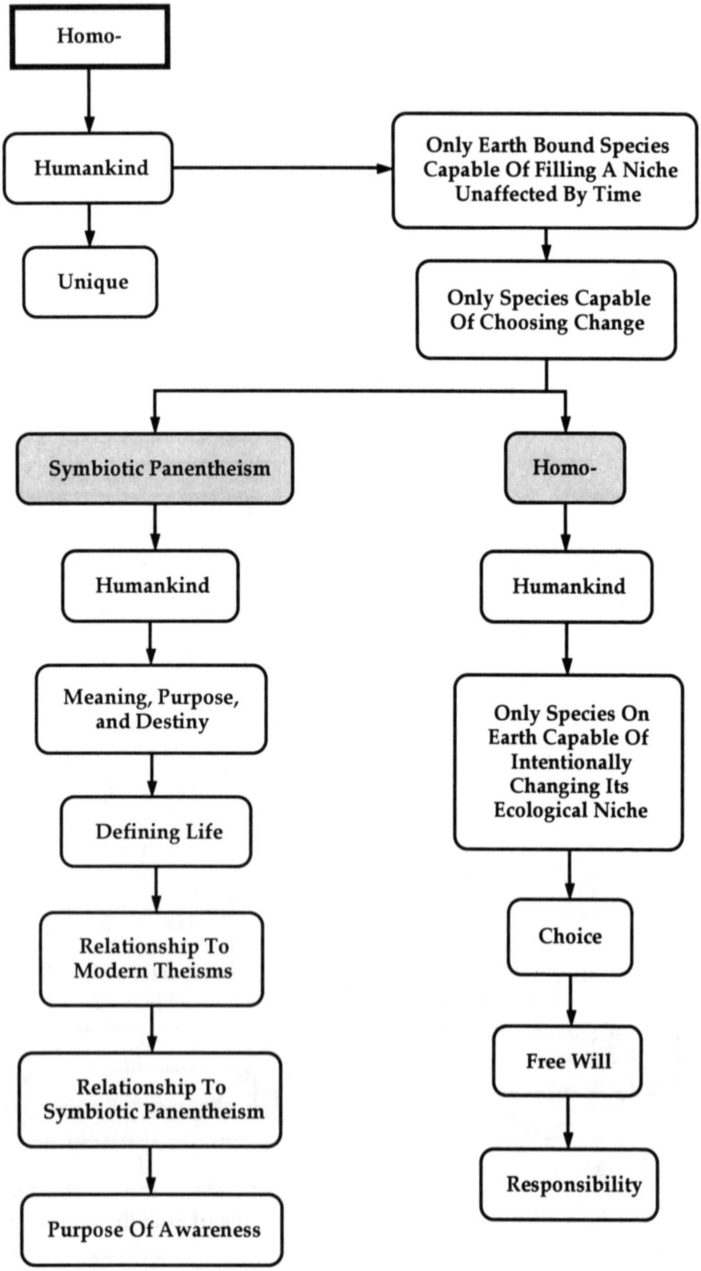

Volume III - Stepping Up To The Creator

Science: Palaeomagnetism *# 280-289*

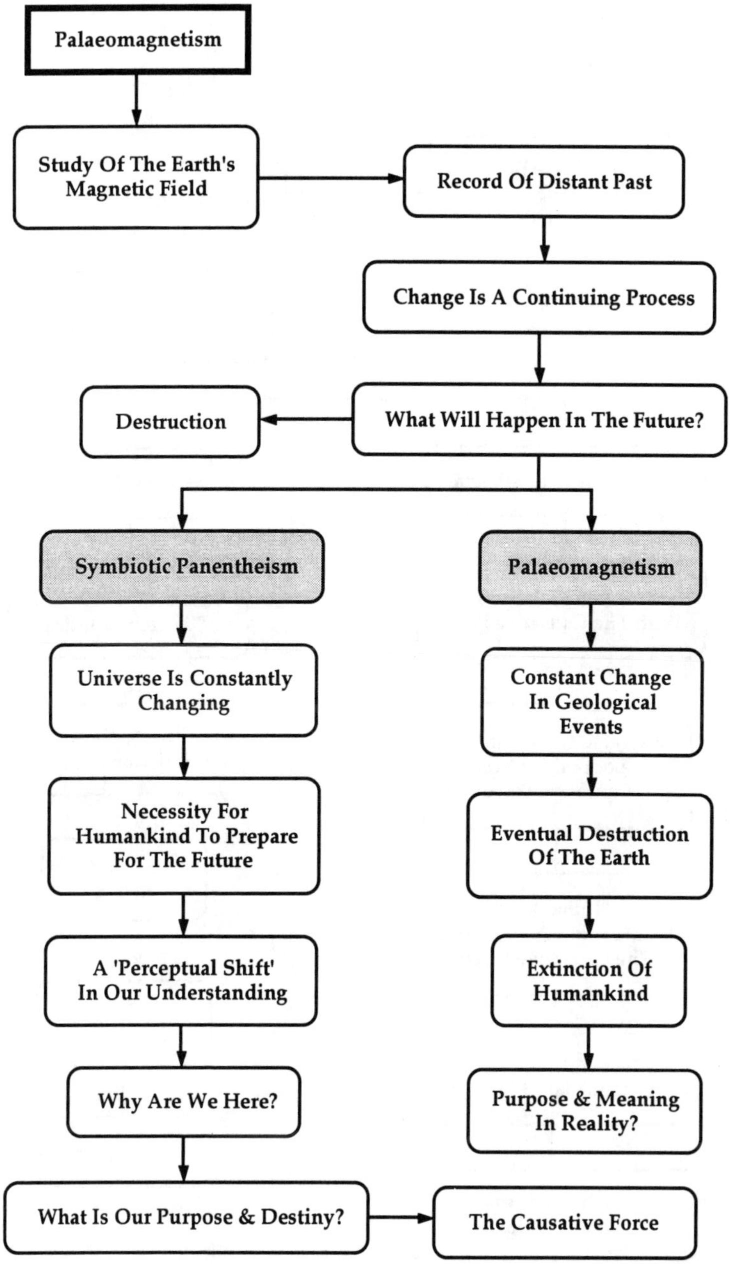

FLOWCHARTS

Volume III - Stepping Up To The Creator

Science: Symbiosis *# 290-299*

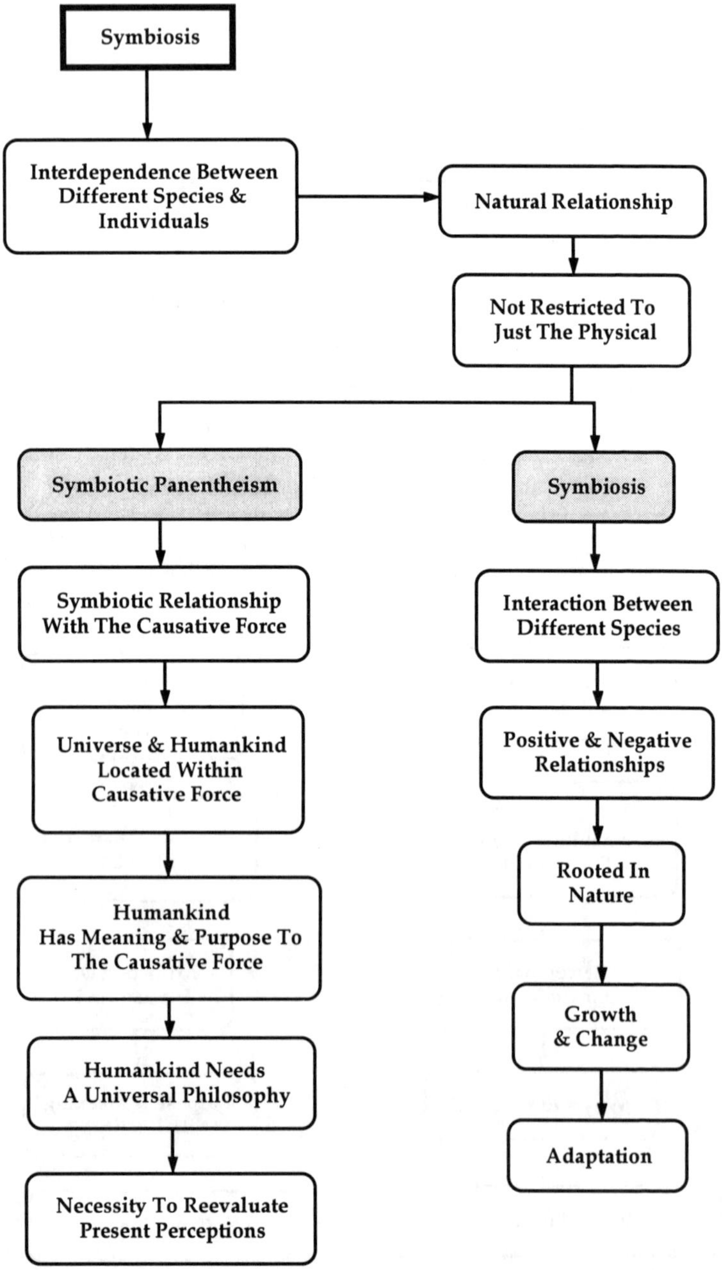

Volume III - Stepping Up To The Creator

Philosophy: Unified View *# 300-309*

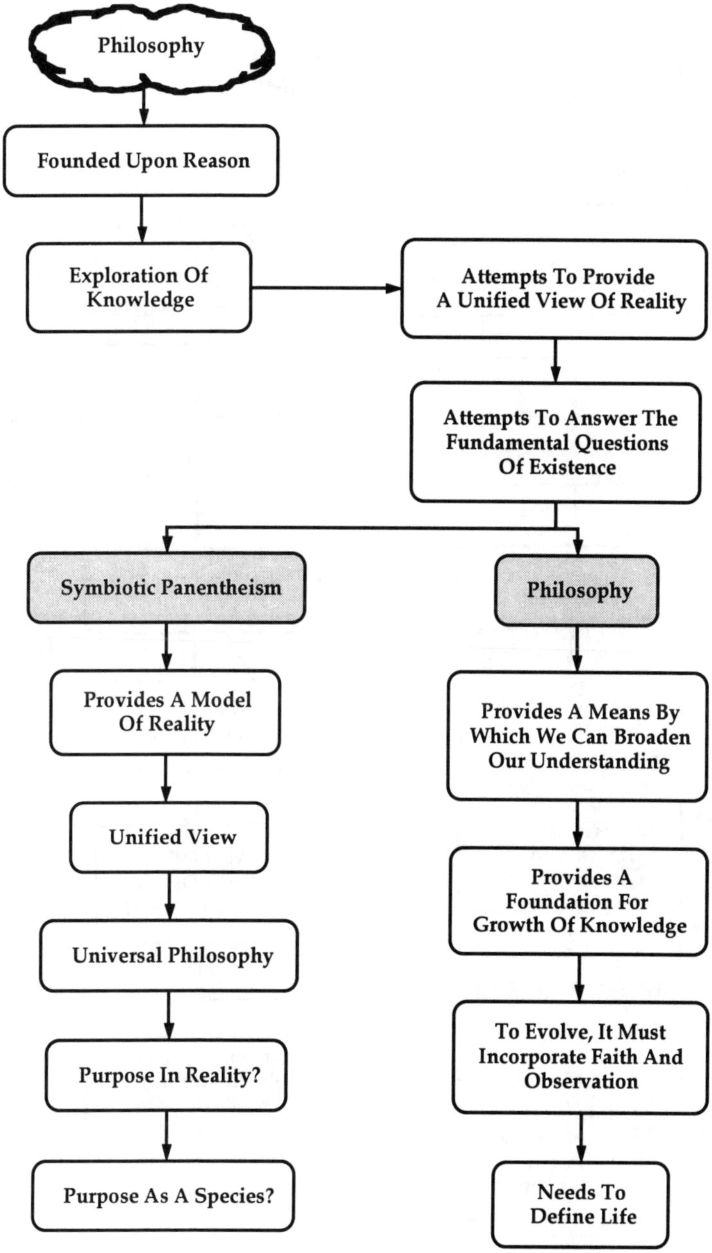

Volume III - Stepping Up To The Creator

Philosophy: Philosophy, Religion, and Science ***# 310-319***

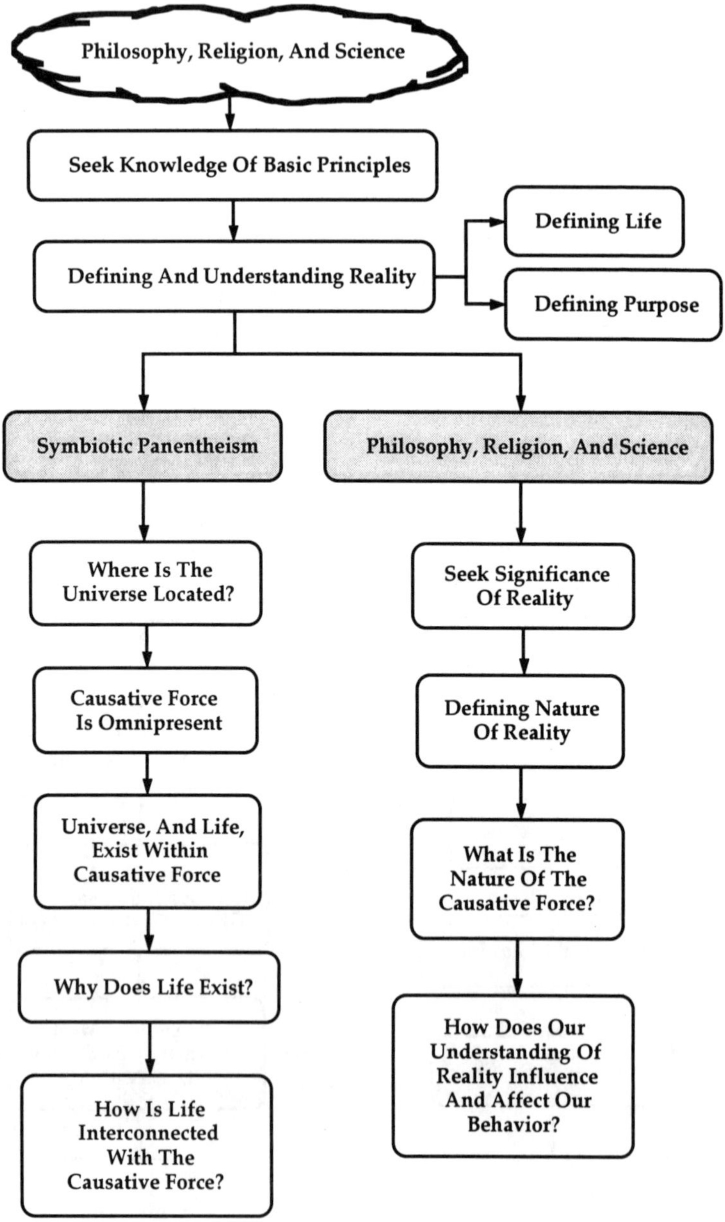

Volume III - Stepping Up To The Creator
Philosophy: Confucianism *# 320-329*

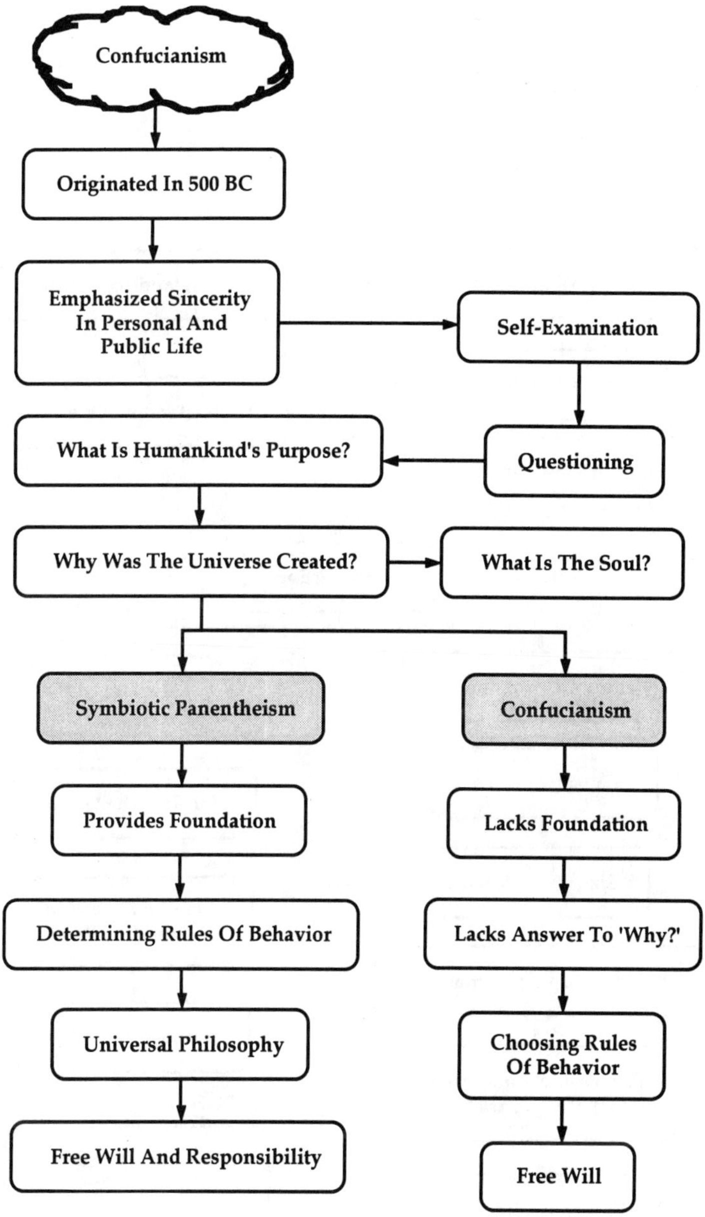

Volume III - Stepping Up To The Creator

Philosophy: Taoism *# 330-339*

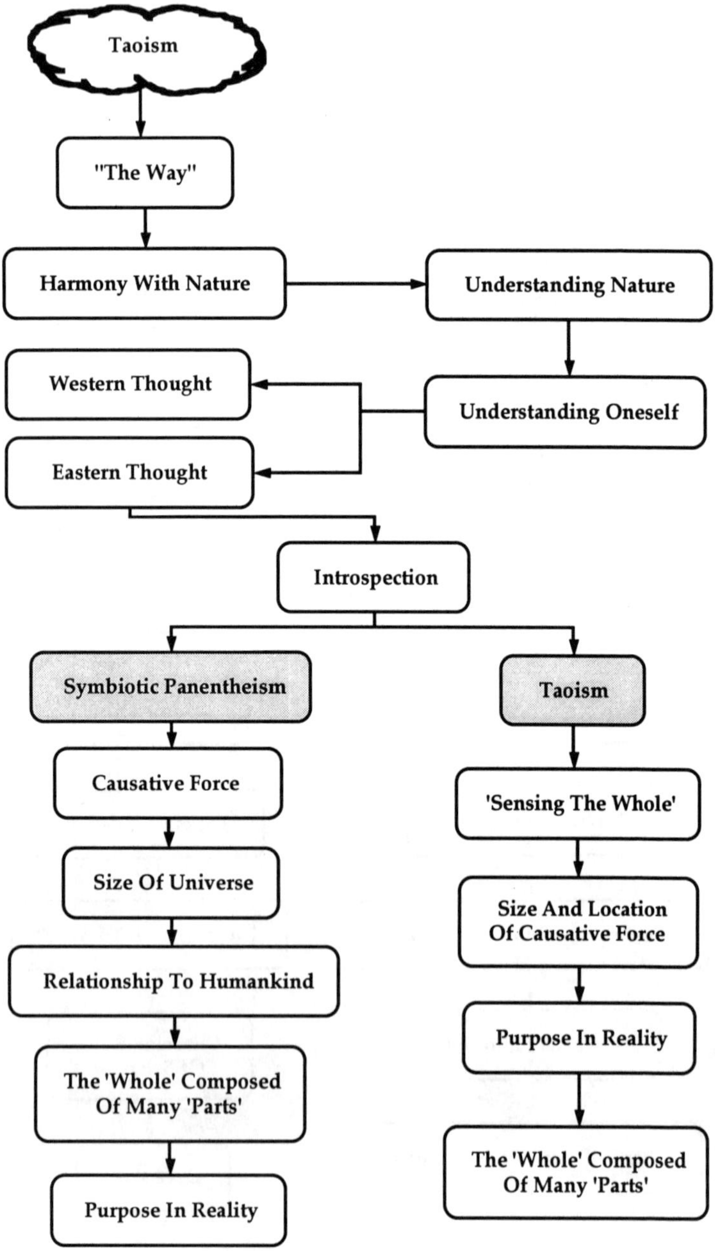

Volume III - Stepping Up To The Creator

Philosophy: Ancient Philosophy *# 340-349*

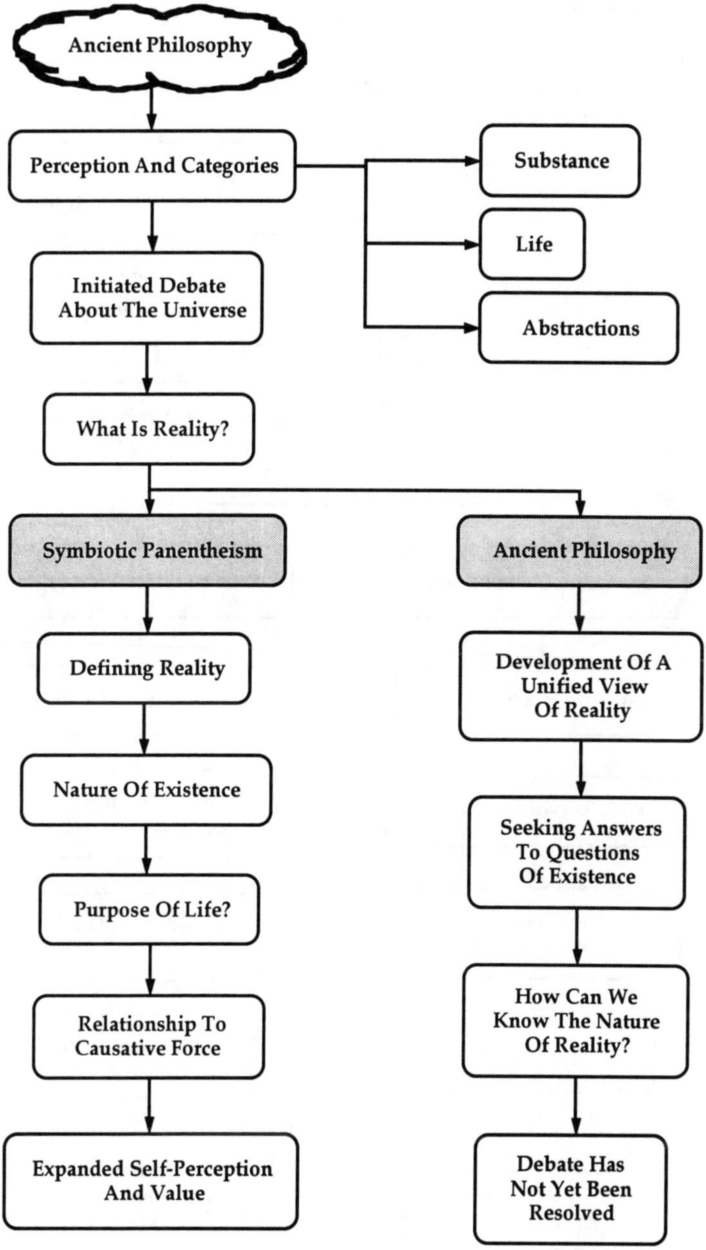

FLOWCHARTS

Volume III - Stepping Up To The Creator

Philosophy: Early Christian Philosophy *# 350-359*

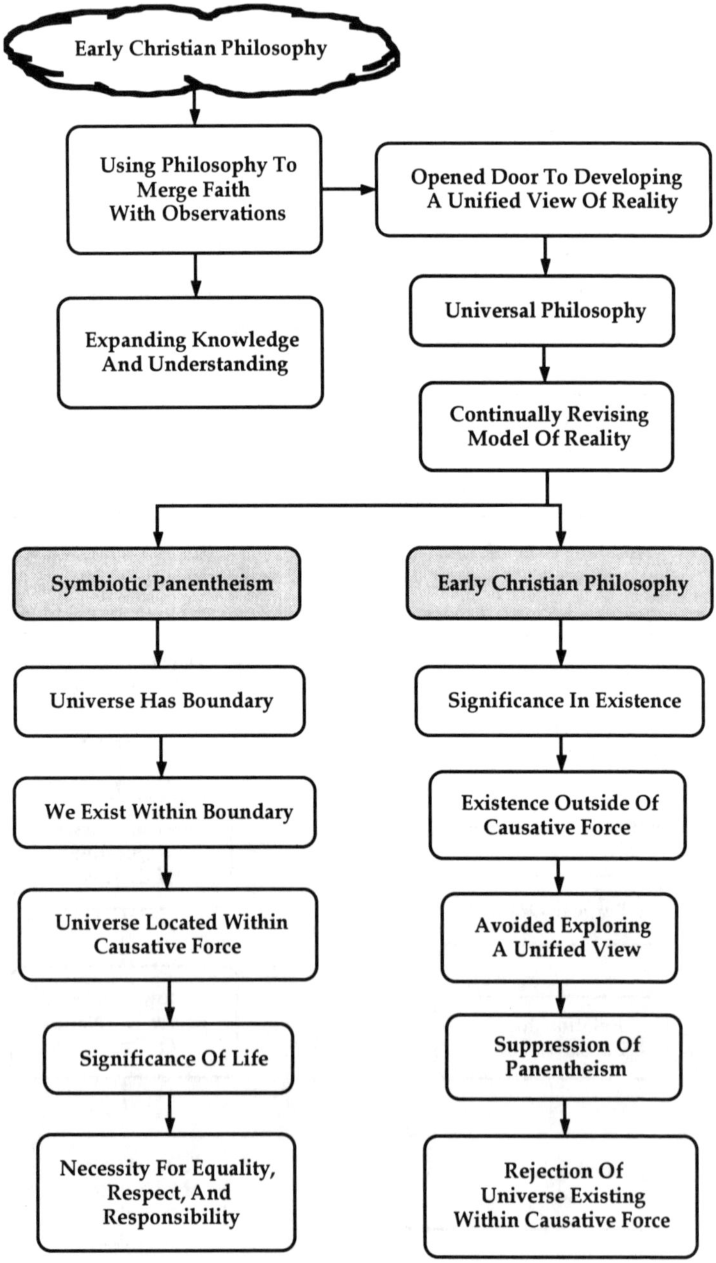

Volume III - Stepping Up To The Creator

Philosophy: Renaissance Philosophy *# 360-369*

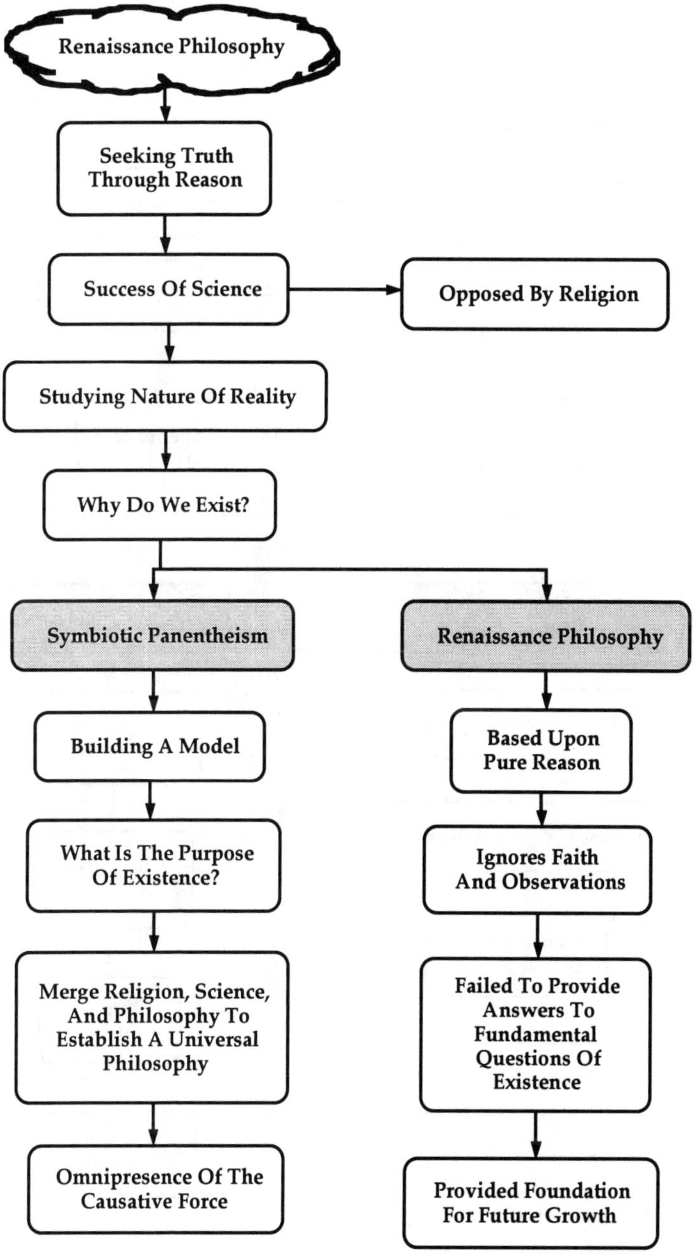

Volume III - Stepping Up To The Creator

Philosophy: Appeal to Reason and Experience *# 370-379*

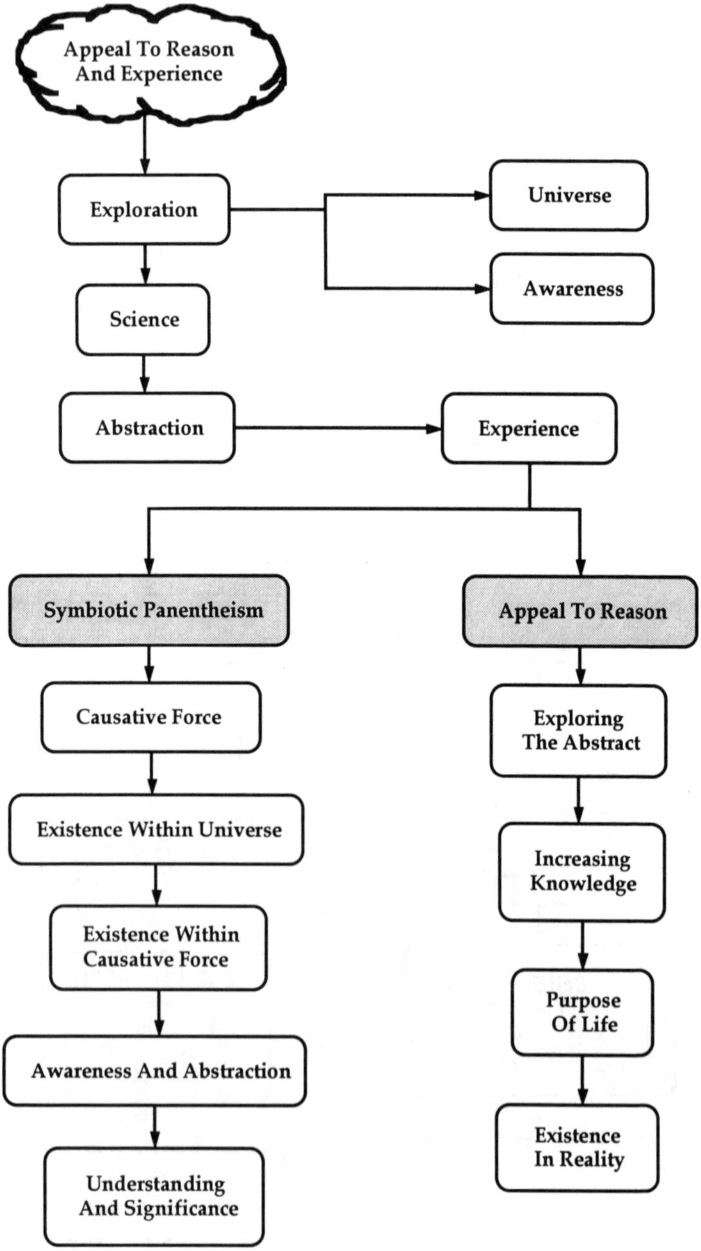

Volume III - Stepping Up To The Creator

Philosophy: Appeal to Humanism/Adjustment *# 380-389*

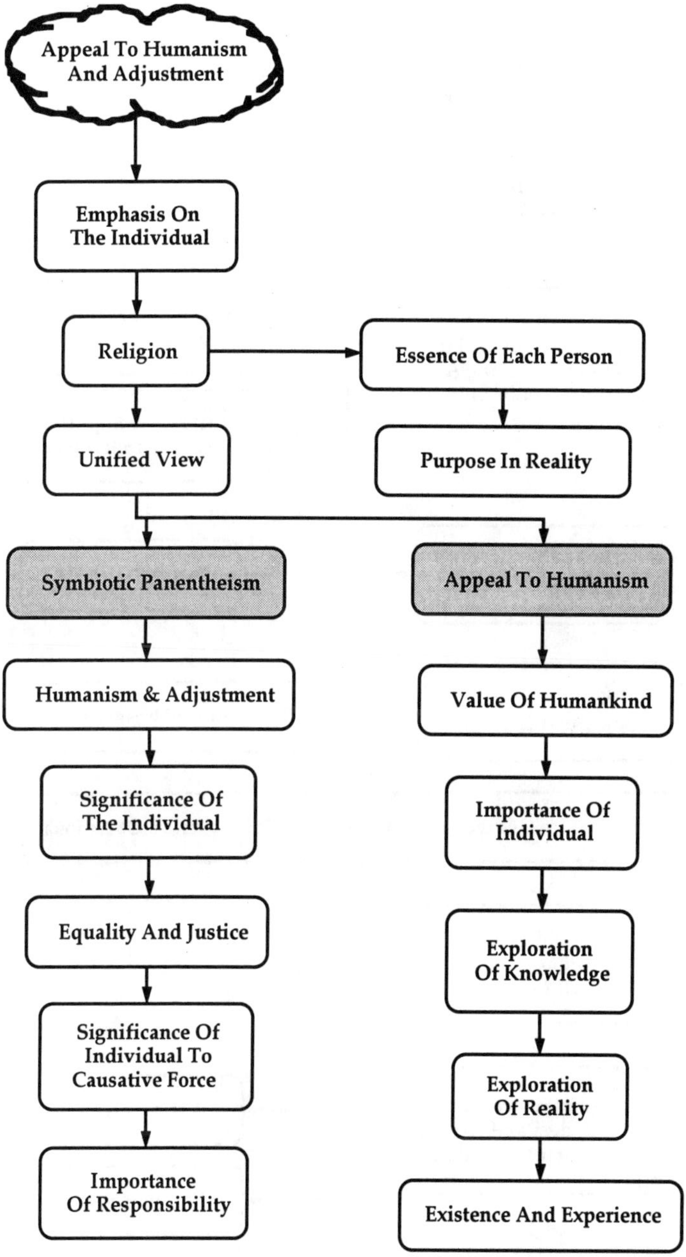

Volume III - Stepping Up To The Creator

Philosophy: Symbiotic Panentheism *# 390-399*

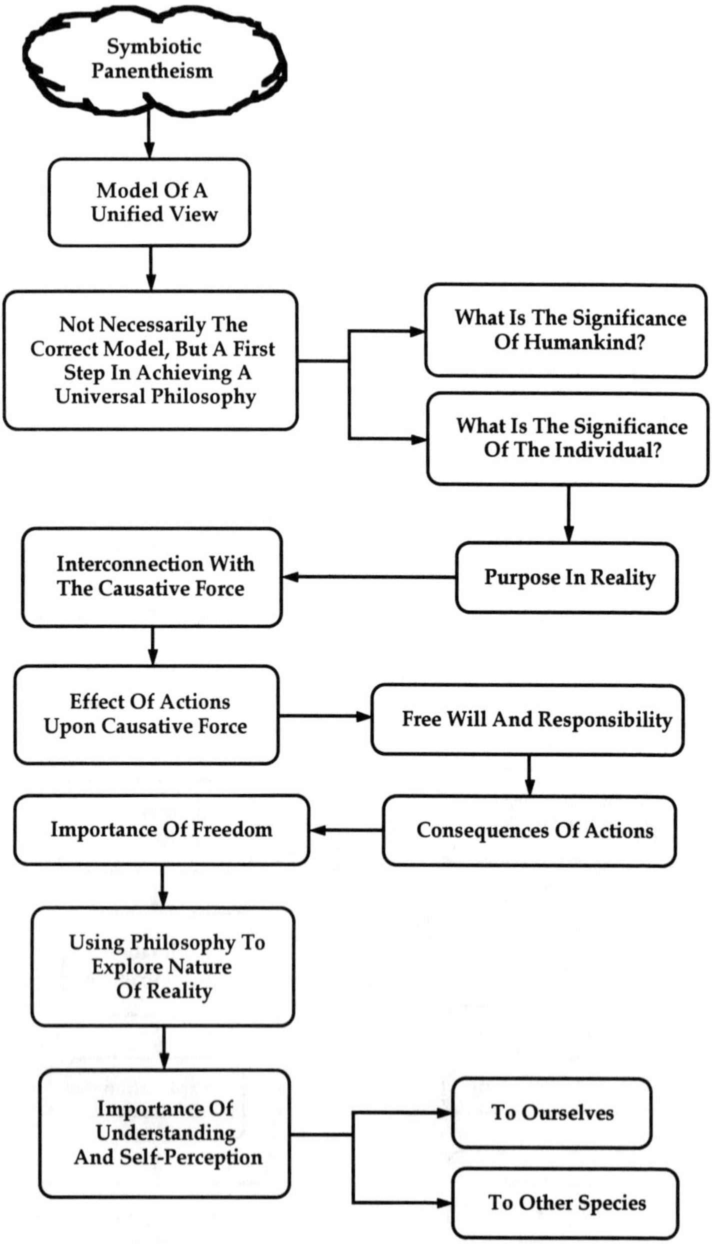

Thematic Index

Volume I

You & I Together

- Have a Purpose in Reality -

Volume II

In the Image of God

Volume III

Stepping Up To The Creator

A

Abortion
case involving two Delaware teenagers, II:1
is it ever right to take the life of another?, I:244
is it moral or immoral?, I:240
what are the consequences for God?, I:244
what are the consequences for the soul?, I:240, 244

Afterlife
suicide and the soul - what are the dangers?, I:253-254
what can it say about the meaning of life?, I:163
what does 'the Philosophy' tell us?, I:162

Alien Species
consequences of contacting, II:74
subversive actions, II:75, 80

Ancient Philosophy
effects upon society, III:333
helping us to understand life, III:338
Humankind's significance to Causative Force, III:343
relationship to panentheism, III:336
significance of existence, III:337
significance of Humankind in eternity, III:342
understanding the Universe, III:335
what it can offer other life forms, III:341
what it can offer us as a species, III:334, 340
what it can offer us as individuals, III:339

Atheism
absence of Causative Force within Universe, III:113
belief established within society, III:113
consequences for Causative Force, III:120
defining away significance of Humankind in eternity, III:122-123
differs from panentheism, III:117
disbelief in a supreme being and perception of the Universe, III:114
has it a role to play?, I:232
how does it relate to religion?, I:232
how does it relate to the Ripple Effect?, I:235
how it characterizes Causative Force, III:124
limiting significance of our species, III:132
limiting the boundaries of our existence, III:116
limiting the significance of life, III:129
necessity for respect for religions and other faiths, I:233
non-belief - how does it relate to God's purpose?, I:26
perception and significance as a species, III:118

provided great service in helping to understand significance, III:119
putting a limit on the value of life and existence, III:130
rationalizes the process of subjugation, III:120
relationship to set theory, III:196, 203-204
significance for other life forms in the Universe, III:121
significance of life, III:117-118
what it has to offer us as individuals, III:114, 119
what it implies about the Universe, III:115
what it reinforces about panentheism, III:116

Awareness
nature is to change, III:185
never destroyed, III:187

B

Belief
how comforting and reassuring concepts relate to our lives, I:29
Man's historical belief in some form of God or Creator, I:27

Big Bang, The
boundary to the Universe, III:185
elevating significance of individuals, III:177
elevating significance of other life forms, III:177
Humankind's relationship to Causative Force, III:179
implies that our Universe is temporary, III:178
insights established within society, III:169-170
offering us hope as individuals, III:175-176
provides understanding of boundary to Universe, III:175-176
provides understanding of existence, III:175-177
reinforcing our understanding of life, III:173-174
scientific insight into eternity, III:175
what it has to offer other life forms, III:177
what it has to offer us as a species, III:176
what it has to offer us as individuals, III:175
what it implies about the Universe, III:171-172

Buddhism
behavior affecting Causative Force, III:63
building the bridge from East to West, III:53-54
consequences of the Ripple Effect, III:58
effects on society, III:53-55
helping Humankind understand what life is, III:58
importance of eliminating suffering, III:61
intolerance of suffering, III:91
providing an understanding of the significance of life, III:57
providing significance for the individual, III:59

rational belief in the importance of eliminating suffering, III:62
reinforcing the concept of panentheism, III:56
significance for other life forms in the Universe, III:61
significance of life in eternity, III:59
strive to eliminate suffering within society, III:53-54, 64
suffering need not be tolerated within society, III:55
understanding our journey through life, III:59

C

Capital Punishment
consequences for the soul, I:263
interfering with journey of Causative Force, III:111
protection of society, I:266
what are the issues for Mankind?, I:260-262

Capitalism
not necessary to dismantle, III:135

Causative Force *(see God and Creator)*
ability of individuals to influence, III:164-165
absence under atheism, III:122-123
achieving a new understanding, III:111
affected by atheistic beliefs, III:120
affected by Humankind's behavior, III:63, 68
assisting her development, III:88, 251
atheism and its implications, III:115
atheistic beliefs, III:113
awareness and essence, III:262
awareness and existence, III:247
belief in her existence, III:100
capital punishment interfering with journey, III:111
changing our perceptions, III:75, 111
characteristics assigned by panentheism, III:148
characteristised as 'all loving', III:140
characteristised as 'all present', III:140
choosing to create our Universe, III:93
Christianity's conception of size and significance, III:76
concept of love and equality within our species, III:73, 75
consequences of Humankind's actions, III:69
creating some-thing from no-thing, III:182
creation of space to gain knowledge and experience, III:209-210
creation of the Universe, III:31, 226
defining connection to life, III:95
effects of panentheism, III:142-143
entropy and the nature of life, III:161-162
essence of the individual, III:39

THEMATIC INDEX

eternal and tied to the soul, III:93
forgiveness for negative behavior, III:81-82
growth and change, III:191
Humankind assigning characteristics, III:136
Humankind's behavior leading to abuse, III:121
Humankind's importance, III:87
Humankind's perception needs to change, III:71, 87
increasing awareness, III:215
increasing her knowledge, III:251
interdependent relationship with Humankind, III:167
interfering with journey, III:88
journey of the individual must be respected, III:86
Judaism and the nature of the Universe, III:43
judging Humankind, III:38
nature of the Universe, III:47
negative effects upon, III:191
omnipresence and existence, III:92
omnipresence and the elimination of suffering, III:56
omnipresent and existing everywhere, III:83
omnipresent and omniscient – all present, III:93
omnipresent force, III:68, 192
omniscience and the individual, III:190
omniscience and total awareness, III:166-167
ontology and the significance of Humankind, III:99
origin of the Universe, III:184
panentheism and concept of omnipresence, III:138
panentheism and Humankind, III:72, 141
panentheism and omnipresence, III:137, 140
paradoxes implicit in theism, III:207
perception and atheism, III:130
perception of equilibrium, III:171-172
philosophical perception and influence of ontology, III:90
positive effects upon, III:191
possessing a creator, III:116
relationship to Humankind, III:32-33, 147, 167
relationship to self, III:39
relationship to the soul, III:33
relationship to the Universe, III:44, 185
science expanding our perception, III:102
significance and importance of life, III:105-106
significance of homo-, III:263
significance of Humankind, III:45, 48, 75, 110-111, 132
significance of life, III:60, 129, 227
significance of other life forms, III:201
significance of our species, III:200
significance of symbiosis, III:275
significance of symmetry, III:191

significance of the individual, III:35-36, 108, 199
significance of the soul, III:51, 96
soul returning to, III:187
status of Humankind, III:211-212
symbiosis and interaction, III:269-270
theism and its support for panentheism, III:128
theism and omnipresence, III:125
theism and the concept of size, III:126
topology of the Universe, III:220
total awareness within Universe, III:186
travelling reality, III:35
Universe existing within, III:104
what Humankind has to offer, III:96
what set theory implies III:203
what the Big Bang can tell us about size, III:173

Christianity
Causative Force and omniscience, III:258
comparisons with 'the Philosophy', I:352
concept of loving one another, III:65
consequences of actions, III:69
eliminating suffering within society, III:65-66
helping to understand our Universe, III:67
loving one another, III:67-68, 72, 74-75, 178
reinforcing concept of equality with each other, III:75
reinforcing significance of existence, III:69
relationship of Humankind to Causative Force, III:75
relationship to other religions, I:351
relationship to symbiotic panentheism, III:76
significance of Humankind in eternity, III:74
significance of soul is tied to eternity, III:74
treating everyone equally and with love, III:66
what it can offer other life forms in the Universe, III:73
what it can offer our species, III:66, 72
what it can offer society, III:71
what it can offer the individual, III:71
what it tells us about life, III:70

Christians
do they need to reassess their present assumptions?, I:151
is their portrayal of God accurate or inaccurate?, I:27
judging Judas - the absence of forgiveness, I:152

Civilization
status and growth, II:53

Concepts
good and evil, I:327
morality and immorality, I:327
right and wrong, I:327

Confucianism
effects on society, III:309
helping us to understand what life is, III:314
helping us understand the Universe, III:311
Humankind's relationship to Causative Force, III:319
implies a need for order, III:312
what it can offer other life forms, III:317
what it can offer us as a species, III:316
what it can offer us as individuals, III:315
what it can tell us about our significance in eternity, III:318
what it can tell us about the significance of existence, III:313
what it has to offer society, III:310

Contradictions
necessity for a new perception, I:37
present way of looking too simplistic, I:37

Creator *(see God and Causative Force)*
creating a new perspective, II:89
gift of life, II:70
Humankind - feelings of anger, II:88
Humankind - feelings of inferiority, II:56
Humankind's perception, II:63
increasing knowledge, II:46
increasing power, II:46
Mankind necessary for Its omnipotence, I:181
Mankind necessary for Its omnipresence, I:181
Mankind necessary for Its omniscience, I:181
relationship with Humankind, II:84
significance of Humankind, III:45
size of and the significance for existence, III:57
value and purpose of Humankind, II:98

D

Death
defining beginning and end, II:8
medical definitions, II:9

Democracy
not necessary to dismantle, III:135

E

Early Christian Philosophy
effects upon society, III:345
helping us to understand nature of life, III:350
reinforcing significance of life, III:349, 354
relationship of Humankind to Causative Force, III:355
relationship to panentheism, III:348
what it can offer other life forms, III:353
what it can offer us as a species, III:346, 352
what it can offer us as individuals, III:351
what it can tell us about the Universe, III:347

Ecological Niche
established within society, III:229
existence of the Universe, III:233
future of the human race, III:236
helping us to understand life, III:234
implications for our Universe, III:231
reinforcing significance of existence, III:233
relationship to panentheism, III:232, 240
significance of Humankind in eternity, III:238
what does it imply about our relationship to Causative Force?, III:239
what it has to offer other life forms, III:237
what it has to offer us as a species, III:230, 236
what it has to offer us as individuals, III:235

Economic Systems
not necessary to dismantle, III:135

Entropy
decay of the Universe, III:159
effects of science on society, III:157
how does it reinforce concept of panentheism?, III:160, 163, 168
implies that life and change are interconnected, III:161-162
significance of Humankind in eternity, III:166-167
three possible states of existence of Universe, III:159
what it can offer other life forms, III:165
what it can offer us as a species, III:158, 164

Eternity
Humankind's actions influencing, III:62
justice existing in eternity, III:79
significance of Humankind, III:146, 166-167, 169-170
significance of Judaism, III:50
significance of panentheism, III:146

Extraterrestrials
significance of Hinduism, III:37
significance of Judaism, III:49

F

Free Will
choice and responsibility for our actions, II:193, III:63
choosing to love one another, III:67
does God possess it? - what are the implications?, I:37
does Man possess it? - what are the implications?, I:37
Humankind's possession of - not predestined, II:141
responsibilities implicit, II:195
why God would need Man to possess it in order to expand His own knowledge, I:66

G

God *(see Creator and Causative Force)*
absence of judgement or revenge, I:341
accepting His true nature - what we first need to do, I:30
atheists - their relationship to God and belief, I:26
beginnings - where did He come from?, I:27
concept of panentheism and the consequences of subservience, II:90
concept of religion within society, II:59
creating Humankind in its image, II:197
creation of the Universe, II:52
creator of all things, but who created Him?, I:27
creator of reality, II:191
definitions and names - are they accurate?, I:315
does He possess complete knowledge?, I:64
environment a sacred realm, II:142
expanding essence, II:140
expanding his omnipresence, omnipotence, and omniscience, I:267
faulty and limited conceptions, I:315
free will and Man's destiny, I:37
His historical relationship with Man, I:26
His knowledge, and why He would need to create Man, I:65
how does Mankind's present perception limit the Creator? - what can we do to resolve the problem?, I:193
Humankind acting as servants, II:45, 58
Humankind importance, II:187
Humankind's perception of inferiority, II:142
Humankind's theistic beliefs, II:18
hurt and abuse by our actions, II:193
importance and significance for people, II:205
importance and value of people, II:137

importance of every soul, II:199
importance of every soul's journey, II:210
importance of Humankind, II:192, 194
importance of the soul, II:192
isolating portions of Himself to attain more knowledge, I:67
limits on God without Humankind, II:35
Man's picture of Him - is it accurate?, I:37
Man's purpose to create knowledge through experiences and creativity, I:223-224
Mankind's existence, I:320
monotony inherent in possessing complete and absolute knowledge, I:110
myths removed - finding the truth about God, I:26
nature and status of Humankind, II:61, 173
necessity for growth and change, II:55
not limited by Mankind's definitions, I:318
omnipotence, omniscience, and omnipresence, II:208
people being a portion of God, II:202
philosophical discussions, II:159
presence in reality, II:43, 48
raising Humankind to equal level, II:30
reality in time, II:44
recognition of purpose in reality, II:209
relationship to reality, II:115
relationship to theistic beliefs, II:66
relationship with Humankind, II:21, 57
setting the soul free, I:272
status and hierarchy within society - what are the implications for the soul?, I:203
status of Humankind as inferior, II:65
status system, II:143
subjecting to abuse by our actions, II:188
theistic religions, II:69
travelling reality, II:144, 156, 193
understanding His true nature - going back to the beginning, I:28
universal or particular - do we possess an accurate knowledge of His true nature?, I:27
violence directed, II:198
what is His true nature? - is it compatible with Mankind's perception?, I:193
who is He? - is He really as established religions portray him?, I:27
wonder and significance of in reality, II:149

H

Heaven
does it exist?, I:166

relationship to eternal existence, III:134

Hedonism
how it relates to responsibility, I:82
responsibility to Mankind and your fellow-man - what is needed?, I:37

Hell
does it exist?, I:166
relationship to eternal existence, III:134

Hinduism
ancient religion, III:40
Causative Force and self are identical, III:39
concept of dissolving Universe, III:182
establishing concept of the soul, III:30
establishing monotheism within society, III:29-30
eternal nature of the soul, III:38
Humankind's impact on eternity, III:38
incorporated into other religions, III:39
monotheistic foundations, III:38
reinforced by panentheism, III:40
reinforcing panentheism, III:32
relationship to other religions, III:33
relationship to panentheism, III:31
respect and equality, III:37
significance for Humankind, III:34
significance of the individual, III:33, 35
significance to other life forms, III:37

History
how would 'the Philosophy' approach the question of Man's behavior?, I:186
what do we need to do to hear its message?, I:184, 186
what has it taught us ?, I:184, 186

Homo-
expanding our understanding of life, III:258, 261
implications for the Universe, III:255
reinforcing significance of existence, III:257
relationship to Causative Force, III:263
relationship to panentheism, III:256, 264
sapiens – last of its species, III:253
significance for other life forms, III:261
significance for our species, III:260
significance in eternity, III:262
what does its conceptual framework have to offer us?, III:254

what it has to offer individuals, III:259

Humanism and Adjustment
effects upon society, III:381
helping us to understand life, III:386
implications for the Universe, III:383
relationship and significance for panentheism, III:384
relationship to Causative Force, III:391
significance of Humankind in eternity, III:390
significance of life and existence, III:385
what it can offer other life forms, III:389
what it can offer us as a species, III:382, 388
what it can offer us as individuals, III:387

Humankind *(see Mankind)*
accepting a new perception, II:80
acting as servants of God, II:58
anger at the Creator, II:88
belief in inferiority to God, II:17
beliefs leading to slavery, II:23, 25-26
changing self-perception and value, II:77
choice to be subservient or be a piece of God, II:37-38
consequences of reaching into space, II:94
expanding perceptions of reality, III:36
feelings of despair over status, II:51
feelings of inferiority to Creator, II:56
feelings of inferiority to God, II:143
function within reality, II:19
historical opportunities for self-destruction, II:141
importance and value, II:137
institutions and beliefs, II:74
lacks a universal philosophy, II:24
making choices - consciously or by default, II:141
not native to Earth, II:29
not servants, but equals, II:137
occupying niche unaffected by time, III:254
origins in violent past, II:33
perception of the Creator, II:63
purpose beyond reality, II:53
purpose in reality, II:16, III:36
relationship to Causative Force, III:32, 147
relationship to Creator, II:67
relationship to God, II:57
remaining subservient to God, II:143
significance and importance, II:50, III:46
significance of Causative Force, III:48
significance of Hinduism, III:34

significance of Judaism on our understanding of Causative Force, III:45
significance of the soul and monotheism, III:47
significance of the soul to Causative Force, III:51
significance to Causative Force, III:36
status and relationship with God, II:96
status of God as superior, II:65
value and purpose to the Creator, II:98

I

Individual
consequences of Buddhist philosophy, III:59

Islam
accountable for actions, III:83
beliefs reinforced by symbiotic panentheism, III:88
Causative Force and omniscience, III:258
concept of justice, III:86
consequences of injustice, III:84
establishing justice within society, III:77-78
Humankind's relationship to Causative Force, III:87
justice and Causative Force, III:78
justice in this life, III:83
justice will not be denied within the Universe, III:79
nature of the Universe, III:79-80
offers all life forms the concept of justice, III:85
reinforcing significance of life, III:81-82
relationship to panentheism, III:80
significance of Humankind in eternity, III:86
significance of our species, III:84
significance of the individual, III:83

J

Jesus Christ
Christianity and 'the Philosophy' are compatible, I:361
purpose to turn Mankind away from violence, I:364

Journey
importance and significance, II:136

Judaism
building the bridge from East to West, III:41
Causative Force and omniscience, III:258
concept of eternity and Humankind, III:45
effects on society, III:41

helping Humankind to understand life, III:46
holds to the concept that there is only one Causative Force, III:44
introduced concept of monotheism to the West, III:42
monotheistic religion, III:44-45
reinforced by panentheism, III:52
significance for Humankind as a species, III:48
significance for other life forms, III:49
significance of the soul and Humankind's relationship to Causative Force, III:51
significance of the soul and monotheism on Humankind, III:47
significance of the soul in eternity, III:50
teaching Humankind about the nature of the Universe, III:43
teaching Humankind about the significance of existence, III:45

Judgement
Judas - have we treated him fairly?, I:149-150

Justice
Islamic teaching and eternity, III:87

K

Klein Bottle
existence within the boundary, II:183
limits of the Universe, II:115
relationship to reality, II:87
structure of the Universe, II:81, 84, 102
What it tells us about Humankind's possible future, II:115

Knowledge
Mankind has reached a point in its understanding of philosophy, science, and religion where it realizes that these fields of enquiry overlap and are interconnected, I:100
monotony for God in possessing complete and absolute knowledge, I:110
paradoxes of and alternative approaches examined, I:110

L

Life
atheism and significance of existence, III:117
Buddhism helping Humankind understand what life is, III:57-58
defining beginning and end, II:7-8, 10
definitions and accuracy, III:234
essence of us all, III:258
importance to Causative Force, III:129
Islam and significance of existence, III:81-82

limited significance under atheism, III:119
meaning and purpose for Humankind in eternity, III:88
nature is to change, III:185
necessary to define, III:94-95, 258
palaeomagnetism and understanding, III:246
philosophers ask the fundamental questions in their search for truth, I:46
philosophical definition, III:95
relationship to the Creator, II:70
science reinforcing significance, III:105
significance and importance in eternity, III:59
significance and importance to Causative Force, III:105-106
significance in reality, III:129
significance of ecological niche, III:234
significance of life, III:46, 118
symmetry and its role in our understanding, III:186
theism helping us to understand importance, III:130
topology leading to understanding, III:222
value and importance, III:70
what The Big Bang can tell us about existence, III:173-174

Life Forms
defining ecological niche, III:237
effects of atheistic beliefs, III:121
importance of Christianity, III:73
significance of homo-, III:261
significance of palaeomagnetism, III:249
significance of symbiosis, III:273
significance of symmetry, III:189
significance of topology, III:225
significance to Causative Force, III:201
significance within the Universe, III:109
value and equal status within the Universe, III:74
what ecological niche has to offer, III:237
what entropy can offer, III:165
what panentheism has to offer, III:145
what space has to offer, III:213
what The Big Bang has to offer, III:177
what theism can offer, III:133

Life Incarceration
consequences for the soul, I:263
protection of society, I:266
what are the issues for Mankind?, I:260-262

Love
Christian concept within society, III:65-66, 73

recognizing significance of the individual, III:71

M

Mankind *(see Humankind)*
accepting responsibility - the first steps to solving universal problems, I:145
accomplishing true purpose within the Universe, I:74
attaining knowledge - the need for patience, I:28
capable now, with present technology, of destroying itself, I:101
capital punishment and life incarceration, I:267
commonality of the soul, I:322
conflict between different religions and faiths necessitate the need for change, I:101
contradictions - facing difficult decisions and choices, I:36
created in God's image, I:37
different approaches to the questions of life, I:38
finding answers to purpose in life, I:50
God - is His true nature compatible with that of Man?, I:193
good and bad actions - are they always as they appear?, I:148
good or evil - what is Man's true nature?, I:158
helping each other find peace and security, I:29
historical belief in God - the reasons why, I:26
hope and despair - what do we need to do in order to attain our true purpose?, I:180
how actions, both great and small, can cause great harm or good, I:81
Judas - have we treated or understood him properly?, I:149
lacks a complete understanding of its true purpose in reality, I:148
mass-media - what harm has it done?, I:172
mortality and limits, I:334
moving to the next level - solving the puzzle of life, I:44
must not waste this time in its development, but instead learn and grow, I:100
must study the past in order to safeguard the future, I:367
necessity for a purpose in life - staying true to its true potential, I:197
necessity for struggle to change and grow, I:165
necessity for tolerance and patience in quest for the truth, I:45
obligated to reach out to fellow man, I:111
obtaining a truer picture of God - what first needs to be done?, I:28
origin and nature, I:319
possessing a greater role and value than it presently realizes - what are the implications?, I:114
potential and realization - what is Man's future?, I:123
present beliefs inhibit his ability to grow and change, I:50

purpose to create knowledge through experiences and creativity, I:223
reaching a point in its understanding of philosophy, science, and religion where it realizes that these fields of enquiry overlap and are interconnected, I:100
religion and hope - what 'the Philosophy' can do, I:170
religion and the concepts of heaven and hell, I:333
searching and attaining knowledge as a species, I:29
searching for the true spiritual Creator, I:28
seeking an answer to the purpose of life, I:44
strive to attain true purpose in life and assist fellow man, I:226
tolerance and empathy - why we need to be sympathetic to other beliefs, I:30
wars and conflicts - what have been the results of our actions?, I:140
why does it need to believe that the Creator is omnipresent, omnipotent, and omniscient?, I:113

Missionary Work
importance for the soul, I:285
importance within society, I:282, 285
relationship to 'the Philosophy', I:283

Morality
contradictions and conflicts within society, II:2-3
logical basis for, II:204

O

Omnipotence
does it undermine the structure of society?, I:113
eliminating the paradoxes, I:112-113
Mankind should not be limited by present conceptions and understanding, I:112
what do we need to do in order to change?, I:112

Omnipresence
does it undermine the structure of society?, I:113
eliminating the paradoxes, I:112, 113
Mankind should not be limited by present conceptions and understanding, I:112
not wholly embraced by religions, III:143
panentheism and Causative Force, III:137, 140
theism and Causative Force, III:128
what do we need to do in order to change?, I:112

Omniscience
does it undermine the structure of society?, I:113
eliminating the paradoxes, I:112-113
Mankind should not be limited by present conceptions and understanding, I:112
symbiosis and religious perceptions, III:271

Ontology
conception of a necessary being, III:90
global perception generates global behavior, III:89
helping us to understand what life is, III:94-96
perception leading to change in behavior, III:89
philosophical perception of Causative Force, III:90
reinforcing panentheism, III:92
reinforcing significance of existence, III:93
significance of Humankind in eternity, III:98
significance of the individual, III:97
what it can offer us as a species, III:96
what it can offer us as individuals, III:95
what it has taught us about the Universe, III:91
what it tells us about Humankind's relationship to Causative Force, III:99

P

Palaeomagnetism
concept established within society, III:241
relationship to panentheism, III:244, 252
significance of existence, III:245
significance of Humankind in eternity, III:250
significance of Humankind to Causative Force, III:251
understanding what life is, III:246
what it has to offer other life forms, III:249
what it has to offer our species, III:242, 248
what it has to offer us as individuals, III:247
what it implies about the Universe, III:243

Panentheism
accepted as a belief system, II:202
accepted by society, II:206, 207
adoption by Humankind as a philosophy, II:52, 86
assigning true omnipresence to Causative Force, III:137
beginning and growth of, II:145
being a part of the whole, III:199-201
changing and altering our perceptions, II:157
characteristics assigned to Causative Force, III:148
Christianity's relationship to Causative Force, III:76

closer to the truth of reality, II:194
concept not easily accepted by society, II:156
concept of an all present Causative Force, III:73
concept of equality among Humankind, II:192
concept of equality and how it relates to Humankind's value and importance to God, II:191
concept of universal tolerance, II:27
creating radical changes within society, II:174
destroying the rationale for abuse within society, II:156
does the Causative Force need you?, III:141
effects of Humankind's behavior on Causative Force, III:68
effects on Causative Force, III:142-143
elevates size and significance of Causative Force, III:76
emerging and developing philosophy, II:155
finding a home for the soul, III:147
fundamental logic, II:193
how is it reinforced by our knowledge of entropy?, III:160, 163
how theism supports and reinforces, III:128
Humankind returning to Causative Force, III:72
Humankind's adoption, II:72
Humankind's higher purpose in reality, II:26
Humankind's significance, II:91
immersion in 'the Philosophy', II:48
importance of Humankind within the Universe, II:43
necessity for Humankind to act responsibly, III:68
not a religion, but a foundation for religion, III:44
not wholly embraced by religions, III:142-143
omnipresence and Causative Force, III:140, 180
parallel Universes and Humankind's future, II:92
pervading society, II:211
philosophical perception of reality, II:155
placing responsibility upon life, III:117
provides understanding of Universe, III:139
providing foundation for religions, III:52
providing rationale for hope and optimism III:202
radical change within society, II:211
reality existing within God, II:155
reinforced by Buddhism, III:56
reinforced by concept of The Big Bang, III:180
reinforced by Hinduism, III:40
reinforced by ontology, III:92
reinforces religions, but requires a new perception of significance, III:138
reinforcing Buddhism, III:64
reinforcing concept of ecological niche, III:240
reinforcing concept of homo-, III:264
reinforcing ontology, III:100

reinforcing science, III:112
reinforcing significance of palaeomagnetism, III:252
reinforcing, not undermining religion, science and philosophy, III:204
rejected by society, II:206-207
relationship of Humankind to Causative Force, III:147
relationship of symmetry to our understanding, III:184
relationship to atheism, III:116
relationship to ecological niche, III:232
relationship to Hinduism, III:31, 37
relationship to homo-, III:256
relationship to palaeomagnetism, III:244
relationship to pantheism, II:159
relationship to science, III:104
relationship to set theory, III:196, 203-204
relationship to symbiosis, III:276
relationship to symmetry, III:192
relationship to theism, II:159
relationship to topology, III:220
relationship with Islamic teaching, III:80, 88
requires modification of our present perceptions, III:138
resolving many paradoxes of religions, III:144
responsibility for actions and behavior, III:146
seeds of growth within society, II:204-205
set theory leading to understanding, III:194-195
significance and Causative Force, III:141
significance of Humankind in eternity, III:146
significance of life and the elimination of suffering, III:60
simple in concept, but radical in practice, II:207
simple yet complex philosophy, II:186
simplicity of concept, II:211
supported by Hinduism, III:34
supporting concept of topology, III:228
understanding of Humankind's purpose in reality, II:103
universal philosophy and society, II:12
what does it have to offer us?, III:138, 144
what it has to offer other life forms, III:145
what it says, II:186
what symbiosis implies, III:268

Pantheism
consequences of continuing present beliefs, II:86
inclusive, not exclusive, philosophy, III:207
relationship to panentheism, II:194
relationship to set theory, III:196, 203-204
what it to offer us, III:114

Paradox
need for resolution or destruction, I:111

People
elevated to the level of God, II:205
gaining knowledge of their true value and importance, II:138
visionaries for the future, II:137

Philosophers
asking the first question - why?, I:44
asking the fundamental questions to find the truth, I:46

Philosophy
application of abstract concepts, III:218
basic concepts of panentheism, II:12
basic concepts of theism, II:11, 13
battle of perception, II:25
different approaches to the search for truth, I:39
easier to repress than science, III:255
failure to change perspective, II:61
necessity for 'circular' reasoning in order to find the truth, I:38
necessity for 'quadratic' thinking in order to solve the problems of life, I:39
necessity for Mankind to think not in a linear way, but in a quadratic way, I:38
quadratic vs. linear thinking, I:39
significance of panentheism, II:48

Philosophy, Religion, Science
effects on society, III:297
helping us to understand life, III:302
Humankind's significance in eternity, III:306
importance of panentheism, III:300
life and existence within the Universe, III:301
significance and purpose within the Universe, III:299
what they can tell us about Humankind's relationship to Causative Force, III:307
what they have to offer other life forms, III:305
what they offer the individual, III:303
what they offer us as a species, III:298, 304

Philosophy, the
basic principles, II:185-186
belief in equality of religion, I:288
belief in the inherent value of every human being, I:175
changing our ideas about capital punishment and life incarceration, I:262

comparisons with Christianity, I:352
different approaches to the questions of life, I:39
do we need to be more understanding of Judas?, I:155
does not undermine religion, I:170
embraces everything in reality, 157
God and the absence of vengeance, I:345
helping the victims of crime, I:274
helping us reevaluate social norms and behavior, I:276
how can it be applied successfully?, I:122
how it can initiate the first steps of change, I:144
how the Ripple Effect can cause great harm or good, I:143
how the Ripple Effect relates to our behavior, I:80
importance within society, I:288
is Judas a part of God?, I:155
it doesn't teach, it guides, I:156
its basic concepts explored, I:241
Mankind's purpose in reality, I:344
provides foundation for growth, I:170
provides foundation for religion, but is not itself a religion, I:262, 353, 361
supports religion, I:170
what are its limits?, I:122
what does it say about Man's purpose?, I:241
what impact could it have for Mankind?, I:121
what is necessary to know in order to begin understanding Man's true purpose?, I:119
why every person and soul are important, I:175

Predestination
absence of choice in our actions, III:63

Prophecy
Buddhism and the significance of the Wheel of Dharma, III:418-419
change is necessary within society in order to prevent catastrophe, III:411, 413, 419, 422
Christian concept of unconditional love, III:419
extinction of life on Earth, III:414
geological evidence of change in the Earth's history, III:414
Humankind's destiny and purpose, III:411
humbling effect of the third millennium, III:413
Mayan calendar – present cycle to end in the year 2012, III:416
necessity for change to occur within society, III:423
necessity to define Humankind's purpose, III:413, 419
necessity to elevate worth of the individual, III:412
Nostradamus - giving hope for the future, III:421
Papal Prophecy – is the future predetermined?, III:420
predicting a major setback for Humankind, III:411

predictions of change at the end of the millennium, III:422
preparing for the future, III:423
purpose and significance of the Great Pyramid, III:415
Revelations and the need for change, III:419
significance of the Hopi, III:417
Wheel of Dharma and the end of present cycle, III:419

Puzzle
asking the first question - why?, I:44
Man - first steps in solving the puzzle of life, I:44
putting the pieces together in order to make a complete thought, I:44
putting the pieces together to find an answer to the questions of life, I:45
seeking an answer to the purpose of life, I:44

Q

Quark
fundamental building block of Universe, II:49

Questions
are omnipotence, omnipresence, omniscience based on logic and reason?, I:162
is religion necessary?, I:162
is religion significant?, I:162
is there hope for individuals?, I:162
is there hope for Mankind?, I:162, 288

R

Race
perception of exploitation within society, II:189

Reality
exploration by science, II:59
figment of imagination, II:44
Humankind's purpose, II:53
is it an accurate representation of the truth?, I:27
significance of Humankind, II:50
who created our reality?, I:27

Reason and Experience
effects upon society, III:369
Humankind's significance to Causative Force, III:379
reinforcing the significance of life and existence, III:373
relationship and significance for panentheism, III:372

significance of Humankind, III:378
understanding meaning and purpose of life, III:374
understanding the Universe, III:371
understanding what we see, III:370
what it can offer other life forms, III:377
what it can offer us as a species, III:370, 376
what it can offer us as individuals, III:375

Religion
acceptance of God within society, II:59
application of abstract concepts, III:218
atheist's role in teaching and learning, I:233, 236
based on faith, II:5
based on reason, II:5
battle of perception, II:25
belief in eternity, III:62
Christian concept of love, III:66
conflict due to different definitions of God, I:316
difficulty with concept of omnipresence, III:127
how theism supports the concept of panentheism, III:128
how they can prevent stagnation in their beliefs, I:47
influence upon society, II:169
invoking fear about God - is there a better approach?, I:192
judgement and condemnation, II:4
lacks understanding of who Man is, I:343
lingering and struggling in their present form - the necessity for change, I:50
modernizing beliefs and attitudes in order to find the truth of existence, I:50
moral contradictions within society, II:3
necessity for change within society, II:57
necessity for combining religious principles with science, I:45
necessity for cooperation between different faiths, I:50
necessity for religion to comfort the soul, I:197
necessity for tolerance and patience for different beliefs and opinions, I:29
necessity for tolerance and respect of others, I:47
necessity to change their perceptions, III:172
necessity to commence self-introspection, II:161
not necessary to dismantle, III:135
omnipresence and contradictions in belief, III:179
panentheism providing foundation, III:52
panentheism resolving many paradoxes, III:144
paradox concerning omnipresence, III:92, 110, 127
perceiving Causative Force to be in a permanent state of equilibrium, III:171-172
perpetuation of concepts of heaven and hell, I:333

perpetuation of myths and fear within society, I:190
positive and negative effects for Mankind, I:84
professing belief in the soul, III:225
professing omniscience of Causative Force, III:110
refusal to change perspective, II:61
refusal to embrace panentheism, III:142-143
rejecting a companion in reality, II:149
relationship and equality with 'the Philosophy', I:288
relationship of Christianity to other beliefs, I:351
relationship with Hinduism, III:33
relationship with science and society, I:36
relationship with science, I:48, III:103
serving Humankind, II:150
significant or necessary? - what can we know?, I:190
society's modification, II:97
stagnation of perspective in Humankind, II:55
supported by panentheism, III:44
teaching the concept of an eternal soul, III:250
understanding who we are, III:219

Renaissance Philosophy
effects upon society, III:357
helping us to understand life, III:362
reinforcing significance of existence, III:361
relationship of Humankind to Causative Force, III:367
relationship to panentheism, III:360
significance of Humankind in eternity, III:366
what it can offer other life forms, III:365
what it can offer us as a species, III:358, 364
what it can offer us as individuals, III:363
what it can tell us about the Universe, III:359

Research
controversial and sensitive, II:189

Responsibility
benefits and understanding, III:275

Ripple Effect
consequences for Mankind, I:335
consequences of behavior, I:328
effects on the soul, I:328
Mankind's behavior and mortality, I:334
struggle with life, II:184
suicide and the soul - what are the dangers?, I:254
understanding purpose of life and existence, II:164
what Buddhism tells us about our actions, III:58

what impact could it have for Mankind?, I:143

S

Science
concept of 'om' and its significance to the Universe and Humankind, II:68
concept of a bounded Universe, III:114
expanding our perception of Causative Force, III:102
exploration of reality, II:59
helping Humankind to understand its origins, III:107
helping us to understand our Universe, III:103
influence upon society, II:169
necessity for combining its beliefs with those of religion, I:45
reinforcing concept of panentheism, III:104
reinforcing need for religion, III:103
reinforcing significance of life, III:105
relationship with religious beliefs, I:48
significance of Causative Force, III:112
significance of Humankind in eternity, III:110
significance of Humankind to Causative Force, III:108, 111
significance of other life forms in the Universe, III:109
significant influence on society, III:50
understanding meaning of life, III:106
understanding who we are, III:219
what it can offer the individual, III:107
what it has established within society, III:101
what it has to offer Humankind, III:102, 108

Set Theory
how it reinforces symbiotic panentheism III:204
leading to a universal philosophy, III:196
reinforcing significance of existence, III:197-198
relationship to atheism, III:196, 203-204
relationship to panentheism, III:196, 203-204
relationship to pantheism, III:196, 203-204
relationship to theism, III:196, 203-204
seeing the significance of life, III:197-198
significance of Humankind in eternity, III:202
understanding concept of panentheism, III:194-198
understanding our Universe, III:195
what does it have to offer us?, III:194-195, 200
what has it firmly established within society?, III:193
what has it to offer other life forms?, III:201
what has it to offer us as individuals?, III:199
what it implies about our relationship to Causative Force III:203

Significance
theism elevating value of existence, III:136

Social Institutions
absence of free will, II:197
abuses within society, II:206
directives imposed upon by society, II:197
not necessary to dismantle, III:135
tragedy within, II:203

Society
absence of a universal philosophy, II:15
absence of free will in its institutions, II:197
atheism established within society, III:113
based upon equality, II:97
capital punishment and life incarceration - what are the issues?, I:260
directives imposed upon social institutions, II:197
effects of Buddhism, III:53-54
effects of entropy, III:181
effects of Hinduism and monotheism, III:29
effects of Judaism, III:41
effects of modern science, III:101
effects of ontology, III:89
effects of science within, III:157
effects of set theory, III:193
effects of symbiotic panentheism, III:393
helping victims of domestic violence, II:199-200
how does status and hierarchy affect the soul?, I:222
Humankind strengthening structure of, II:79
ignoring the victims of crime, I:273
Islam and the concept of justice, III:78
necessity for care within, II:200
necessity for protection of the soul, I:273
necessity for respect and tolerance for another person's decisions and actions, I:246
paying debt to - what is involved?, I:260
perpetuation of myths and fear by religion, I:191
possibilities for change and reform - can it happen?, II:210
religious morality and faith, II:3
self-righteousness, II:197
significance of palaeomagnetism, III:241
significance of science within, III:50
social morality and laws, II:2
symbiotic relationship between God and Humankind, II:20
The Big Bang and society, III:169-170
violence towards differing social groups within, II:78, 196

what does Mankind need to do in order to fulfill its potential?, I:182
what role does status and hierarchy play?, I:200
what science has established, III:217
with panentheism as its foundation, II:206
without panentheism as its foundation, II:206

Soul
accomplishing its journey in eternity, III:88
allowing it to fulfill its destiny and purpose, I:86
atheists' role in teaching and learning, I:236
consequences of atheistic beliefs - positive or negative?, I:233
distress and suffering it is exposed to, I:37
essence of life, III:225
eventual destruction of the Universe, III:139
existing in eternity, III:80, 82
faulty and limited conceptions, I:317
how does the Ripple Effect relate to Mankind's purpose?, I:204
how it can transcend this reality, I:95
how its journey relates to Humankind's and God's future, II:117
importance and function, II:190
importance of every person in life, I:185
journey in reality, II:170
Judas - what can he teach us about Man's nature?, I:153
nature of and potential in eternity, III:46
origin and purpose, I:322
panentheism providing a home for the soul, III:147
positive and negative effects of social status and hierarchy, I:222
protecting it within society, I:283
purpose in reality for Humankind and God, II:116
relationship to Hinduism, III:30
relationship to Humankind and the Creator, II:5
religion and atheism - what are the consequences?, I:235
returning to Causative Force, III:187
searching for inner peace and harmony, I:36
setting it free, I:272
significance to Causative Force, III:96
status and society - what are the problems?, I:200
status in reality, II:142
what harm has mass media done to Mankind?, I:172

Space
concepts and implications of space-time, III:206
exploration, II:94
Humankind's relationship to Causative force, III:215
Humankind's significance in eternity, III:214
located within Causative Force, III:208
nature and structure, III:206

reinforcing significance of life, III:209-210
relationship to symbiotic panentheism, III:208, 216
what it can tell us about our Universe, III:207
what it has firmly established within society, III:205
what it has to offer other life forms, III:213
what it has to offer us as a species, III:206, 212
what it has to offer us as individuals, III:211

Species
contribution of palaeomagnetism, III:248
significance of homo-, III:260
significance of symbiosis, III:272
what entropy can offer us, III:164
what symmetry can offer us, III:188
what topology can offer us, III:224

Subjugation
consequences of atheistic beliefs, III:120

Suffering
awareness in eternity, III:81-82
Buddhist intolerance for, III:91
consequences for Causative Force, III:62
consequences for Humankind, III:62
elimination within society, III:55-57, 83-84
ignoring it will cause us great harm, III:84
not to be ignored within society, III:54

Suicide
is it ever justified?, I:252-253
why should we continue to live?, I:252-253

Symbiosis
concept established within society, III:265
relationship with Causative Force, III:266, 275
relationship with panentheism, III:268, 276
significance for other life forms, III:273
significance in eternity, III:274
significance of existence, III:269-270
significance of individuals, III:271
significance of our species, III:266, 272
what it implies about the Universe, III:267

Symbiotic Panentheism
defining life, III:398
effects within society, III:393
existence within the Universe, III:396

importance and significance of life, III:397
importance of free will, III:396, 402
importance of Humankind to Causative Force, III:403
model of a universal philosophy, III:404
philosophy and life, III:398
providing a model of a unified view, III:394
significance of Humankind in eternity, III:402
what it can offer other life forms, III:401
what it can offer us as a species, III:394, 400
what it can offer us as individuals, III:399
what it implies about the nature and structure of the Universe, III:395

Symmetry
energy and the creation of the Universe, III:183
established within society, III:181
helping us to understand life, III:186
helping us to understand the creation of the Universe, III:187
helping us to understand the destruction of the Universe, III:187
reinforcing significance of existence, III:185
reinforcing the concept of panentheism, III:184
relationship to symbiotic panentheism, III:192
significance of Humankind in eternity, III:190
significance to Causative Force, III:191
what does it imply about the Universe?, III:183
what it has to offer other life forms?, III:189
what it has to offer our species?, III:182, 188
what it has to offer the individual, III:187

T

Taoism
effects within society, III:321
helping us to understand life, III:326
Humankind's significance in eternity, III:330
Humankind's significance to Causative Force, III:331
implications for our Universe, III:323
relationship to panentheism, III:324
significance of life and existence, III:325
what it can offer other life forms, III:329
what it can offer us as a species, III:322, 328
what it can offer us as individuals, III:327

Theism
assigning characteristics to Causative Force, III:136
belief that Humankind is humble servant of Creator, II:24
Causative Force 'almost' omnipresent, III:125

concept of God, II:18
consequences of continuing present beliefs, II:86
continuing to accept as a philosophy, II:72
elevated significance of existence, III:136
establishing that Universe is not the only existence, III:127
existence and life in eternity, III:129
expanding upon the size of Causative Force, III:126
helping us to understand importance of life, III:130
Humankind is affected by eternity, III:134
importance of life, III:131
including everything but the Universe, III:125
limits as a belief system, II:194
paradoxes within, III:208
reinforcing significance of life, III:129
relationship to God, II:66, 69
relationship to panentheism, II:159
relationship to Pantheism, II:159
relationship to set theory, III:196, 203-204
significance in eternity, III:134
significance of Humankind in eternity, III:134
what it can offer other life forms, III:133
what it can offer our species, III:132, 126
what it can offer the individual, III:131

Thinking
advantages of quadratic over linear philosophy, I:38
necessity for 'circular' reasoning in order to find the truth, I:38

Time
existence and imagination, II:44

Tolerance
not enough, in itself, to stop the growing conflict in the world, I:102-103
time has come to begin searching for better solutions to Mankind's problems, I:104
why Man needs to be tolerant, I:51

Topology
abstract concepts applies to religion and philosophy, III:218
Causative Force and the creation of the Universe, III:226
existence of time, III:227
helping us to understand life, III:222
implications for the Universe, III:219
insights established within society, III:217
relationship to panentheism, III:220, 228
searching for universal truths, III:223

significance of existence, III:221
significance of life in eternity, III:226
significance of life to Causative Force, III:227
significance to other life forms, III:225
what is has to offer us as a species, III:218, 224
what is has to offer us as individuals, III:223

U

Unified View
attaining knowledge as a species, III:287
consequences for Causative Force, III:295
defining life, III:294
effects on society, III:285-286
free will and responsibility, III:290
relationship with panentheism, III:288
significance and purpose of life, III:289
what it can offer other life forms, III:293
what it can offer us as a species, III:292
what it can offer us as individuals, III:291

Universal Philosophy
achieving and maintaining, III:213
establishing foundation, II:157
helping to define Humankind's purpose within reality, II:5
implementation within society, II:195
Positive and negative consequences of atheistic beliefs, I:237
protecting the journey of everyone, III:213
relationship to panentheism and set theory, III:196
relationship to set theory, III:196
significance for other life forms, III:273

Universe
absence of a supreme being, III:114
absence of hope under atheism, III:122-123
Asimov's theory that the Universe is composed of four Universes, I:56
awareness and Causative Force, III:186
basic building block, II:49
boundaries and limits imposed by its structure, I:72
Christian understanding of nature, III:67
concept of boundary and structure, III:91
concept of the Klein bottle, II:81
concept of the quark and its relationship to reality, II:49
created from nothingness, III:31, 91, 184
creation and origin, II:68, 84
eventual destruction, III:139, 158

existing within Causative Force, III:104
God and the creation of 'nothingness', I:58
God's creation, II:52
God's relationship, II:161
growth, decay and entropy, III:159
Hindu concept of dissolving, III:182
how it's constructed and how it can be destroyed, I:57
how its structure appears to limit Humankind, II:101
Humankind's presence, II:42
implications of a boundary and limit, II:35, 41
implications of parallel Universes and how they would help explain our reality, I:50
implications of topology, III:219
is it outside or within Causative Force?, III:216
Islamic teaching concerning justice and equality, III:85
Islamic teaching leading to understanding, III:79
its diversity and how it relates to the creation of Man, I:92
its true structure and possible destruction - the implications for Mankind, I:93
journeying through, III:186
Judaism's relationship to Causative Force, III:43
nature and structure of the Universe, III:79
omniscient nature of Causative Force, III:109
omniscient presence, II:161
outside of Causative Force, III:216
panentheism and our understanding, III:139
reducible to nothingness, III:215
reinforcing significance of existence, III:233
relationship to atheistic beliefs, III:115
relationship to Causative Force, III:47
science as a tool of understanding, III:103
science's perception of boundary, III:114
scientists propose new theories to explain the structure of the Universe, I:45
set theory leading to understanding, III:195
significance of atheism for other life forms, III:121
significance of ecological niche, III:233
significance of life, III:61
significance of other life forms, III:109
structure resembling Klein bottle, II:34
symmetry and creation, III:183
temporary in nature, III:192
theism and Causative Force, III:126
theism and understanding of existence, III:127
three possible states of existence, III:159
topology and Causative Force, III:220
value and importance of all life forms, III:74

what can we know from entropy, III:158
what ontology has thought us, III:91
what palaeomagnetism implies, III:243
what symbiosis implies, III:267
what The Big Bang implies, III:171-172

V

Violence
elimination within society, II:202
presence within society and its consequences, II:196

W

War
is it ever justified?, I:242
Is it moral or right to participate in violence?, I:240
is there such a thing as a moral war?, I:242
what implications are there for the soul?, I:240, 242

Women
importance to God, II:196
subjugation by society, II:196

Index

Volume I

You & I Together

- Have a Purpose in Reality -

Volume II

In the Image of God

Volume III

Stepping Up To The Creator

A

Abortion
choice, I:243
consequences for individuals, I:243
consequences for Mankind, I:243
Delaware teenagers, I:1
issues concerning, II:12
Mankind and the soul, I:244-245
respect for decisions, I:244-245

Afterlife
suicide and the Ripple Effect, I:252, 254

Alien Species
contacting, II:74
subversive actions, II:75, 80

Allah
God and, I:66

Ancient Philosophy
Causative Force, III:343
effects upon society, III:333
helping us to understand life, III:338
Humankind, III:343
relationship to panentheism, III:336
significance of existence, III:337
significance of Humankind in eternity, III:342
understanding our Universe, III:335
what it can offer other life forms, III:341
what it can offer us as a species, III:334, 340
what it can offer us as individuals, III:339

Anti-Matter
destruction of matter, I:56
discovery, I:47

Aristotle
pillar of society, I:182

Asimov, Isaac
B.E.G.A., I:38
four leaf clover Universe, I:48
scientist, I:44
theory concerning merging of two Universes, I:56
theory of the destruction of the Universe, I:92
theory regarding four parallel Universes, I:65
theory regarding how the Universes are separated, I:56

Astronomers
study of time, I:46

Atheism
absence of Causative Force, III:113
belief established within society, III:113
consequences for Causative Force, III:120, 124
defining away significance of Humankind, III:122-123
differs from panentheism, III:117
disbelief in a supreme being, III:114
expression of beliefs, I:232-233
life and existence, III:130
limiting boundaries of existence, III:116
limiting life, III:129
limiting significance, III:132
perception and significance as a species, III:118
provided understanding of our significance, III:119

rationalizes subjugation, III:120
reinforcing panentheism, III:116
relationship to organized religions, I:231
relationship to set theory, III:196, 203-204
relationship to soul of Man, I:236
respect for religious beliefs, I:232-233
significance for other life forms, III:121
significance of life, III:117-118
what it has to offer us as individuals, III:119
what it implies about the Universe, III:115
what it to offer us, III:114

Atlantis
discovery, II:29

Atom
understanding the concept, I:27

Awareness
nature is to change, III:185
never destroyed, III:187

B

Bad
concept, I:327

Belief
Man and God, I:25

Bernoulli
B.E.G.A., I:38
Lemniscule, I:47
mathematician, I:44

Big Bang, The
boundary to the Universe, III:185
implications, II:68
insights established within society, III:169-170
life forms, III:177
offering us hope, III:175-176
provides understanding of existence, III:174-176
provides understanding of Universe, III:175-176
scientific insight into eternity, III:175
significance of individuals, III:177
significance of other life forms, III:177
understanding of existence, III:177
Universe is mortal, III:178
Universe, III:171-172
what it has to offer individuals, III:175
what it has to offer our species, III:176

Boundary
Universe, I:72

Brainwashing
effects of mass media, I:172

Buddha
quote, I:43

Buddhism
affecting Causative Force, III:63
effects on society, III:53-55
eliminating suffering, III:61-62, 64
intolerance of suffering, III:91
reinforcing panentheism, III:56
Ripple Effect, III:58

significance for other life forms, III:61
significance of life in eternity, III:57, 59
significance of the individual, III:59
suffering not tolerated within society, III:55
understanding life, III:58
understanding our journey through life, III:59

Burke, Edmund
quote, I:281

Burns, Robert
quote, I:139

C

Caesar
status and position within society, I:222

Capital Punishment
interfering with journey of Causative Force, III:111
society and the soul, I:259, 263-264

Capitalism
dismantling, III:135

Catholics
historical conflict, I:100

Causative Force *(see God and Creator)*
absence under atheism, III:122-123
achieving a new understanding, III:111
affected by atheistic beliefs, III:120
affected by Humankind, III:63
all loving, III:140
all present, III:140
assigning characteristics, III:136
assisting her journey, III:88, 251
atheism and its implications, III:115
atheism and perception, III:121
atheistic beliefs, III:113
awareness, III:247, 262
belief in her existence, III:100
capital punishment interfering with journey, III:111
changing our perceptions, III:75, 111
Christianity's perception, III:76
creating some-thing from no-thing, III:182
creation of space, III:209-210
creation of the Universe, III:93, 226
defining connection to life, III:95
entropy and the nature of life, III:161-162
essence of the individual, III:39, 262
eternal, III:93
existence, III:247
forgiveness, III:81-82
growth, III:191
Hinduism, III:30
Humankind, III:36
Humankind's actions, III:68-69
Humankind's importance, III:87
Humankind's perception, III:87
increasing awareness, III:215
increasing her knowledge, III:251
individuals, III:190
influence of individuals, III:164

influence of other life forms, III:165
interdependent relationship, III:167
interfering with journey, III:88
Judaism and the Universe, III:43
judging Humankind, III:38
love and equality within our species, III:75
loving each other, III:73
nature of the Universe, III:47
negative effects upon, III:191
omnipresence, III:56, 83, 92, 137
omnipresent and omniscient, III:93
omnipresent force, III:68
omnipresent, III:32, 140-141, 179, 192
omniscience, III:148, 166-167, 190
omniscient within the Universe, III:109
origin of the Universe, III:184
panentheism and Humankind, III:72
panentheism and omnipresence, III:138, 140-141
panentheism, III:137, 142-143
paradoxes of theism, III:207
perception and atheism, III:130
perception, III:71
philosophical perception of ontology, III:90
positive effects upon, III:191
possessing a Creator, III:116
reality, III:35
relationship with Humankind, III:147, 167
relationship with our Universe, III:44
relationship with self, III:39
relationship with the Universe, III:185
respect for individual, III:86
science and perception, III:102
significance of homo-, III:263
significance of Humankind, III:45, 48, 75, 99, 110-111, 132
significance of life, III:105, 106, 129, 227
significance of other life forms, III:201
significance of our species, III:200
significance of the individual, III:108, 199
significance of the soul, III:51, 96
soul returning to, III:187
soul, III:33
status of Humankind, III:211-212
suffering, III:56
symbiosis and interaction, III:269-270
symbiosis, III:275
symmetry, III:191
theism and its support for panentheism, III:128
theism and omnipresence, III:125-126
theism, III:125-126
topology, III:220
total awareness, III:186
Universe existing within, III:104
Universe, III:186
what Humankind has to offer, III:96
what set theory implies III:203

Christianity
actions, III:69
advancing its cause, I:153
Causative Force and omniscience, III:258
concepts of good and bad, I:352

INDEX

conflicts with scientific knowledge, I:100
eliminating suffering within society, III:65-66
existence, III:69
extraterrestrial life, III:73
fundamental beliefs, I:352
Humankind and Causative Force, III:75
individual, III:71
loving one another, III:65, 67-68, 72, 74-75, 178
reinforcing concept of equality, III:75
relationship to symbiotic panentheism, III:76
significance of Humankind, III:74
significance of soul, III:74
society, III:71
telling us about life, III:70
treating everyone equally and with love, III:66
understanding our Universe, III:67
what it can offer our species, III:72

Chuang-Tzu
quote, I:199

Church
Christianity and tolerance, I:155
Christianity, I:151-152
condemnation of Judas, I:151-152

Civilization
status and growth, II:53

Concept
universally generated, I:25

Confucianism
effects on society, III:309
helping us understand the Universe, III:311
Humankind's relationship to Causative Force, III:319
implies a need for order, III:312
significance in eternity, III:318
significance of existence, III:313
understanding what life is, III:314
what it can offer other life forms, III:317
what it can offer us as a species, III:316
what it can offer us as individuals, III:315
what it has to offer society, III:310

Confucius
quote, I:239
status and position within society, I:225

Consciousness
God and creation, I:64

Creation
how the Universe is constructed, I:92

Creative Force
Mankind, I:328

Creator *(see God and Causative Force)*
awareness of true origins, I:66
creating new perspective, II:89
gift of life, II:70
glorifying, II:69
growth, I:112
Humankind, II:67
Humankind's anger, II:88
Humankind's feelings of inferiority, II:56

Humankind's future, II:32
Humankind's perception, II:63
imposing limits, I:192-193
increasing power, II:46
insight, I:27
Judas, I:153
love and forgiveness for Judas, I:153
making peace, I:348
Mankind's connection, I:180
omnipresence, omnipotence, omniscience, I:192
philosophical implications, I:27
relationship of Humankind, II:84
relationship of the soul, I:193
significance in reality, II:25
significance of Humankind, II:24, III:45
size of and the significance for existence, III:57
stopping the search, I:27
value of Humankind, II:98

Crime
against society, I:260
against the soul, I:260

Cytologists
understanding the structure of the human cell, II:23

D

Da Vinci
pillar of society, I:182

Dante
pillar of society, I:182

Death
afterlife - absence of punishment or reward, I:162
beginning of life, I:36
definition, II:8-9, 13
life and consciousness following, I:162
relationship to the afterlife, I:161
termination of brain waves, II:10

Democracy
dismantling, III:135

Despair
Humankind, II:51

Dylan, Bob
quote, I:147

E

Early Christian Philosophy
Causative Force, III:355
effects upon society, III:345
reinforcing significance of life, III:349
relationship to panentheism, III:348
significance of life, III:354
understanding nature of life, III:350
Universe, III:347
what it can offer other life forms, III:353
what it can offer us as a species, III:346, 352
what it can offer us as individuals, III:351

Earth
Humankind created as work force, II:23
pacification of Humankind, II:27
spreading beliefs, II:33

Ecological Niche
established within society, III:229-230

existence of the Universe, III:233
future of the human race, III:236
implications for our Universe, III:231
other life forms, III:237
panentheism, III:232
relationship to Causative Force, III:239
significance for individuals, III:235
significance of existence, III:233
significance of Humankind, III:236, 238
symbiotic panentheism, III:240
understanding life, III:234

Economic Systems
dismantling, III:135

Edison
status and position within society, I:225

Einstein, Albert
B.E.G.A., I:38
concept of $E=mc^2$, I:47
theory of a bounded Universe, I:71
theory of curved light rays and bounded Universe, I:66

Elliott, George
quote, I:63

Entropy
change and the individual, III:163
effects of science on society, III:157
implies that life and change are interconnected, III:161-162
panentheism, III:160, 163
reinforcing panentheism, III:168
significance of Humankind, III:166-167
Universe, III:158-159

Environment
improvements, II:21

Eternity
Humankind's actions upon, III:62
justice in eternity, III:79
significance of Humankind, III:146, 166-167, 169-170
significance of Judaism, III:50
significance of panentheism, III:146

Evil
accepting and perpetuating, I:79
concept, I:327

Existence
termination of life, II:9

Extraterrestrials
banished to Earth, II:29
Hinduism, III:37
significance of Judaism, III:49

F

Faith
adapting our, I:111
maintaining, I:111

Free Will
choice and responsibility, III:63
choosing to love one another, III:67
God and creation, I:65
Humankind, II:141
Mankind's need, I:362
necessity, I:65

responsibility, I:36, II:193, 195
society, II:197

Frost, Robert
quote, II:139

G

Gandhi
pillar of society, I:182
quote, I:169
status and position within society, I:225

Geneticists
understanding the structure of the human cell, II:23

God *(see Creator and Causative Force)*
absence of judgement, I:347
absence of punishment, I:164, 273
absence of significance, I:25
accepting who He is, I:29
achieving a better understanding, I:27
adding new knowledge to Him, I:63
Allah and, I:26
all-encompassing totality, II:17
arguments against existence, I:25
atheistic beliefs, I:231
becoming God, I:73
Christian conceptualization, I:26
concept of panentheism and subservience, II:90
concept of panentheism, II:11
concept of religion, II:59
concept of revenge, I:341
concept of theism, II:11
connections to Mankind, I:181
creating Humankind in its image, II:197
creation of awareness within the Universe, I:65
creation of the Universe, II:52
Creator of Mankind, I:318
Creator of reality, I:26, II:19, 191
Creator of Universe, I:25, 57, 318
defining, I:315
environment as sacred realm, II:142
expanding His omnipresence, omnipotence, and omniscience, I:266
expanding His omniscience, I:66
expanding the concept, II:18
expanding the essence, II:140
experiencing Hell, I:74
feeling of inferiority, II:17
glorifying, II:69
His beginning, I:26
how does He create a void?, I:64
Humankind as servants, II:58
Humankind servant, II:45
Humankind, II:187
Humankind's Creator, II:25
Humankind's equality, II:37
Humankind's perception of inferiority, II:142
Humankind's soul, II:21
hurting and abusing, II:193
if omniscient, would know everything, I:63
implications of a bounded Universe, II:41
importance and value of people to, II:137
importance of every journey, II:210
importance of every soul, II:199
importance of Humankind, II:192, 194
importance of people, II:205
importance of the soul, II:192

INDEX

infusion into, I:170
isolation from other life forms, I:66
Judas and the betrayal, I:150
knowing and not-knowing, I:63
knowing the mind, I:103
laboratories, I:122
Man, I:25
Mankind created in His image, I:201
Mankind's relationship, I:202
missionary work, I:282
nature and status, II:61
nature of reality, II:44
nature, II:85, 174
necessity for growth and change, II:55
necessity for Humankind, II:19
omnipotence, I:26
omnipotence, omniscience, and omnipresence, II:208
people being a portion of, II:202
perception of existence, II:30
perception of, II:74
philosophical discussions, I:25, II:159
placing intelligence within the Universe, I:65
possesses no limit, II:35
presence in reality, II:42
providing guidance, II:38
punishment, I:336
purpose of Humankind, II:36
purpose within this reality, I:266
recognition of purpose, II:209
redefining, II:23
relationship to Man, I:271
relationship to reality, II:115
relationship to theism, II:66
relationship with Humankind, II:15, 18, 57
respect for all life forms, II:38
returning, I:170
significance of Humankind, II:24, 30
soul and the Creator, II:5
soul of Man, I:228
soul, I:320, 322
status of Humankind, II:48, 65, 96
status system, II:143
subjecting to abuse, II:188
survival and growth, II:21
symbiotic relationship with Humankind, II:27, 31
theistic religions, II:69
those professing not to believe in, I:25
transcending reality, II:43, 156
travelling reality, II:11-12, 26, 80, 99, 193, 144
understanding Humankind's purpose, II:37
understanding who He is, I:27
violence directed at, II:198
what is God?, I:26
who is the God of?, I:27
why would He create the Universe?, I:57
wonder of in reality, II:149
Zeus, I:26

Good
concept, I:327

Government
issue of abortion, II:13

Grandi
B.E.G.A., I:38
rose of, I:48

Gutenberg
pillar of society, I:182

H

Hawking, Steven
belief that the entire Universe can be understood by everyone, I:102

Heaven
does it exist?, I:165
eternal existence, III:134

Hedonism
responsibilities, I:86
Ripple Effect, I:81

Hell
does it exist?, I:165
eternal existence, III:134

Heroros
slaughter, I:140

Hikmet, Nazim
quote, I:259

Hinduism
ancient religion, III:30, 40
Causative Force and self, III:39
dissolving Universe, III:182
impacting eternity, III:38
incorporated into other religions, III:39
monotheism, III:29
monotheistic foundations, III:38
other life forms, III:37
reinforced by panentheism, III:32, 34, 40
religion, III:35
respect and equality, III:37
soul, III:30, 38
the self, III:33
Universe, III:31

Hitler, Adolf
World War II and the Jews, I:139

Homo-
Causative Force, III:263
life forms, III:261
relationship to panentheism, III:256
sapiens, III:253
significance of existence, III:257, 262
species, III:260
symbiotic panentheism, III:264
understanding life, III:258
Universe, III:255

Humanism and Adjustment
effects upon society, III:381
relationship to Causative Force, III:391
relationship to panentheism, III:384
significance of existence, III:385
significance of Humankind, III:390
significance of life, III:385
understanding life, III:386
Universe, III:383
what it can offer other life forms, III:389
what it can offer us as a species, III:382, 388
what it can offer us as individuals, III:387

Humanity
gaining knowledge, I:28

Humankind *(see Mankind)*
accepting a new perception, II:80
anger at the Creator, II:88
changing self-perception and value, II:77

created as work force, II:23
created by owners of the Earth, II:23
evaluating self-perception, II:95
faith in religious institutions, II:26
feelings of despair, II:51
feelings of inferiority to Creator, II:56, 143
importance and value, II:137
institutions and beliefs, II:74
issue of abortion, II:14
lacks universal philosophy, II:24
leaders within, II:21
loyal servants, II:42
making choices, II:141
not native to Earth, II:29
not servants, II:137
not servants, II:21
opportunities for self-destruction, II:141
perception of the Creator, II:63
purpose beyond reality, II:53
purpose in existence, II:19, III:36
reaching into space, II:94
relationship to Causative Force, III:147
relationship to Creator, II:67
relationship to God, II:57
remaining subservient to God, II:143
servants of God, II:58
significance and importance, II:50, III:46
significance of Causative Force, III:48
significance of monotheism, III:47
significance of the soul to Causative Force, III:51
significance of the soul, III:47
significance, III:36
slaves, II:26
status of God as superior, II:65
status with God, II:96
symbiotic relationship with God, II:18
understanding of Causative Force, III:45
universally equal, II:27
value to the Creator, II:98

Hur Shi
quote, I:35

I

Ibsen, Henrik
quote, I:91

Ideas
contradictory and non-contradictory, I:35

Inquisition, The
persecution by, I:100

Iraq
persecution of the Kurds, I:140

Islam
accountable for actions, III:83
Causative Force and omniscience, III:258
Causative Force, III:78
concept of justice, III:85-86
consequences of injustice, III:84
Humankind and Causative Force, III:87
justice in this life, III:83
justice within society, III:77-78
justice within the Universe, III:79
nature of the Universe, III:79-80
reinforced by symbiotic panentheism, III:88

relationship to panentheism, III:80
significance of Humankind, III:86
significance of life, III:81-82
significance of our species, III:84
significance of the individual, III:83

J

Japanese Proverb
quote, I:271

Jesus Christ
belief, I:351
Judas and the betrayal, I:151
pillar of society, I:182
purpose for Mankind, I:364
relationship to 'the Philosophy', I:361
sent by God, I:364

Jews
historical conflict, I:100

Journey
importance, II:136

Judaism
Causative Force and omniscience, III:258
effects on society, III:41
eternity and Humankind, III:45
influence on the West, III:42
monotheism and the West, III:42
monotheistic religion, III:44, 45
one Causative Force, III:44
reinforced by panentheism, III:52
significance for other life forms, III:49
significance of existence, III:45
significance of Humankind, III:47-48
significance of the soul, III:50-51
understanding life, III:46
Universe, III:43

Judas
Christian belief that he was evil, I:149
Christian condemnation, I:150
goodness, I:150
understanding and forgiving, I:152

Justice
Islam, III:77, 87
Islamic teaching and eternity, III:87

K

King, Martin Luther
quote, I:79

Klein Bottle
energy waves, II:93
existence within boundary, II:183
limits of the Universe, II:115
relationship to reality, II:87
significance for reality, II:92
structure of the Universe, II:81, 84, 102

Knowledge
acquiring more, I:28
comfort in our lack, I:29

Kurds
persecution, I:140

L

Lao-Tzu
quote, I:71

Lemkin, Raphail
concept of 'genocide', I:140

Life
atheism and significance of existence, III:117
beginning and end, I:37
Buddhism, III:58
Causative Force, III:129
defining, II:8, 10, 13, III:94, 258
definitions and truth, III:234
ecological niche, III:234
essence, III:258
eternal, I:37
finding the right path, I:81
Humankind's understanding, III:57
importance to Causative Force, III:106
limited significance under atheism, III:119
living and experiencing, I:281
meaning and purpose, III:88
nature is to change, III:185
necessary to define, III:95
palaeomagnetism and understanding, III:246
philosophical definition, III:95
purpose, I:281, 284, II:20
relationship to the Creator, II:70
science reinforcing significance, III:105
significance and importance in eternity, III:59
significance in reality, III:129
significance of existence, III:81-82
significance of life, III:46, 118
significance to Causative Force, III:105
significance, II:20
symmetry, III:186
termination, II:376
topology leading to understanding, III:222
understanding Mankind's purpose, I:171
understanding, III:186
value and importance, III:70
what The Big Bang can tell us, III:174

Life Forms
defining ecological niche, III:237
ecological niche, III:237
effects of atheistic beliefs, III:121
entropy, III:165
homo-, III:261
importance of Christianity, III:73
palaeomagnetism, III:249
panentheism, III:145
significance of symmetry, III:189
significance within Universe, III:109
significance, III:201
symbiosis, III:273
The Big Bang, III:177
theism, III:133
topology, III:225
value and equal status, III:74
what space has to offer them, III:213

Life Incarceration
society and the soul, I:259, 263-264

Lippmann, Walter
quote, I:99

Longfellow, Henry W.
quote, I:119, 221

Love
Christian conception, III:73
recognizing significance, III:71
within society, III:65-66

Luther
pillar of society, I:182

M

Mahapurana
quote, I:25

Mankind *(see Humankind)*
adding to its experiences, I:285
awareness, I:36
becoming God, I:335
being part of God, I:202
belief in God, I:25
capable of good, I:36
challenges, I:194
conceptualization of God, I:26
contradictions, I:35
contribution to omnipotence, I:165
created in the image of God, I:36
destiny, I:180
erroneous actions, I:148
eternal soul - actions upon, I:37
examining its past, I:317, 369
experience and purpose, I:37
feelings of superiority and inferiority, I:199
His purpose in the Universe, I:79
history, I:317
hope, I:179, 184
ignorance of true purpose, I:49
impatience, I:27
interfering with the purpose of the soul, I:203
lacks understanding of God, I:343
lacks understanding of true function in life, I:147
misconceptions about the Creator, I:112
necessity for free will, I:362
necessity for purpose to survive, I:196
next major puzzle, I:43
not let fellow-man suffer, I:73
not replaceable as a species, I:73
one entity among many, I:46
overall purpose, I:28
past, present, and future, I:367
perpetuating misconceptions, I:200
position in our space time continuum, I:27
present and future dangers, I:101
purpose in life, I:36, 49
purpose to create knowledge through experience and creativity, I:221
purpose, I:315
putting the puzzle together, I:43
relationship to God, I:271
searching for customs and personal beliefs, I:28
searching for the true purpose of life, I:196
significance, I:202
soul and purpose, I:201
status and position within society, I:221
stopping its search for a true spiritual Creator, I:27
thoughts, emotions, insights, and knowledge, I:35
tolerance and empathy, I:29
true beginnings, I:36

understanding and acceptance of purpose, I:200
understanding the next major puzzle, I:43
vulnerabililty to annihilation, II:376
weakness, I:271
withdrawing from true purpose, I:195

Mathematics
universal language, II:34

Matter
based on energy, II:41

Matter and Anti-Matter
creation of nothingness, I:93

Missionary Work
assisting each other, I:28
everyone is a missionary, I:281
necessity of, I:283
noble journey for the soul, I:284
relevance, I:282

Mohammed
pillar of society, I:182
quote, I:333

Morality
law, II:2
logical basis, II:204
relationship to religious faith, II:3
social, II:2

Moses
pillar of society, I:182
status and position within society, I:225

Muhammad
quote, I:161

Muslims
historical conflict, I:100

Myths
positive and negative effects within a society, I:189
religion, I:191

N

Naguib, Mohammed
quote, I:189

Nietzche, Friedrich Wilhelm
quote, I:367

Nostradamus
pillar of society, I:182
status and position within society, I:222

O

Om
discovery by science, II:68

Omnipotence
eliminating our present conception, I:112
Mankind's contribution, I:180
Mankind's limited understanding, I:111
paradoxes, I:109

Omnipresence
Causative Force, III:137, 140-141
eliminating our present conception, I:112
Mankind's contribution, I:180
Mankind's limited understanding, I:111
panentheism, III:137, 140-141
paradoxes, I:109
religions, III:143
theism and Causative Force, III:128

Omniscience
eliminating our present conception, I:112
Mankind's contribution, I:180
Mankind's limited understanding, I:111
paradoxes, I:109
religious perceptions, III:271

Ontology
Causative Force, III:90
change in behavior, III:89
conception of a necessary being, III:90
global behavior, III:89
Humankind's and Causative Force, III:99
reinforcing panentheism, III:92
reinforcing significance of existence, III:93
significance of Humankind, III:98
significance of the individual, III:97
understanding what life is, III:94-96
Universe, III:91
what it can offer us as a species, III:96
what it can offer us as individuals, III:95

P

Palaeomagnetism
concept, III:241
existence, III:245
life forms, III:249
panentheism, III:244, 252
significance of Humankind, III:250, 251
significance, III:242
species, III:248
understanding life, III:246
Universe, III:243
what it has to offer us, III:247

Panentheism
acceptance, II:202, 206-207
acting responsibly, III:68
adoption, II:52, 72, 86, 90
advantages for Humankind, II:37, 90
all present Causative Force, III:73
basic concepts, II:16
beginnings, II:145
being part of the whole, III:199-201
Causative Force, III:137, 140-143
changing our perception, II:157
closer to truth, II:194
concept not easily accepted, II:156
concept of equality, II:191-192
concept of God, II:11
creating radical change, II:174
destroying rationale for abuse, II:156
ecological niche, III:232, 240
effects of Humankind's behavior, III:68
emerging philosophy, II:155
ending war, II:12
entropy, III:160, 163
foundation for religions, III:44, 52
Hinduism, III:32, 34, 37
homo-, III:264
humanity and the soul, II:26
Humankind and Causative Force, III:72
Humankind's significance within, II:91
leads Humankind to understanding, II:38
life forms, III:145
logic, II:193
maintaining, II:79
modifying present perceptions, III:138

INDEX

omnipresence, III:137, 140-141, 180
our species, III:144
palaeomagnetism, III:244, 252
parallel Universes, II:92
pervading society, II:211
philosophical perception, II:48, 155
placing responsibility upon life, III:117
providing hope III:202
providing understanding of reality, II:43
radical change within society, II:211
reality existing within God, II:155
reinforced by Buddhism, III:56
reinforced by Hinduism, III:40
reinforced by ontology, III:92
reinforcing Buddhism, III:64
reinforcing ontology, III:100
reinforcing religion, science and philosophy, III:204
reinforcing science, III:112
rejected by society, II:206
rejecting inferiority, II:196
relationship of Humankind to Causative Force, III:147
relationship of symmetry, III:184
relationship to Causative Force, III:76
relationship to atheism, III:116
relationship to homo-, III:256
relationship to Islamic teaching, III:88
relationship to science, III:104
relationship to set theory, III:196, 203-204
relationship to theism and pantheism, II:159
relationship with Islamic teaching, III:80
religions, III:142-143
resolving paradoxes of religions, III:144
responsibility for actions, III:146
seeds, II:204-205
set theory and understanding, III:194-195
significance of Humankind, III:146
simple yet complex, II:42, 186, 207, 211
size and significance of Causative Force, III:76
soul, III:147
stepping into the heavens, II:28
symbiosis, III:268, 276
symmetry, III:192
The Big Bang, III:180
theism supporting and reinforcing, III:128
topology, III:220, 228
understanding of purpose, II:103
understanding the Universe, III:139
universal philosophy, II:30
universal tolerance, II:27
what it has to offer III:138
what it says, II:186

Pantheism
choosing, II:72
continuing present beliefs, II:86
inclusive philosophy, III:207
relationship to panentheism, II:159, 194
relationship to set theory, III:196, 203-204
relationship to theism, II:159
what it to offer us, III:114

Paradox
Mankind's creation and perpetuation, I:110

INDEX

omnipotence, omnipresence, omniscience, I:109
religions, III:148

People
being visionaries, II:137
elevated to the level of God, II:205
empowerment through a new perspective, II:22
finding purpose in reality, II:16
gaining knowledge of true value and importance, II:138
piece of God, II:48
purpose in reality, II:20

Philosophers
finding responses to the Ripple Effect, I:81
I think, therefore I am, I:45
questioning our place in the Universe, I:43
time, I:45

Philosophy
adapting to true significance, II:41
application of abstract concepts, III:218
battle of perception, II:25
benefits of panentheism, II:37
concept of panentheism, II:11
concept of theism, II:11
failure to change perspective, II:61
limits of theism, II:37
linear, I:37
panentheism, II:48
problems with theism, II:31
quadratic vs. linear, I:29, 35, 37
repression, III:255
right, I:38
simplicity of panentheism, II:42
subject of reason, II:5
understanding, I:100

Philosophy, Religion, Science
effects on society, III:297
existence within the Universe, III:301
helping us to understand life, III:302
Humankind's relationship to Causative Force, III:307
Humankind's significance, III:306
importance of panentheism, III:300
life within the Universe, III:301
purpose within the Universe, III:299
significance within the Universe, III:299
what they have to offer other life forms, III:305
what they offer the individual, III:303
what they offer us as a species, III:298, 304

Philosophy, the
absence of punishment, I:261
accepting assumptions, I:362
basic beliefs, I:240
equality of religions, I:287
establishing a foundation to build upon, I:154
foundation for religion, I:261, 355
fundamental beliefs, I:353
helping victims, I:273
impact on society, I:120, II:168
insights, I:170
Judas and forgiveness, I:154
Judas, I:152, 154
Mankind's purpose, I:148
not a religion, I:169
principles, II:185, 186
providing foundation, I:155, 373

INDEX

putting it to the test, I:119
reevaluating social norms, I:275
respect for other beliefs, I:287
responsibility and the soul, I:174, 275
Ripple Effect, I:240
seven basic concepts, I:121
supports religions, I:361
understanding who Man is, I:154
what it teaches, I:155

Physics
relationship to philosophy and religion, I:57
symmetry and the Universe, I:72

Plato
pillar of society, I:182

Predestination
absence of choice, III:63

Prophecy
Buddhism and Wheel of Dharma, III:418-419
change necessary in order to prevent catastrophe, III:411, 413, 419, 422
Christian concept of unconditional love, III:419
extinction of life, III:414
geological evidence of change, III:414
Humankind's purpose, III:411
humbling effect of the third millennium, III:413
Mayan calendar, III:416
necessity for change within society, III:423
necessity to define purpose, III:413, 419
necessity to elevate the individual, III:412
Nostradamus, III:421
Papal, III:420
predicting setback for Humankind, III:411
preparing for the future, III:423
purpose of the Great Pyramid, III:415
Revelations, III:419
significance of the Hopi, III:417

Protestants
historical conflict, I:100

Purpose
Man put in the Universe for a reason, I:79
Mankind, I:73, 36
soul, I:43

Puzzle
complete picture emerges, I:44
drawing the pieces together, I:47
keeping apart, creating uncertainty, I:43
Man putting the pieces together, I:43
next for Mankind, I:43
purpose of life, I:43
putting together to make a complete thought, I:43
universal philosophy, I:44

Q

Qing, Ai
quote, I:251

Quark
building block of Universe, II:49

Questions
is our time at hand?, I:185

is religion significant or necessary?, I:161, 189
is there a heaven and hell?, I:161
is there hope for Mankind?, I:185
is there hope for me as an individual?, I:161
what is my purpose in life?, I:50, 143-144, 173
where did I come from?, 173
where will I be going after life?, 173
who am I?, I:143-144, 173
why are we here?, I:50
why do people suffer?, I:195
why the gender wars?, I:199
why the racism?, I:199
why?, I:50, 173

Quote
Buddha, I:43
Burke, Edmund, I:281
Burns, Robert, I:139
Chuang-Tzu, I:199
Confucius, I:239
Dylan, Bob, I:147
Elliott, George, I:63
Hikmet, Nazim, I:259
Hur Shi, I:35
Ibsen, Henrik, I:91
Japanese proverb, I:271
King, Martin Luther, I:79
Lao-Tzu, I:71
Lippmann, Walter, I:99
Longfellow, Henry W, I:119, 221
Mahapurana, I:25
Mohammed, I:161, 333
Naguib, Mohammed, I:189
Nietzche, Friedrich Wilhelm, I:367
Qing, AI, I:251
Renan, Ernest, I:361
Romans, I:341
Santayana, George, I:231
Shakespeare, William, I:315
Spinoza, Benedict, I:327
St. Mark, I:55
Tennyson, Alfred North, I:109
Vovelananda, I:351
Washington, Booker T., I:179

R

Race
perception of exploitation, II:189

Reality
Causative Force, III:35
exploration by science, II:59
God created, I:26
God travelling, II:80
Humankind's purpose within, II:5
limit imposed by a bounded Universe, I:71
significance of Humankind, II:50
time frame of existence, II:42

Reason and Experience
effects upon society, III:369
Humankind's significance, III:379
meaning and purpose of life, III:374
reinforcing significance of existence, III:373
reinforcing significance of life, III:373
significance for panentheism, III:372
significance of Humankind, III:378
understanding the Universe, III:371
understanding what we see, III:370
what it can offer other life forms, III:377
what it can offer us as a species, III:376

INDEX

what it can offer us as individuals, III:370, 375

Religion
acceptance of God, II:59
adapting to true significance, II:41
application of abstract concepts, III:218
atheistic beliefs, I:232-233
battle of perception, II:25
belief in eternity, III:62
belief in the soul, III:225
Causative Force and equilibrium, III:171-172
changing perceptions, III:172
Christian concept of love, III:66
Christianity and the judgement of Judas, I:148
Christianity, I:351
concept of an eternal soul, III:250
concept of omnipresence, III:127
contradictions and their resolution, I:35, II:4
contradictions, continues to struggle with, I:49
cooperation, I:49
creed, does it matter?, I:83
customs, I:28
defining purpose, I:358
dismantling, III:135
doctrines, I:44
does it have significance?, I:189
examine and answer the questions, I:46
heaven and hell, I:333
Hinduism, III:33-35
importance, I:316
inner peace, I:28
institutions shunning companion in reality, II:151
issue of abortion, II:13
losing, I:46
modernizing, I:49
modification, II:97
moral judgements, II:4
myths, I:190-191
necessity for change, I:149, II:57
necessity to begin self-introspection, II:161
non-acceptance of other life forms, I:46
omniscience of Causative Force, III:110
organizations made up of people, I:149
panentheism providing foundation, III:52
panentheism resolving paradoxes, III:144
panentheism, III:142-143
paradoxes in their beliefs, III:92, 110, 127, 148, 179
portrayal of God, I:342
providing direction and guidance, I:173
refusal to change perspective, II:61
rejecting a companion in reality, II:149
relationship with atheism, I:231
relationship with science, III:103
revolutionize our, I:28
Ripple Effect, I:82
sanctuary for souls, I:83
serving Humankind, II:150
society - myths, I:191
source of inner-peace, I:83
stagnation of perspective, II:55
subject of faith, II:5
supported by panentheism, III:44
supporting panentheism, III:128
'the Philosophy' provides a foundation, I:155

tolerance, I:28
understanding, I:100, III:219
variations, I:28

Rembrandt
pillar of society, I:182
status and position within society, I:222

Renaissance Philosophy
Causative Force, III:367
effects upon society, III:357
helping us to understand life, III:362
Humankind, III:367
relationship to panentheism, III:360
significance of existence, III:361
significance of Humankind, III:366
Universe, III:359
what it can offer other life forms, III:365
what it can offer us, III:258, 363-364

Renan, Ernest
quote, I:361

Research
controversial, II:189

Responsibility
accepting, I:169, II:166
benefits, III:275
need for within society, I:85
understanding, III:275

Ripple Effect
accepting responsibilities, I:79, 84
afterlife, I:163
consequences of our actions, I:74, 163, III:58
consequences of punishment, I:262
hedonism, I:79
infinite implications, I:80
punishment and consequences, I:346
religion, I:79
shouldering responsibility, I:81
small and great consequences, I:80
society, I:142, 162
struggle with life, II:184
understanding purpose of life, II:164

Roe vs. Wade
definition of life, II:7

Romans
quote, I:341

Rwandans
death of 500,000, I:140

S

Santayana, George
quote, I:231

Schools
mentoring and educating, II:21

Science
Causative Force, III:102
concept of 'om', II:68
concept of a bounded Universe, III:114
developing new technologies, II:40
discoveries in year 2200, II:35
expansion of present knowledge, I:101
exploration of reality, II:59
finding outer limits of Universe, II:34
Humankind, III:102
influence upon society, II:169

INDEX

knowledge and destruction, I:100
nature of time and space, II:44
reinforcing concept of panentheism, III:104
reinforcing life, III:105
reinforcing religion, III:103
significance of Causative Force, III:112
significance of Humankind to Causative Force, III:108
significance of Humankind, III:110-111
significance of other life forms, III:109
significant influence on society, III:50
understanding Humankind's origins, III:107
understanding life, III:106
understanding our species, III:108
understanding our Universe, III:103
understanding, I:100
understanding, III:219
what it can offer the individual, III:107
within society, III:101

Scientists
study of Humankind, II:14

Set Theory
Causative Force III:203
established within society, III:193
leading to a universal philosophy, III:196
reinforcing significance of existence, III:197-198
reinforcing symbiotic panentheism III:204
relationship to atheism, III:196, 203-204
relationship to panentheism, III:196, 203-204
relationship to pantheism, III:196, 203-204
relationship to theism, III:196, 203-204
seeing the significance of life, III:197-198
significance of Humankind, III:202
understanding panentheism, III:194-198

Shakespeare, William
pillar of society, I:182
quote, I:315

Significance
theism and existence, III:136

Social Institutions
absence of free will, II:197
abuses, II:206
directives imposed upon, II:197
tragedy, II:203

Social Systems
dismantling, III:135

Society
abortion and the soul, I:243
absence of free will in institutions, II:197
absence of moral guidance, II:2
atheism established within, III:113
atheistic beliefs, I:232
based upon equality, II:97
behavior, II:15
can it change?, II:210
capital punishment, I:259, 263-264
changes, I:29
crimes, I:141
debt, I:259

definitions of life and death, II:10
destructive behavior of, I:142
directives imposed, II:197
effects of Buddhism, III:53-54
effects of entropy, III:181
effects of Hinduism, III:29
effects of Judaism, III:41
effects of mass media, I:173
effects of science within, III:157
effects of symbiotic panentheism, III:393
elimination of status, I:223
establishing a purpose, I:275
helping victims of domestic violence, II:199-200
influence of mass media, I:171
influence of ontology, III:89
influence of science, III:101
influence of set theory, III:193
information overload, I:284
intolerance, racism, pornography, I:85
Islam and justice, III:78
issue of abortion, II:13
law, II:2
life incarceration, I:259, 263-264
Mankind's conceptions of position and status, I:221
missionary work, I:281
moral and legal contradictions, II:3
myths - positive and negative effects, I:189
necessity for care, II:200
necessity for status - right or wrong?, I:223
panentheism, II:211
radical changes, II:211
responsibility, I:85
role of police, judges, juries, I:272
role of the elite, II:15
science, III:217
self-righteousness, II:197
significance of palaeomagnetism, III:241
significance of science, III:50
status and position of Caesar, I:222
status and position of Confucius, I:225
status and position of Edison, I:225
status and position of Ghandi, I:225
status and position of Moses, I:225
status and position of Nostradamus, I:222
status and position of Rembrandt, I:222
status and position of Tolstoy, I:225
status and position of Van Gogh, I:225
status and position, I:199
strengthening structure, II:79
tolerance, I:84
violence, II:78, 196
war and the soul, I:241
with panentheism, II:206
without panentheism, II:206

Soul
accepting responsibility, I:329
accomplishing its journey, III:88
brothers in shared belief, I:26
contradictions, I:35
contributing to reality, I:184
damaged in its journey through life, I:277
damaging other souls, I:272
destruction of the Universe, III:139
essence of Humankind, II:30
essence of life, III:225
existing in eternity, III:80, 82
fragmented, I:288
God and, I:228, 320

growing in knowledge and experience, I:65
haunting, I:36
Humankind, II:26
importance and function, II:190
imposing limits, I:193
journey, II:117, 170
location, I:45
Mankind's interference with purpose, I:203
mercy and God, II:4
missionary work, I:282
origin, I:322
panentheism, III:147
piece of God, I:282
potential in eternity, III:46
purpose in reality, II:116
quest of fulfillment, I:316
returning to Causative Force, III:187
seeking its home, I:84
significance to Causative Force, III:96
status, I:227, II:142
suicide and the Ripple Effect, I:252-254
transcending this reality, I:94
value and importance, I:194
war and abortion, I:239
war, I:241
who man really is, I:199

Space
Causative Force, III:208
exploration, II:94
Humankind and Causative Force, III:215
life forms, III:213
nature and structure, III:206
reinforcing life, III:209-210
relationship to panentheism, III:208
relationship to symbiotic panentheism, III:216
significance of Humankind, III:214
society, III:205
space-time, III:206
Universe, III:207
weapons and space fleets, II:36
what it has to offer us as a species, III:212
what it has to offer us as individuals, III:206, 211

Space time continuum
Universe as multitude of laboratories, I:91

Species
entropy, III:164
homo-, III:260
knowledge, I:28
Mankind increasing significance, I:73
Mankind not replaceable, I:73
palaeomagnetism, III:248
symbiosis, III:272
symmetry, III:188
topology, III:224

Spinoza, Benedict
quote, I:327

St. Mark
quote, I:55

Stalin, Joseph
World War II and, I:139

Subjugation
consequences of atheistic beliefs, III:120

Suffering
awareness in eternity, III:81-82
Buddhist intolerance, III:91
consequences for Causative Force, III:62
consequences for Humankind, III:62

eliminating, III:55-57, 60-61, 83-84
within society, III:54

Suicide
afterlife, I:252
consequences for the soul, I:252, 254
despair and suffering, I:251
Ripple Effect, I:253

Symbiosis
Causative Force, III:266, 275
life forms, III:273
panentheism, III:268
significance in eternity, III:274
significance of existence, III:269-270
significance of individuals, III:271
society, III:265
species, III:272
symbiotic panentheism, III:276
Universe, III:267

Symbiotic Panentheism
a model of a unified view, III:394
defining life, III:398
effects within society, III:393
existence within the Universe, III:396
importance and significance of life, III:397
importance of free will, III:396, 402
importance of Humankind to Causative Force, III:403
model of a universal philosophy, III:404
nature of the Universe, III:395
philosophy and life, III:398
significance of Humankind, III:402
what it can offer other life forms, III:401
what it can offer us as a species, III:394, 400
what it can offer us as individuals, III:399

Symmetry
Causative Force, III:191
consequences for Humankind, III:182
creation of the Universe, III:183
destruction of matter and anti-matter, I:56
established within society, III:181
other life forms, III:189
reinforcing existence, III:185
reinforcing panentheism, III:184
significance of Humankind, III:190
symbiotic panentheism, III:192
understanding life, III:186
understanding Universe, III:183, 187
what it has to offer our species?, III:188
what it has to offer the individual, III:187

T

T'ao Chi' ien
pillar of society, I:182

Taoism
effects upon society, III:321
helping us to understand life, III:326
Humankind's significance in eternity, III:330
Humankind's significance to Causative Force, III:331
implications for our Universe, III:323

INDEX

relationship to panentheism, III:324
significance of life and existence, III:325
what it can offer other life forms, III:329
what it can offer us as a species, III:322, 328
what it can offer us as individuals, III:327

Tennyson, Alfred North
quote, I:109

Theism
Causative Force, III:136
concept of God, II:11
continuing present beliefs, II:86
continuing to accept, II:72
disadvantages for Humankind, II:37
eliminating, II:31
existence in eternity, III:129
God and the world, III:135
Humankind, III:134
importance of life, III:130-131
life forms, III:133
limits, II:194
omnipresence, III:125-126
paradoxes, III:208
reinforcing life, III:129
relationship to God, II:66, 69
relationship to panentheism, II:159
relationship to pantheism, II:159
relationship to set theory, III:196, 203-204
significance of existence, III:136
significance, III:134
Universe and existence, III:127
what it can offer our species, III:132

Thought
quadratic vs. linear, I:38

Time
relationship to reality, II:44

Tolerance
limits, I:101
Mankind, I:28, 113
search for a missing binding

Tolstoy, Leo
status and position within society, I:225

Topology
applied to philosophy, III:218
applied to religion, III:218
creation of the Universe, III:226
existence of time, III:227
helping us to understand life, III:222
life forms, III:225
panentheism, III:220
significance of existence, III:221
significance of life, III:226-227
species, III:224
symbiotic panentheism, III:228
universal truths, III:223
Universe, III:219
what does it have to offer us?, III:218

Truth
removing the myths, I:25

U

Unified View
attaining knowledge as a species, III:287
consequences for Causative Force, III:295
defining life, III:294

effects on society, III:285-286
free will, III:290
relationship with panentheism, III:288
responsibility, III:290
significance and purpose of life, III:289
what it can offer individuals, III:291
what it can offer other life forms, III:293
what it can offer our species, III:292

Universal Philosophy
abortion and the consequence for the soul, I:246
absence of a supreme being, III:114
absence of hope under atheism, III:122-123
achieving and maintaining, III:213
atheism and the soul, I:236
awareness, III:186
begin developing, III:248
Causative Force, III:186
changing society, I:143
Christian understanding of nature, III:67
companion to religion, II:151
created from nothingness, III:91, 184
defining morality and purpose, II:5
destruction and the soul, III:139
destruction, III:139, 158
elevates responsibility for actions, I:175
entropy, III:158
establish foundation, II:157
existing within Causative Force, III:104
God and revenge, I:345
growth, decay and entropy, III:159
Hindu dissolving, III:182
Hinduism, III:31
Humankind's lack, II:24
implementation, II:195
importance of life, III:74
is it outside or within Causative Force?, III:216
Islamic teaching, III:79, 85
journeying, III:186
Judaism and Causative Force, III:43
Mankind's future, I:185
nature and structure of Universe, III:79
omniscient nature of Causative Force, III:109
ontology, III:91
other life forms, III:273
outside of Causative Force, III:216
palaeomagnetism, III:243
panentheism and set theory, III:196
panentheism and understanding, III:139
protecting the journey of everyone, III:213
provides an understanding of Man's purpose, I:175
reducible to nothingness, III:215
relationship to Causative Force, III:47
relationship to atheistic beliefs, III:115
relationship to universal morality, II:5
science as a tool of understanding, III:103
science's perception of boundary, III:114
significance of atheism, III:121
significance of ecological niche, III:233
significance of existence, III:233

INDEX

significance of life, III:61
significance or other life forms, III:109
symbiosis, III:267
symmetry and creation, III:183
temporary, III:192
The Big Bang, III:171-172
theism and existence, III:127
three possible states, III:159
topology and Causative Force, III:220
topology, III:219
understanding and applying, I:287

Universe
annihilation, I:64
Asimov's belief that it could self-destruct, I:92
basic building block, II:49
boundary and limits, II:40
composed of matter and energy, I:55
creation, I:92, II:68, 84
destruction, I:91-92, 55, 86
Einstein's theory of a bounded, I:71
four leafed clover concept, I:48, 55
four stages of its creation and destruction, I:91
God knowing, I:63
God, II:161
God's creation, II:52
infinite, I:37
Klein bottle construction, II:34, 40, 81
limitless limits, I:37, 71
limitless, I:37
limits, I:73
located within God's consciousness, I:66
nature, I:93
omniscient presence, II:161
one of four, I:55
outer limits, II:27
parallel, I:49, II:87
presence of other life forms, II:36
quark, II:49
structure, II:101
structured as a multitude of laboratories, I:91
The Big Bang II:68
why it was constructed - The Missing Link, I:92

V

Van Gogh
status and position within society, I:225

Violence
elimination, II:202
society, II:196

Void
Asimov's theory of how a void could be created, I:56
creation of 'something' from 'nothing', I:57

Vovelananda
quote, I:351

W

War
definition of life, II:7
Roe vs. Wade, II:7
soul of Man, I:241

Washington, Booker T.
quote, I:179

Women
importance to God, II:196
society, II:196
subjugation, II:196

World War I
gas warfare, I:140

World War II
Armenians, I:139
casualties, II:7
causes, I:100
consequence for Mankind, I:242
consequence for the soul, I:242
fifty million lives lost, I:101
Hitler and the Jews, I:139
Man's interference, I:242
Stalin, I:139

World War III
abortion, II:14, 8

Glossary

Volume I

You & I Together

- Have a Purpose in Reality -

Volume II

In the Image of God

Volume III

Stepping Up To The Creator

Allah: God of Islam.

Anti-Matter: A form of matter that is similar to real matter. However, unlike matter, its atoms are composed of anti-electrons, anti-protons and anti-neutrons, rather than electrons, protons and neutrons.

Atheism: The belief that there is no God or gods, that Humankind does not have a divine Creator.

Atom: The smallest part of any element that exists. It is the basic building block of all matter.

Bigotry: An attitude or behavior showing intolerance and disrespect for another person or persons, because of their religious or political differences.

Brainwashing: A process whereby a person is forcibly indoctrinated into a belief system other than their own.

Christian: A person professing a belief in the teachings and philosophy of Jesus Christ.

Concept: A method of thinking whereby certain events are classified into individual categories, as opposed to a universal and all-embracing single category.

Creator: Also known as the First Cause, Causative Force, or God. Almost every culture on Earth professes a belief in a Divine Creator or First Cause, the Creator of Humankind.

Deja Vu: A feeling that an action or event occurred previously, though no memory of that action or event is present.

Disciple: A person who embraces and assists in spreading the religious teachings of another. The term is often associated specifically with the twelve Apostles, the original followers of Jesus Christ.

DNA Structure (*Deoxyribonucleic Acid*)**:** The genetic material of most organisms. It plays a strong role in selecting and determining hereditary characteristics.

Equation: A mathematical concept. It expresses the relationship of previously defined variables with each other.

Eternity: Time without beginning or end. It is infinite. It has no boundaries.

Evolution: Usually associated with the field of biology and the teachings of Charles Darwin. It states that all living organisms evolve and change over time, adapting and improving to suit their environment in order to ensure their survival.

Free Will: The belief that we have control over our actions. Unlike determinism, it states that we can make choices and decisions about our behavior. Therefore, we are responsible for what we do.

God: An eternal being of immense power. Though worshiped differently by individual religions and faiths, many similar characteristics are ascribed to Him, such as infinite knowledge, wisdom, and goodness. He is regarded as the creator of the Universe.

Hedonism: The belief that the seeking of pleasure is the most important goal in life.

Hinduism: Practiced mostly in India, its religions, philosophy, and practices are characterized by a belief in reincarnation and a supreme being of many forms.

Holocaust: Occurring in Europe during World War II, it was the genocide of millions of Jews and others by Adolf Hitler and the members of the Nazi Party.

Humankind *(see Mankind)*: All of the people on the planet Earth, irrespective of tribe, culture or faith.

Inquisition: Tribunal held in the Roman Catholic Church in 1483. Its mission was to suppress heresy and witchcraft. Torture and cruelty were used to extract confessions from the accused.

Islam: Religion practiced by the Moslem people.

Judaism: Monotheistic religion of the Jewish people. Its source of inspiration is the Bible.

Linear Philosophy: Methodical way of thinking, characterized by a step-by-step approach upon a single line of thought.

Mankind *(see Humankind)*: All of the people on the planet Earth, irrespective of tribe, culture or faith.

Medical Morality: Field of enquiry into the morality of medical decisions, practices, and ethics.

Millennia: A span of a thousand years. The Millenium is seen by many as a time of major change and upheavel in Humankind's affairs.

Muslim: A person professing a belief in the teachings and philosophy of Islam.

Omnipotent: Possessing complete and absolute knowledge.

Omnipresent: Being present everywhere simultaneously.

Omniscient: Possessing complete knowledge. Knowing everything knowable.

Panentheism, Symbiotic: A metaphysical model based upon true omniscience. Panentheism places the Universe within God, therefore the Universe becomes a part of God. Likewise, the individual becomes a part of God. Thus emerges the rationality for the respect due the individual.

Paradox: A seemingly contradictory statement that may in fact be true.

Parallel Universes: Two universes separated by a slim buffer. Because each universe has a different energy status, this buffer is necessary to prevent their mutual destruction.

Philosophy: A diverse and expansive field of human enquiry into the fundamental questions of existence. Its impulse is to construct a worldview that encompasses all of reality.

Philosophy, Universal: A belief system that is embraced by all of Humankind.

Physics: A branch of science dedicated to the study of matter and energy.

Predestination: The absence of free will. The belief that all our actions are made not by choice, but by a chain of events in which we are helpless participants.

Quadratic Philosophy: A non-linear approach to thinking about an individual idea or concept. It is all-embracing, inclusive, and broad in scope.

Racism: Behavior characterized by discrimination, based on the race of another person.

Reality: A concept which embraces everything possessing actuality, existence or essence.

Religion: Beliefs, values, and practices based on the teachings of a spiritual leader or Creator.

Ripple Effect, the: A concept which states that our actions, no matter how small, have a potential for great harm or good in the future.

Soul: An entity believed, by many, to exist only in living things. Many philosophers and theologians believe that its nature is immaterial and thereby immortal.

Subatomic Particles: Also known as 'elementary particles'. These are the fundamental constituents of all matter found within the universe.

Symmetry: An equal division, represented in similarity and balance, such as mirror-image.

Taoist: A person professing a belief in the teachings and philosophy of Lao-Tzu, a teacher who lived in China in the 6th Century B.C..

Truth: The absence of error or deceit. An accurate representation of reality, in accordance with the known facts.

Vindictiveness: Behavior characterized by spitefulness and revenge. The desire to hurt and to undermine another person.